Virtualizing and Tuning Large-Scale Java Platforms

VMware Press is the official publisher of VMware books and training materials, which provide guidance on the critical topics facing today's technology professionals and students. Enterprises, as well as small- and medium-sized organizations, adopt virtualization as a more agile way of scaling IT to meet business needs. VMware Press provides proven, technically accurate information that will help them meet their goals for customizing, building, and maintaining their virtual environment.

With books, certification and study guides, video training, and learning tools produced by world-class architects and IT experts, VMware Press helps IT professionals master a diverse range of topics on virtualization and cloud computing. It is the official source of reference materials for preparing for the VMware Certified Professional Examination.

VMware Press is also pleased to have localization partners that can publish its products into more than 42 languages, including Chinese (Simplified), Chinese (Traditional), French, German, Greek, Hindi, Japanese, Korean, Polish, Russian, and Spanish.

For more information about VMware Press, please visit **vmwarepress.com**.

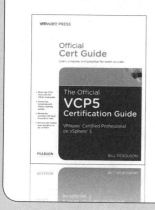

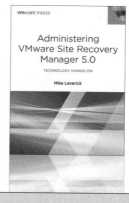
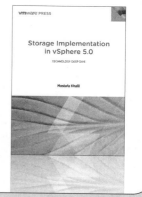

Virtualizing and Tuning Large-Scale Java Platforms

Emad Benjamin

vmware® PRESS

Upper Saddle River, NJ • Boston • Indianapolis • San Francisco
New York • Toronto • Montreal • London • Munich • Paris • Madrid
Capetown • Sydney • Tokyo • Singapore • Mexico City

Virtualizing and Tuning Large-Scale Java Platforms

Warning and Disclaimer

Corporate and Government Sales

ASSOCIATE PUBLISHER
David Dusthimer

ACQUISITIONS EDITOR
Joan Murray

VMWARE PRESS PROGRAM MANAGER
Anand Sundaram

SENIOR DEVELOPMENT EDITOR
Christopher Cleveland

MANAGING EDITOR
Sandra Schroeder

SENIOR PROJECT EDITOR
Tonya Simpson

COPY EDITOR
Keith Cline

PROOFREADER
Debbie Williams

BOOK DESIGNER
Gary Adair

COVER DESIGNER
Chuti Prasertsith

COMPOSITOR
Bumpy Design

EDITORIAL ASSISTANT
Vanessa Evans

I dedicate this book to my beloved wife, Christine,
and our two beautiful boys, Anthony and Adrian.
They fill my life with plenty of joy and inspiration.
Thank you Lord for all your blessings.

Contents

Best Practices

Preface

This book is the culmination of 9 years of experience in running Java on VMware vSphere, both at VMware and at many of VMware's customers. In fact, many VMware customers run enterprise-critical Java applications on VMware vSphere and have achieved better total cost of ownership (TCO) and service level agreements (SLAs). In my first book, *Enterprise Java Applications Architecture on VMware*, the topic of Java virtualization was covered well, both from a high-level architecture perspective and with in-depth technical chapters on sizing and best practices. To keep that first book more affordable, a decision was made to hold back some of the chapters for a second book, what you are reading now. These two books are complementary in many ways. The first book has a few high-level chapters for architects, engineers, and managers considering Java virtualization for the first time and asking the high-level question "why." This book is all about how and what to tune for optimal performance.

Limiting the scope of the first book was a good idea; the book was thus made available quickly for those launching their first Java virtualization projects. It has been almost 2 years since the release date of that first book, and since then nearly 300 customer interactions have helped to further analyze the guidance offered. Some of these interactions have included large-scale Java platforms of significant scale and have significantly contributed to the greater level of detail in this book. This book discusses in detail the sizing and tuning of both small-scale and large-scale virtualized Java platforms—100 Java Virtual Machines (JVMs) to 10,000 JVMs and a JVM heap range of 1 to 128GB. This recent experience, combined with my 15 years of tuning Java platforms, is presented in this book in such way to summarize what is most practical and immediately applicable to the vast majority of Java workload types. You can retrofit the advice, deployment configuration, and garbage collection (GC) tuning knowledge gained from this book to effectively combat GC poor behavior or to design and size your Java platform overall. The best practices highlighted throughout this book apply to physical environments, virtual environments, or both.

Motivation for Writing This Book

I have spent the past 9 years at VMware in various capacities ensuring that all internal enterprise Java applications were virtualized to showcase to VMware customers the benefits of the approach. In that time, I came to believe that a lot of the best practices that we learned from empirical evidence in production environments should be shared with the VMware community. I received lots of feedback requesting that I document many of the lessons learned and the various tips and tricks needed to successfully run enterprise Java applications on VMware. This served as the motivation for the first book, *Enterprise Java Applications Architecture on VMware* (https://www.createspace.com/3632131).

Continuing on from the motivation of the first book, this book (the second book) focuses on what to tune, how far you can tune it, and how large virtualized Java platforms can be. In essence, the first book had a reasonable mix of the "why virtualize" and "what/how to virtualize." In contrast, this book examines "how large of a scale you can virtualize and how far you can drive the platform tuning."

It was quite exciting to write the first book, as we were trying to let the broader VMware customer base know that Java virtualization absolutely works and provides significant advantages. In this current book, we want to help those customers who are saying, "Now help me take it to the next level of scale." We have spent the past 2 years helping customers virtualize many large-scale JVM platforms, some as big as 10,000 JVMs, and others in the big data platform space (with multiple terabytes of data kept in memory within a set of clustered JVMs). Before you dive into this book, though, remember this: Although this book presents many best practices, these practices represent optimal configuration guidance; they are not mandatory requirements. In our experience, we have found that most enterprise Java applications virtualize readily without having to worry about too many specific configurations. In fact, of any enterprise-level production application, Java applications are prime "low-hanging fruit" candidates for virtualization. By sharing the lessons we learned, we hope that you can avoid some of the pitfalls we encountered in our efforts to virtualize large-scale Java platforms.

Wanting to cover how best to deploy Java platforms in virtual environments (while also addressing misconceptions that the virtual platform is the problem), we built best practices that apply equally to both physical and virtual environments. By design, this book contains sections that cover best practices for physical and virtualized Java platforms, so as to enable customers to correct any problems on their physical Java platform before they virtualize. Of course, this is not mandatory; customers may choose to keep the legacy aspect of their physical Java deployment as they migrate to virtualization. However, at least they have been made aware of the design and deployment deficiencies of their physical Java platform should they wish to correct it in the future.

This is an important exercise to go through, allowing us to highlight the problem was actually customers' own physical environments. Customers could thus understand the cost of maintaining the legacy aspect of their physical Java platform. For example, we often discover that many Java physical platforms were poorly architected with the wrong deployment topology, many times with sprawling thousands of unnecessary JVMs. When we speak with customers, we walk them through the best practices and ensure that these environments are sized and tuned correctly, regardless of whether they leave their Java applications on physical environments or migrate to virtual. Again, customers can choose to ignore our prescriptions and deploy the legacy aspect of their Java physical platform onto the virtual equivalent without much change or intrusion on the codebase and platform. However, customers these days are pretty cognizant of the value of the best practices we (and many others) have embraced to improve the Java deployment paradigm while migrating to virtual platforms.

The lessons learned fall into the following general categories:

- Things will go wrong in production; it is just a matter of when. So, you want to meticulously consider what could go wrong and have a roll-forward and a rollback plan. The planning exercise helps to further solidify the QA test plan. Note that this is not specific to a virtualized environment. In fact, it is an equally stringent requirement whether you are dealing with a physical or a virtual infrastructure. However, the reality is that virtualization gives you the mechanisms to quickly deal with issues (in contrast to a physical case in which you are restricted to the amount of flexibility you have to move around your compute resources).

- Enterprise Java applications are the low-hanging fruit when it comes to virtualization.

- Everyone operated in various silos at each of the Java tiers and did not necessarily speak the same language in terms of technology and organizational logistics. This was certainly the modus operandi under the old physical (nonvirtualized) paradigm, with these technology and organizational silos having been formed over the past decades. However, cross-team collaboration was a big part of virtualizing Java on VMware; it drove a lot of the teams to talk to each other to facilitate a best-of-breed design. Teams from both application development and operations came to the table many times.

- Customers sometimes seek to rationalize the legacy aspects of their environment. As a consequence, customers pay additional administrative cost associated with sprawling JVMs in the physical environment; if not remedied, these costs carry over into the virtualized system. For example, do you really need those 1GB heap space 5000 JVMs? Couldn't they be consolidated? Absolutely, they can be, and we show you how you can save by reducing your licensing costs and improving administration (because you will have fewer JVMs to manage).

- Performance issues. Customers often race to the conclusion that any problem must be a virtualization issue or a GC issue. In reality, though, virtualization is not the issue, but the GC may sometimes be an issue. If a GC issue exists, though, it is not specific to virtualization, and in fact the issue is almost always equally present in the physical deployment.

- Big in-memory databases on physical Java platforms (1TB memory cluster, really!)? Absolutely, if the prime objective is to service transactions at any cost, but at the highest speed possible, this is the right architecture for you. I found that many customers were skeptical about this. The fact that they attempted to size these types of environments without regard for the underlying platform gave them a poor start. You must pay attention to the server machine architecture when sizing these data platforms (as discussed later). The other poor practice I found with some customers is that they attempted to size these environments to have 30 or so JVMs. Well, that is not the right approach, because maintaining chatter between that many JVMs at a high rate can make latency worse overall. Quite simply, these are latency-sensitive memory-bound workloads and perform better using a deployment paradigm of fewer larger JVMs. If you were to compare the performance of an in-memory database system that had 30 JVMs versus one with 8 much larger JVMs, the configuration with 8 larger JVMs would be better. Of course, the caveat here is that the larger JVMs are sized correctly for NUMA optimization and the appropriate GC tuning has been applied.

- Can big in-memory databases really perform when virtualized? Over the past couple of years, I have seen an increase in customers virtualizing Java application servers. Specifically, large-scale platforms with thousands of JVMs are being virtualized. One unique category of workload is in-memory data management systems that require terabytes of memory and are latency sensitive. With these in-memory data clusters, we find that although there are fewer JVMs, they do tend to be of large heap space, ranging in JVM size from 8 to 128GB (and usually fewer than 12 JVMs). Of course, there is nothing magical about the number 12, it could be as low as 3, or as high as 30. However, the more JVMs you have, the more potential latency issues you risk because of the additional network hops. Later in the book, you will learn how to size and tune these workloads.

Many Java application developers know the development process well, know how to write Java code, and know how to tune the JVM. However, too often that information stays with developers and is not shared with (or translated for) application administrators. Often, the skills needed to run Java platforms are split between Java developers and administrators, without a single person understanding both purviews. This silo-ing of understanding is changing, though, as more individuals begin to understand how to write Java code, deploy it, tune the JVM, and recognize the full breadth of virtualization and the intricacies of the server hardware architecture. So, another goal of this book is to encourage readers to follow this career path as they develop this skill-set profile.

I sincerely hope this book helps those with backgrounds in Java development, operations infrastructure, and virtualization. You can use this book both as a guide to combat day-to-day situations and as an aid to help you compose a strategic architectural map of your Java platform.

Prerequisites

This book assumes a high-level understanding of Java, JVM GC, server hardware architecture, and virtualization technologies. The information herein relates to running large-scale Java platforms. Although you might want to brush up on virtualization before delving into the material in this book, most senior Java specialists will quickly learn enough about virtualization and virtualizing Java applications from this book alone. In fact, by learning the answer to the following question, you will gain enough background on virtualization to continue through this book. This is the question asked on day one by folks new to virtualizing Java: "Is Java both operating system and hypervisor independent?"

This text assumes that the reader has some background in the Java language and specifically JVM architecture. The book does its best to summarize the JVM architecture, and specific JVM tunings, but it is not a replacement for a book dedicated to Java tuning. Suffice it to say, vSphere administrators who are new to JVM tuning should be able to learn enough from this book to hold technical conversations with their Java counterparts. In addition, vSphere and Java administrators can apply the tuning advice in this book and modify it as it applies to their environment. The various chapters on JVM tuning advice have been written in such a way that they are less overwhelming than those found in other Java books, enabling vSphere and the Java administrators to have a quick and effective go-forward design and tuning strategy. Many VMware customers running Java have applied the tuning parameters discussed in this book and have gained immediate performance improvements.

What You Need to Know First

The fact that you are reading this book means that you are halfway to correcting your Java platform. Perhaps you have already concluded that tuning Java platforms cannot be ignored/minimized. However, even if you have just dabbled with VMware virtualization and Java tuning to some degree on physical systems, you are ready for this book. As a refresher (or an introduction for those new to the material), the following sections briefly introduce important concepts related to virtualizing and tuning large-scale Java platforms.

Is a 4GB Java Heap the New 1GB? Why?

In the past 2 years, I have conducted more than 290 customer calls and workshops where it was evident that 40% of workloads running on Java platforms were deployed on JVMs that were 1 to 4GB in size. I continue to see a huge number of less than 1GB JVMs, approximately another 40% within the customer base I interact with. The remaining 20% varies from 4 to 360GB. Yes, a 360GB JVM is due to a monitoring system that cannot horizontally scale out and so the customer is forced to have a single JVM. Although this might seem unbelievable, it is the reality of Java production platforms today. However, the JVMs with 1GB of heap cause a sprawl of JVMs instances, and that becomes its own management headache. For example, you might want to service 1TB of total heap space, which would then mean thousands of JVM instances if you allow only a 1GB JVM heap. How can that possibly make any sense? Couldn't you get the 1TB serviced with 250 JVMs of 4GB each? Of course you could, but because of your organization's legacy rules from the old 32-bit JVM days, you continue to spin JVMs that are less than 1GB. More realistically, though, the notion that larger JVMs may have larger GC pauses is ill conceived. That belief is not entirely true, but not completely false either. Yes, larger pauses will occur, but with recent advancements in 64-bit JVM and concurrent mark-sweep (CMS) GC, the days of larger and less-pause-sensitive JVMs have arrived. Not only has GC gotten a lot better, but also the underlying server hardware has gotten better to support 4GB heap spaces. In fact, 4GB is a unique and magical number because JVMs these days automatically treat the 4GB heap space as 32-bit address space within a 64-bit JVM to save on memory usage. This is possible because a 32-bit address range is within 4GB. In fact, the JVM using the -XX:+UseCompressedOops option can be applied to Java heap spaces of up to 32GB.

After reading this book, you will understand that alternatives and workloads suited for larger JVMs exist. Clearly, I am not advocating larger JVMs for everyone, but a 4GB JVM is really not that big anymore. Keep in mind that I *am* advocating a more reasonable number of JVMs, even if that means increasing the heap size. And remember, if you have a vendor that says that you will incur a performance cost when moving from 32-bit to 64-bit JVMs, this is not entirely true. Our compression optimization experiences have mostly disproved the notion that migrating from a 32-bit to a 64-bit JVM causes performance degradation. Consider, for instance, servicing 1TB in 250 JVMs versus 1000 JVMs. Ask the vendor how much you save by not having to run 750 JVMs (because you went from a 1GB JVM heap to a 4GB JVM heap). The cost savings would include some of the 750 GC cycles that you no longer use in addition to the underlying CPU cores that you free up. You also save because you do not have to pay for additional licenses.

The latter chapters in this book delve into various sizes of JVMs and when you would use one versus the other.

Why Should I Bother with Virtualization? What Are Some Key Benefits?

Perhaps 5 years ago, we still had some customers asking the "why virtualize" question. In recent years, though, the benefits of virtualization have become widely understood as virtualization has pretty much become the standard. This standard is based on VMware virtualization technology, mostly because of it robustness and its fifth-generation maturity.

Virtualization offers the following key benefits:

- **Mature, proven, and comprehensive platform**: VMware vSphere (http://www.vmware.com/products/datacenter-virtualization/vsphere/overview.html) is fifth-generation virtualization (many years ahead of any alternative). It delivers higher reliability, more advanced capabilities, and greater performance than competing solutions.

- **High application availability:** High-availability infrastructure remains complex and expensive. But VMware integrates robust availability and fault tolerance right into the platform to protect virtualized applications. Should a node or server ever fail, all the VMs are automatically restarted on another machine.

- **Wizard-based guides for ease of installation:** VMware's wizard-based guides take the complexity out of setup and configuration. You can be up and running in one-third the deployment time of other solutions.

- **Simple, streamlined management:** VMware lets you administer both your virtual and physical environments from a "single pane of glass" console right on your web browser. Time-saving features such as auto-deploy, dynamic patching, and live VM migration reduce routine tasks from hours to minutes. Management becomes much faster and easier, boosting productivity without adding to your headcount.

- **Higher reliability and performance:** Our platform blends CPU and memory innovations with a compact, purpose-built hypervisor that eliminates the frequent patching, maintenance, and I/O bottlenecks of other platforms. The net result is best-in-class reliability and consistently higher performance (for heavy workloads, two-to-one and three-to-one performance advantages over our nearest competitors).

- **Superior security:** VMware's hypervisor is much thinner than any rival, consuming just 144MB compared with others' 3 to 10GB disk profile. Our small hypervisor footprint presents a tiny, well-guarded attack surface to external threats, for airtight security and much lower intrusion risk.

- **Greater savings:** VMware trumps other virtualization solutions by providing 50% to 70% higher VM density per host—elevating per-server utilization rates from 15% to as high as 80%. You can run many more applications on much less hardware than with other platforms, for significantly greater savings in capital and operating costs.

- **Affordability:** VMware is highest in capabilities, but not cost. Starting at $165 per server, the small business packages consolidate more of your applications on fewer servers, with greater performance—delivering the industry's lowest total cost of ownership (TCO).

To quickly determine and compare the cost of deploying VMware virtualization in your environment, use the VMware cost-per-application calculator at http://www.vmware.com/go/costperappcalc.

Fundamentally, because Java is independent of the operating system, it is the perfect candidate for virtualization because it does not have any hardware dependencies. Java also benefits from the many virtualization features such as high availability (HA) and VMotion (the ability to move VMs from one vSphere host to another without downtime). This type of agility that virtualization adds to a Java platform is fairly critical for Java platforms in general, but more specifically for large-scale Java. In large-scale Java, we often find thousands of JVMs that require constant administration and management (for instance, starting them, stopping them, and upgrading them without downtime). This type of administration activity cannot be feasibly accommodated at such a large scale without virtualization agility, such as VMotion and HA.

Enterprise Java application requirements for dynamic scalability, rapid provisioning, and HA represent a growing concern for development and operations groups today. Achieving these requirements with platforms that are completely based on conventional hardware is complex and expensive. Virtualization is a breakthrough technology that alleviates the pressures that common enterprise Java application requirements may impose on an organization. Features such as horizontal scalability, vertical scalability, rapid provisioning, enhanced HA, and business continuance are some of the key attributes available with the VMware vSphere suite. Chapter 1 examines three categories of large-scale Java platforms so that you can further appreciate the complexities of such systems.

Now that you understand that large-scale Java platforms require agility features of virtualization, and that Java operating system independence makes it a prime candidate for workload virtualization, let's take a closer look at this Java independence from the operating system and the hypervisor.

Should I Virtualize Java Platforms?

For those who don't have time to read this entire section, I can simply answer, "Yes, you should virtualize." After all, Java is independent of the underlying hypervisor, such as VMware's bare-metal hypervisor, and the operating system. For those who want to delve a little more into what this means, though, read on.

The main design tenets of Java are based on a cross-platform language that is operating system independent (as long as there is an operating-system-supported underlying runtime). We know this runtime as the JVM, which has become a permanent fixture of many enterprise application platforms. You could write a Java application and run it on various JVMs on different operating systems (without having to recompile). Of course, many VMware customers have one vendor-targeted JVM in production and so would not have to worry about moving a Java application from one JVM implementation to another. If they chose to do so, however, they could easily do it, primarily because of Java's cross-platform and operating system independence facilitated by a JVM.

So, you can reasonably conclude that the Java applications do not really care which JVM is being targeted for them to run on and are independent of the specific JVM implementation and operating system.

Of course, you might ask, "What about all the different internal behaviors of one JVM versus another?" At the end of the day, they all adhere to the JVM spec, and although some JVM options (-XX, flags, and so on) have different names, they more or less behave in a similar manner. The differences are not in the language, but in the way the Java process can be optimized with various JVM options passed at the Java command line.

Now fast forward to the infrastructure side of things. VMware ESXi is a bare-metal hypervisor that makes it possible to run multiple operating systems on a particular piece of hardware. Infrastructure administrators no longer have to worry about installing one kind of operating system for one piece of hardware versus another. VMware makes the operating system run independently of the underlying hardware (bare metal) and creates a degree of independence between the operating system and the bare metal/hardware.

Although the answer to whether Java is both OS and hypervisor independent is clearly yes, it is due to two degrees of independence. The first degree is that of Java's main tenet of cross-platform and OS independence, and the second degree is that of VMware ESXi hypervisor making the operating system independent of the hardware that it runs on. In fact, when a Java application runs on an operating system that is in an ESXi-based VM, ESXi has no notion of whether it is a Java workload running on the operating system, making the ESX hypervisor completely independent of the workload running on it. A further testament to this is that, because of this independence, no operating system changes are needed when you deploy a Java application on a VM.

Conversely, the JVM doesn't really know that it is running on a VM sitting on an ESXi hypervisor, and to the JVM, the VM appears like any other server with compute resources (CPUs, RAM, and so on) presented to it.

As long as the JVM you are using is supported on the operating system on which your applications are running, there is no need for additional concern about or dependency on support from the downstream VM and ESXi layers.

Figure I-1 illustrates all the layers discussed in this section.

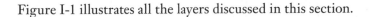

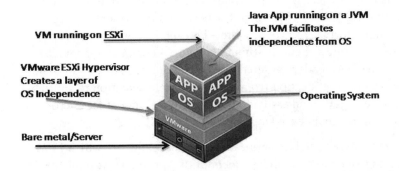

Figure I-1   Enterprise Java Application Running on a VM Virtualized by VMware ESXi

Who Should Read This Book?

This book is targeted at IT professionals who are in search of implementation guidelines for running enterprise Java applications on VMware vSphere in production and in QA/test environments.

The first three chapters are beneficial to CIOs, VPs, directors, and enterprise architects looking for key high-level business propositions for virtualizing enterprise Java applications. The remaining chapters are for developers and administrators looking for implementation details.

How to Use This Book

This book consists of seven chapters, an appendix, and a glossary:

- **Chapter 1, "Introduction to Large-Scale Java Platforms":** This chapter introduces various types of large-scale Java platforms and highlights the unique performance enhancements they require based on their scale.

- **Chapter 2, "Modern Scalable Data Platforms":** This chapter details how modern data platforms are structured.

- **Chapter 3, "Tuning Large-Scale Java Platforms":** This chapter highlights key considerations and provides guidelines to IT architects who are in the process of sizing their enterprise Java applications to run on VMware vSphere. This chapter explains how to obtain the best sizing configuration for your Java applications running on VMware vSphere. You are guided through the process of performance benchmarking on an application and given pointers on what to measure, what is available to be tuned, and how to best determine the optimal size for your Java application.

- **Chapter 4, "Designing and Sizing Large-Scale Java Platforms":** This chapter walks the reader through various approaches in sizing modern virtual Java platforms. It takes the reader through actual methodology of vertical and horizontal scalability as it applies to large-scale Java platforms, while also showing actual sizing examples that can be leveraged on production systems.

- **Chapter 5, "Performance Studies":** This chapter summarizes some of the key highlights from published performance papers.

- **Chapter 6, "Best Practices":** This chapter provides information about best practices for deploying large-scale Java applications on VMware, including key best-practice considerations for architecture, performance, designing and sizing, and high availability. This information is intended to help IT architects successfully deploy and run Java environments on VMware vSphere.

- **Chapter 7, "Monitoring and Troubleshooting Primer":** This chapter summarizes what to do when you hit a bottleneck or a performance issue while virtualizing Java. It provides a helpful summary for your use out in the field.

- **Appendix, "FAQs":** This appendix is a collection of many questions from VMware customers that the author has encountered over the years. It is always helpful to quickly ramp up on any technology by reading FAQs.

- **Glossary**

About the Author

Emad Benjamin has been in the IT industry for the past 20 years. He graduated with a Bachelor of Electrical Engineering degree from the University of Wollongong. Early in his career, he was a C++ software engineer. Then, in 1997, he took on his first major project using Java and has focused on Java ever since. For the past 8 years, his main concentration has been Java on VMware vSphere. Emad is a featured speaker at VMworld, Spring-One, UberConf, NFJS, and various other Java user groups around the world. Currently, Emad is a principal architect in the Global Center of Excellence focused on VMware virtualization, providing training and evangelism to various corners of the world.

About the Technical Reviewer

Michael Webster is a VMware Certified Design Expert (VCDX-066) on vSphere 4 and 5, vExpert 2012–2013, and the owner of IT Solutions 2000 Ltd., which delivers project management, ITIL-based VMware operational readiness, and technical architecture consulting services to enterprise and service provider clients around the world. He has been using VMware products since 1998 and has been designing and deploying VMware solutions since 2002. He specializes in the design and implementation of virtualization solutions for Unix to Linux migrations, business-critical applications, disaster avoidance, mergers and acquisitions, and public and private cloud. Michael has been in the IT industry since 1995 and consulting since 2001. As of February 2012, IT Solutions 2000 Ltd. was granted the VMware Virtualizing Business Critical Applications (VBCA) Competency, making it one of the first companies in the world to achieve this accreditation. IT Solutions 2000 Ltd. is one of very few companies worldwide accredited to deliver projects for all the business-critical applications covered by the VBCA program: SAP, Oracle, MS SQL Server, MS Sharepoint, and MS Exchange. Michael is regularly called on to consult and speak on all aspects of virtualizing business-critical applications at events and for organizations all across the globe. Longwhiteclouds.com was recently voted one of the top 25 virtualization blogs in the world as listed on vSphere-Land.com.

Acknowledgments

I first want to thank my wife, Christine, and our boys, Anthony and Adrian, for their understanding about not spending enough time with them while I was writing this book. Christine, you have been my pillar of strength, always understanding and accommodating.

I also want to thank my parents for sacrificing so much of their life to help me pursue my education and career, and to thank my brothers and sisters for their encouragement. I also want to thank Christine's family for their love and support.

I want to also thank my dear friend, His Grace Mar Awa Royel, Bishop of the Assyrian Church of the East, for his blessings.

I want to extend special thanks to Matt Stepanski, VP of GTS and Steve Beck, Sr. Director of GCOE, for their continuous support and encouragement with the publication of this book.

I want to extend sincere gratitude for Michael Webster's efforts in thoroughly reviewing the book. I greatly appreciate his enthusiasm and ability to promptly review the book, pointing out some key changes.

I would also like to thank my colleagues at VMware who helped make this book a reality: Lyndon Adams, Mark Achtemichuk, John Arrasjid, Scott Bajtos, Stephen Beck, Channing Benson, Jeff Buell, Dino Cicciarelli, Blake Connell, Ben Corrie, Melissa Cotton, Bhavesh Davda, Scott Deeg, Carl Eschenbach, Duncan Epping, Jonathan Fullam, Alex Fontana, Filip Hanik, Bob Goldsand, Jason Karnes, Jeremy Kuhnash, Ross Knippel, Gideon Low, Catherine Johnson, Mark Johnson, Kannan Mani, Sudhir Menon, Justin Murray, Vas Mitra, Avinash Nayak, Mahesh Rajani, Jags Ramnarayan, Raj Ramanujam, Harold Rosenberg, Dan Smoot, Randy Snyder, Lise Storc, Matt Stepanski, Mike Stolz, Guillermo Tantachuco, Don Sullivan, Abdul Wajid, Sumedh Wale, Yvonne Wassenaar, Michael Webster, Mark Wencek, James Williams, and Matthew Wood.

We Want to Hear from You!

As the reader of this book, *you* are our most important critic and commentator. We value your opinion and want to know what we're doing right, what we could do better, what areas you'd like to see us publish in, and any other words of wisdom you're willing to pass our way.

We welcome your comments. You can email or write us directly to let us know what you did or didn't like about this book—as well as what we can do to make our books better.

Please note that we cannot help you with technical problems related to the topic of this book.

When you write, please be sure to include this book's title and author as well as your name, email address, and phone number. We will carefully review your comments and share them with the author and editors who worked on the book.

Email: VMwarePress@vmware.com

Mail: VMware Press
          ATTN: Reader Feedback
          800 East 96th Street
          Indianapolis, IN 46240 USA

Reader Services

Visit our website at www.informit.com/title/9780133491203 and register this book for convenient access to any updates, downloads, or errata that might be available for this book.

Chapter 1

Introduction to Large-Scale Java Platforms

This chapter defines three categories of large-scale Java platforms:

- **Category 1:** Large number of Java Virtual Machines (JVMs) (100s–1000s of JVMs)
- **Category 2:** Smaller number of JVMs with large heap sizes
- **Category 3:** A combination of category 1 consuming data from category 2

In addition, the chapter discusses various trends and outlines technical considerations to help you understand the range of technical issues associated with designing large-scale Java platforms.

Large-Scale Java Platform Categories

Based on field interactions with customers, large-scale Java platforms typically fall into three main categories, as follows:

- **Category 1:** This category is distinguished by its large number of Java Virtual Machines (JVMs). In this category, hundreds to thousands of JVMs are deployed on the Java platform, and these are typically JVMs that function within a system that might be servicing millions of users. I have seen some customers with as many as 15,000 JVMs. Whenever you are dealing with thousands of JVM instances, you must consider the manageability cost and whether opportunities exist to consolidate the JVM instances.

- **Category 2:** This category is distinguished by a smaller number of JVMs (usually 1 to 20) but with large heap size (8GB to 256GB or higher). These JVMs usually have in-memory databases deployed on them. In this category, garbage collection (GC) tuning becomes critical, as discussed in later chapters.

- **Category 3**: The third category is a combination of the first two categories, where perhaps thousands of JVMs run enterprise applications that are consuming data from category 2 types of large JVMs in the back end.

With regard to virtualizing and tuning large-scale Java platforms, four key requirement trends hold true across these three categories:

- Compute-resource consolidation

- JVM consolidation

- Elasticity and flexibility

- Performance

Let's look at each one of these trends in more detail.

Large-Scale Java Platform Trends and Requirements

Compute resource consolidation, JVM instance consolidation, elasticity and flexibility, and performance are some of the major trends that exist within large-scale Java platform migration projects. The following subsections examine each of these in more detail.

Compute-Resource Consolidation

Many VMware customers find that their middleware deployments have proliferated and are becoming an administrative challenge with increasing costs. Customers, therefore, are looking to virtualization as a way of reducing the number of server instances. At the same time, customers are taking the consolidation opportunity to rationalize the number of middleware components needed to service a particular load. Middleware components most commonly run within a JVM with an observed scale of hundreds to thousands of JVM instances and provide many opportunities for JVM instance consolidation. Hence, middleware virtualization provides an opportunity to consolidate twice—once to consolidate server instances and then to consolidate JVM instances. This trend is widespread; after all, every IT shop on the planet is considering the cost savings of consolidation.

One customer in the hospitality sector went through the process of consolidating their server footprint and at the same time consolidated many smaller JVMs with a heap smaller than 1GB. They consolidated many of these smaller 1GB JVMs into two categories: those that were 4GB and others that were 6GB. They performed the consolidation in such a manner that the net total amount of RAM available to the application was equal to the original amount of RAM, but with fewer JVM instances. They did all of this while improving performance and maintaining good service level agreements (SLAs). They also reduced the cost of administration considerably by reducing the number of JVM instances they had to originally manage; this refined environment helped them easily maintain SLAs.

Another customer, in the insurance industry, achieved the same result, but was also able to overcommit CPU in development and QA environments to save on third-party software license costs.

JVM Instance Consolidation

Sometimes we come across customers that have a legitimate business requirement to maintain one JVM for an application and/or one JVM per a line of business. In these cases, you cannot really consolidate the JVM instances because doing so would cause intermixing of the lifecycle of one application from one line of business with another. However, although such customers do not benefit from eliminating additional JVM instances through JVM consolidation, they do benefit from more fully utilizing the available compute resources on the server hardware, resources that otherwise would have been underutilized in a nonvirtualized environment

Elasticity and Flexibility

It is increasingly common to find applications with seasonal demands. For example, many of our customers run various marketing campaigns that drive seasonal traffic toward their application. With VMware, you can handle this kind of traffic burst by automatically provisioning new virtual machines (VMs) and middleware components when needed; you can then automatically tear down these VMs when the load subsides.

The ability to change updating/patching hardware without causing outage is paramount for middleware that supports the cloud era scale and uptime. VMware VMotion enables you to move VMs around without needing to stop applications or the VM. This flexibility alone makes virtualization of middleware worthwhile when managing large-scale middleware deployments. One customer in the financial space, handling millions of transactions per day, used VMotion quite often, without any downtime, to schedule their hardware upgrades; a process that otherwise would be costly to their business because of the required scheduled downtime.

Performance

Customers often report improved middleware platform performance when virtualizing. Performance improvements are partly due to the updated hardware that customers will typically refresh during a virtualization project. Some performance improvement occurs, too, due to the robust VMware hypervisor. The VMware hypervisor has improved considerably in the past few years, and Chapter 5, "Performance Studies," discusses a few performance studies done to showcase some of the heavy workloads that were tested in a virtualized environment.

Large-Scale Java Platform Technical Considerations

When designing large-scale Java platforms, many technical considerations come into play. For example, a good understanding of Java garbage collection (GC) and of JVM architecture, hardware, and hypervisor architectures is essential to building good large-scale Java platforms. At a high level, GC, Non-Uniform Memory Architecture (NUMA), and theoretical versus practical memory limits are discussed. Later chapters provide a more detailed description, but it is imperative to start at a high-level understanding of the issues surrounding large-scale Java platform designs.

Theoretical and Practical Limits of Java Platforms

Figure 1-1 depicts the theoretical and practical sizing limits of Java workloads, critical limits to remember when sizing JVM workloads.

- It is important to highlight that the JVM theoretical limit is 16 exabytes; however, no practical system can provide this amount of memory. So, we capture this as the first theoretical limit.

- The second limit is the amount of memory a guest operating system can support; in most practical cases, this is several terabytes (TB) and depends on the operating system being used.

- The third limit is the ESXi5 1TB RAM per VM, which is ample for any workload that we have encountered with our customers.

- The fourth limit (really the first practical limit) is the amount of RAM that is cost-effective on typical ESX servers. We find that, on average, vSphere hosts have 128GB to 144GB, and at the top end 196GB to 256GB. Certainly from a feasibility standpoint, the hard limit is probably around 256GB. There are, of course, larger RAM-based vSphere hosts, such as 384GB to 1TB; however, these are probably more suited for category 2 types of in-memory database workloads and more likely

suited for traditional relational database management systems (RDBM.
utilize such vast compute resources. The primary reason these systems
large vSphere hosts is because most (with some minor exceptions, such ....acie
RAC) traditional RDBMS do not scale out and mainly scale up. In the case of category 1 and category 2, a scale-out approach is available and so the potential selection of a more cost-effective vSphere host configuration is afforded. In category 1 types of Java workloads, you should consider vSphere hosts with a more reasonable RAM range of less than 128GB.

- The fifth limit is the total amount of RAM across the server and how this is divided into a number of NUMA nodes, where each processor socket will have one NUMA node worth of NUMA-local memory. The NUMA-local memory can be calculated as the total amount of RAM within the server divided by the number of processor sockets. We know that for optimal performance you should always size a VM within the NUMA node memory boundaries; no doubt, ESX has many NUMA optimizations that come into play, but it is always best to stay NUMA local.

If the ESX host, for example, has 256GB of RAM across two processor sockets (that is, it has two NUMA nodes with 128GB (256GB/2) of RAM across each NUMA node), this implies that when you are sizing a VM it should not exceed the 128GB limit for it to be NUMA local.

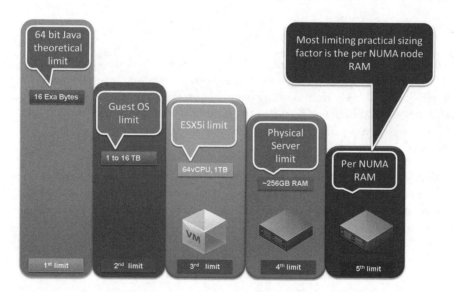

Figure 1-1 Theoretical and Practical Limits of Java Platforms

The limits outlined in Figure 1-1 and the list will help drive your design and sizing decision as to how practical and feasible it is to size large JVMs. However, other considerations come with sizing very large JVMs, such as GC tuning complexity and knowledge needed to maintain large JVMs. In fact, most JVMs within our customer base are in the vicinity of 4GB of RAM for the typical enterprise web application, or what has been referred to in this book as category 1 workloads. However, larger JVMs exist, and we have customers that run large-scale monitoring systems and large distributed data platforms (in-memory databases) on JVMs ranging from 4GB to 128GB. This is also true for in-memory databases such as vFabric GemFire and SQLFire, where individual JVM members within a cluster can be as big as 128GB and total cluster size can be 1 to 3TB. With such large JVMs comes the need to have a better knowledge of GC tuning. At VMware, we have helped many of our customers with their GC tuning activities over the years, even though GC tuning on physical is no different from on virtual. The reason being is that we have uniquely integrated the vFabric Java and vSphere expertise into one spectrum, which has helped our customers optimally run many Java workloads on vSphere. When faced with the decision of whether to vertically scale the size of the JVM and VM, always first consider a horizontal scale-out approach; we have found that our customers get better scalability with a horizontally scaled-out platform. If horizontal scalability is not feasible, consider increasing the size of the JVM memory and hence VM memory. When opting to increase the size of the JVM by increasing the heap space/memory, the next point of consideration is GC tuning and the in-house knowledge you have to handle large JVMs.

NOTE

With regard to the third limit, as of this writing, ESXi 5.1 is the GA released official version; however, by the time this book is published, some of these maximum vSphere limits might change. Double-check official VMware product documentation for the latest maximums. Note, as well, that at these VM limits no cost-effective hardware would need such a large number of vCPUs; however, it is still assuring for those who might need it.

As mentioned earlier in this chapter, in the enterprise today large-scale Java platforms fall into one of three categories. Figure 1-2 shows the various workload types and relative scale. A common trend is that as the size of the JVM increases so, too, does the required JVM GC tuning knowledge.

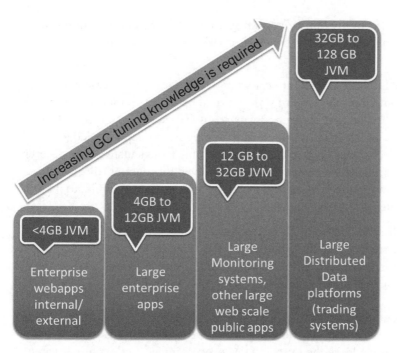

Figure 1-2 GC Tuning Knowledge Requirements Increase with Larger JVMs

It is important to keep the following in mind (from left to right in the figure):

- JVMs with a less than 4GB heap size are the most common among workloads today. The 4GB is a special case because it has the default advantage of using 32-bit address pointers within a 64-bit JVM space (and so has a very efficient memory footprint). These require some tuning, but not a substantial amount. This workload type falls into the realm of category 1 as defined earlier in this chapter. The default GC algorithm on server class machines is adequate. The only time you need to tune these is if the response time measurements do not suffice. In such cases, you want to follow the guidance on GC tuning in Chapter 3, "Tuning Large-Scale Java Platforms," and in Chapter 6, "Best Practices."

- The second workload case is still within category 1, but it is probably a serious user base internal to the organization. In this workload, we typically see heavily used (1,000 to 10,000 users) enterprise Java web applications. In these types of environments, GC tuning and slightly larger than 4GB JVMs are the norm. The DevOps team almost always has decent GC tuning knowledge and has configured the JVM away from the default GC throughput collector. Here we start to see the use of the concurrent mark and sweep (CMS) GC algorithms for these types of workloads to deliver decent response times to the user base. The CMS GC algorithm is offered by the Oracle JVM (formerly Sun JVM). For further details and information about other GC algorithms within the Oracle JVM or IBM JVM, see Chapter 3 and Chapter 6.

- The third workload type could fall into category 2, but it is a unique case within category 2 because sometimes the larger JVMs are used because the application cannot scale out horizontally. Generic category 2 workloads are usually in-memory databases, as mentioned earlier in the chapter. In this category, a deep knowledge of JVM GC tuning is required. Your DevOps team must be able to articulate all the different GC collectors and select those most suited for improved throughput (throughput collectors) (in contrast to latency-sensitive workloads that need CMS GC to deliver better response times).

- The fourth workload type falls into both category 2 and 3. Here there could be a large distributed system, where the client enterprise Java applications are consuming data from the back-end data fabric where a handful or more of in-memory database JVM nodes are running. Tuning GC at expert level is required here.

Other than having to maintain a very large JVM, you must know the workload choices. After all, customers often scale the JVM vertically because they believe it is an easy deployment and that it is best to just leave the existing JVM process intact. Let's consider some JVM deployment and usage scenarios (perhaps something in your current environment or something you have encountered at some point):

- A customer has one JVM process deployed initially. As demand for more applications to be deployed increases, the customer does not horizontally scale out by creating a second JVM and VM. Instead, the customer takes a vertical scale-up approach. As a consequence, the existing JVM is forced to vertically scale and carry many different types of workloads with varied requirements.

- Some workloads, such as a job scheduler, require high throughput, whereas a public-facing web application requires fast response time. So, stacking these types of applications on top of each other, within one JVM, complicates the GC cycle tuning opportunity. When tuning GC for higher throughput, it is usually at the cost of decreased response time, and vice versa.

- You can achieve both higher throughput and better response time with GC tuning, but it certainly extends the GC tuning activity unnecessarily. When faced with this deployment choice, it is always best to split out the types of Java workloads into their own JVMs. One approach is to run the job scheduler type of workload in its own JVM and VM (and do the same for the web-based Java application).

- In Figure 1-3, JVM-1 is deployed on a VM that has mixed application workload types, which complicates GC tuning and scalability when attempting to scale up this application mix in JVM-2. A better approach is to split the web application into JVM-3 and the job scheduler application into JVM-4 (that is, horizontally scaled out and with the flexibility to vertically scale if needed). If you compare the vertical scalability of JVM-3 and JVM-4 versus the vertical scalability of JVM-2 you will find JVM-3 and JVM-4 always scale better and are easier to tune.

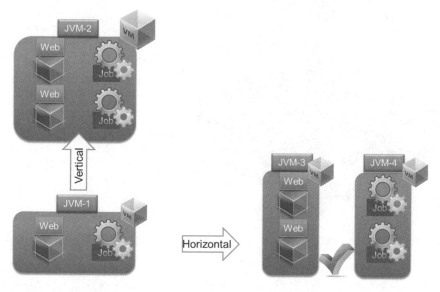

Figure 1-3   Avoiding Mixed Workload Types in the Same JVM

NUMA

Non-Uniform Memory Architecture (NUMA) is a computer memory design used in multiprocessors, where the memory access time depends on the memory location relative to a processor. Under NUMA, a processor can access its own local memory faster than nonlocal memory (that is, memory local to another processor or memory shared between processors).

Understanding NUMA boundaries is critical to sizing VM and JVMs. Ideally, the VM size should be confined to the NUMA boundaries. Figure 1-4 shows a vSphere host made of two sockets, and hence two NUMA nodes. The workload shown is that of two vFabric SQLFire VMs, each VM sized to fit within the NUMA node boundaries for memory and CPU. If a VM is sized to exceed the NUMA boundaries, it might possibly interleave with the other NUMA node to fulfill the request for additional memory that otherwise cannot be fulfilled by the local NUMA node. The figure depicts memory interleaving by the red arrows (dashed curved arrows show the interleaving), highlighting that this type of memory interleaving should be avoided because it may severely impact performance.

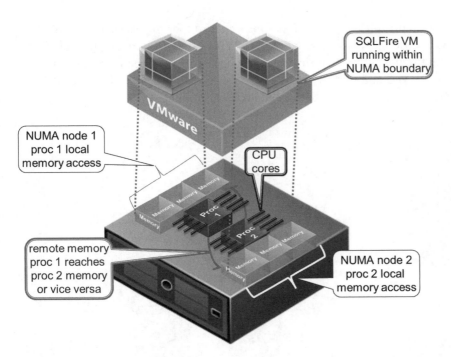

Figure 1-4   Two-Socket Eight-Core vSphere Host with Two NUMA Nodes and One VM on Each NUMA Node

To calculate the amount of RAM available in each NUMA node, apply the equation in Formula 1-1.

NUMA Local Memory = Total RAM on Server /Number of Sockets

Formula 1-1   Per-NUMA Node RAM Size (NUMA Local Memory)

For example, if a server has 128GB of RAM configured on it and has two sockets (as shown in Figure 1-4), this implies that the per-NUMA RAM is 128/2, which equals 64GB. This is not entirely true, however, because ESX overhead needs to be accounted for. So, a more accurate approximation results from the equation shown in Formula 1-2. The formula accounts for the ESXi memory overhead (1GB as a constant, regardless of the size of the server) and a 1% VM memory overhead as 1% of the available memory. The formula is a conservative approximation, and every VM and workload will vary slightly, but the approximation should be pretty close to the worst-case scenario.

> **NUMA Local Memory =**
>
> **[Total RAM on Host- {(Total RAM on Host* nVMs * 0.01)+1GB}] /Number of Sockets**

Formula 1-2   Per-NUMA Node RAM (NUMA Local Memory) with ESXi Overhead Adjustment

The following explains the different parts of the formula:

- **NUMA Local Memory:** The local NUMA memory for best memory throughput and locality, with VM and ESXi overhead already accounted for

- **Total RAM on Host:** The amount of physical RAM configured on the physical server

- **nVMs:** The number of VMs you plan to deploy on the vSphere host

- **1GB:** The overhead needed to run ESXi

- **Number of Sockets:** The number of sockets available on the physical server, 2 socket or 4 socket

---

NOTE

Formula 1-2 assumes the most pessimistic end of the overhead range, especially as you increase the number of VMs—clearly, as you add more VMs you will have more overhead. Despite a lower number of VMs, the approximation of Formula 1-2 is pretty fair and accurate. Also, this assumes a non-overcommitted memory situation. This formula is beneficial for sizing large VMs, which is when NUMA considerations are most pertinent. When sizing large VMs, typically you are trying to maintain fewer than a handful of configured VMs, so this overhead formula accurately applies. In fact, the most optimal configuration for larger VMs that have memory-bound workloads is one VM per NUMA node. If you try to apply this formula to a deployment that has more than six VMs configured, say 10 VMs, the formula can overestimate the amount of overhead needed. More accurately, you can use the 6% rule, which maintains that regardless of the number of VMs, always assume that 6% of memory overhead is ample, whether you have 10 VMs or 20.

If you don't have time to crunch through the formula and want to quickly start configuring, assume about 6% of overhead due to memory. There are many times when not all of this is being used. For example:

Example 1—Using 6% approximation approach: This would imply that if you have a server which has 128GB of physical RAM (two socket hosts, eight cores on each socket) and you choose the 6% overhead approach while configuring two VMs on the host, the total NUMA local memory would be => ((128 * 0.94) – 1) / 2 => 59.7GB per VM available for memory. Because there are two VMs, the total memory offered to the two VMs is approximately 59.7 * 2 => 119.32GB.

You also can apply the approach in Formula 1-2 as shown in Example 2 that follows:

Example 2—Using Formula 1-2 to calculate NUMA local available memory: Again, assuming a 128GB host with two sockets (eight cores on each socket) and two VMs to be configured on it, NUMA local memory = (128 – (128 * 2 * 0.01) - 1) / 2 => 124.44GB. Note that this is for two VMs. If you decide instead to configure 16 VMs of 1vCPU (1vCPU = 1 core), then the NUMA local memory per VM would be NUMA local memory = (128 – (128 * 16 * 0.01) - 1) / 2 => 53.26GB. This probably is overly conservative, and a more accurate representation would be around the 6% overhead calculation approach.

For best guidance, the best approximation of overhead is the 6% of total physical RAM (plus 1GB for ESXi) approach shown in Example 1.

In the preceding example, showing a calculation based on a server having 128GB of RAM, the true local memory would be ((128 * 0.99) – 1GB)/2 => 62.86GB, which is the maximum VM size that can be configured. In this case, you can safely configure two VMs of 62.68GB of RAM and eight vCPUs each, because each of the VMs would be deployed on one NUMA node. Alternatively, you can deploy four VMs if you want to deploy smaller VMs of 62.86GB / 2 => 31.43GB of RAM and four vCPUs each, and the NUMA scheduling algorithm would still localize the VMs to the local NUMA node.

> **NOTE**
>
> On hyperthreaded systems, VMs with a number of vCPUs greater than the number of physical cores in a NUMA node but lower than the number of logical processors (logical processors are usually shown as 2.x of physical cores, but more practically, logical processors are 1.25x of physical cores) in each physical NUMA node might benefit from using logical processors with local memory instead of full cores with remote memory. You can configure this behavior for a specific VM with the numa.vcpu.preferHT flag. For further details, see http://www.vmware.com/pdf/Perf_Best_Practices_vSphere5.1.pdf and the KB article kb.vmware.com/kb/2003582.
>
> It is always advisable to start with vCPUs equal to the number of physical cores and then adjust vCPUs upward when needed, but less than approximately 1.25x of available physical cores.

To further elaborate on the ESXi NUMA scheduling algorithm, Figure 1-5 shows an example of two sockets and six cores on each socket of the server.

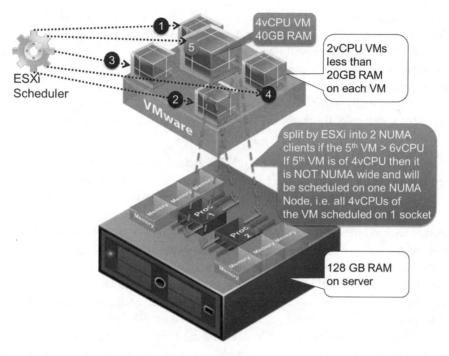

Figure 1-5   ESXi NUMA Scheduling on a Two-Socket Six-Core Server

In this figure, there are initially four VMs of two vCPUs and approximately 20GB RAM on each. The initial ESXi scheduling algorithm will follow a round-robin fashion. First, step 1 occurs (as shown by the black circle with the number 1), and then the next two vCPU VMs are scheduled on the next available empty NUMA node, and then so on (steps 3 and 4) for scheduling the third and fourth VMs. At the point where all four of the 2vCPU 20GB VMs have been scheduled, and as a result of this scheduling, the four VMs will occupy the four cores on each of the sockets, as shown by red pins in this figure (red pins are the pins the four 2 vCPU VMs were initially scheduled ESXi). Moments later, a fifth VM made of four vCPUs and 40GB RAM is deployed, and now ESXi attempts to schedule this VM across one NUMA node. This is because the VM is 4vCPU and is not considered a NUMA-wide VM, so all four of its vCPUs will be scheduled on one NUMA node, even though only two vCPUs are available. What will likely happen in terms of the NUMA balancing awareness algorithm is that the ESXi scheduler will eventually force one of the two vCPU VMs to migrate to the other NUMA node in favor of trying to fit the fifth 4vCPU VM into one NUMA node. The ESXi scheduler behaves like this because it uses a concept of NUMA client and schedules VMs per NUMA client, where the default size of the NUMA client is the size of the physical NUMA node. In this case, the default is 6, so any VM that is 6vCPU and less will be scheduled on one NUMA node because it fits into one NUMA client. If you want to change this behavior, you would have to force the NUMA client calculation to something more granular. The NUMA client calculation is controlled by *numa.vcpu.maxPerClient*, which can be set as Advanced Host Attributes -> Advanced Virtual NUMA Attributes, and if you were to change this to 2, then effectively every socket in our example will have three NUMA clients, so each 2vCPU VM will be scheduled into one NUMA client, and the fifth 4vCPU VM will be scheduled across two NUMA clients, and potentially across two sockets if need be. You seldom need get to this level of tuning, but this example illustrates the power of the NUMA algorithm within vSphere, which far exceeds any nonvirtualized Java platforms.

In general, when a virtual machine is powered on, ESXi assigns it a home node as part of its initial placement algorithm. A virtual machine runs only on processors within its home node, and its newly allocated memory comes from the home node as well. Unless a virtual machine's home node changes, it uses only local memory, avoiding the performance penalties associated with remote memory accesses to other NUMA nodes. When a virtual machine is powered on, it is assigned an initial home node so that the overall CPU and memory load among NUMA nodes remains balanced. Because internode latencies in a large NUMA system can vary greatly, ESXi determines these internode latencies at boot time and uses the information when initially placing virtual machines that are wider than a single NUMA node. These wide virtual machines are placed on NUMA nodes that are close to each other for lowest memory access latencies. Initial placement-only approaches are usually sufficient for systems that run only a single workload, such as a benchmarking configuration that remains unchanged as long as the system is running. However, this approach cannot guarantee good performance and fairness for a datacenter-class system that supports changing workloads. Therefore, in addition to initial placement, ESXi 5.0 does dynamic migration of virtual CPUs and memory between NUMA nodes for improving CPU balance and increasing memory locality. ESXi combines the traditional initial placement approach with a dynamic rebalancing algorithm. Periodically (every two seconds by default), the system examines the loads of the various nodes and determines whether it should rebalance the load by moving a virtual machine from one node to another.

This calculation takes into account the resource settings for virtual machines and resource pools to improve performance without violating fairness or resource entitlements. The rebalancer selects an appropriate virtual machine and changes its home node to the least loaded node. When it can, the rebalancer moves a virtual machine that already has some memory on the destination node. From that point on, the virtual machine allocates memory on its new home node and runs only on processors in the new home node. Rebalancing is an effective solution to maintain fairness and ensure that all nodes are fully used. The rebalancer might need to move a virtual machine to a node on which it has allocated little or no memory. In this case, the virtual machine incurs a performance penalty associated with a large number of remote memory accesses. ESXi can eliminate this penalty by transparently migrating memory from the virtual machine's original node to its new home node.

NOTE

In vSphere 4.1/ESXi 4.1, the underlying physical NUMA architecture is not exposed by the hypervisor to the operating system, and therefore application workloads running on such VMs cannot take specific advantage of additional NUMA hooks that they may provide. However, in vSphere5, the concept of vNUMA was introduced, where through configuration you can expose the underlying NUMA architecture to the operating system, and so NUMA-aware applications can take advantage of it. In Java, the -XX:+UseNUMA JVM option is available; however, it is compatible only with the throughput GC and not the CMS GC. Paradoxically, in most memory-intensive cases where NUMA is a huge factor, latency sensitivity is a big consideration, and therefore the CMS collector is more suitable. This implies that you cannot use CMS and the -XX:+UseNUMA option together. The good news is that vSphere NUMA algorithms are usually good enough to provide locality, especially if you have followed good NUMA sizing best practices—such as sizing VMs to fit within NUMA boundaries for memory and vCPU perspective.

Most Common JVM Size Found in Production Environments

Having discussed thus far the various JVM sizes that you can deploy (in some cases, very large JVMs), it is important to keep in mind that the most common JVMs found in data centers are of 4GB heap size. This may be a fairly busy JVM with 100 to 250 concurrent threads (actual thread count will vary because it depends on the nature of the workload), 4GB of heap, approximately 4.5GB for the JVM process, 0.5GB for the guest operating system, and so a total recommended memory reservation for the VM of 5GB with two vCPUs and one JVM process, as shown in Figure 1-6.

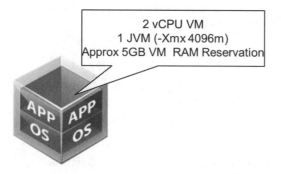

Figure 1-6   Most Common JVM Size Found in Production Environments

Horizontal Scaling Versus Vertical Scaling of JVMs and VMs

When considering horizontal scaling versus vertical scaling, you have three options, as Figure 1-7 shows.

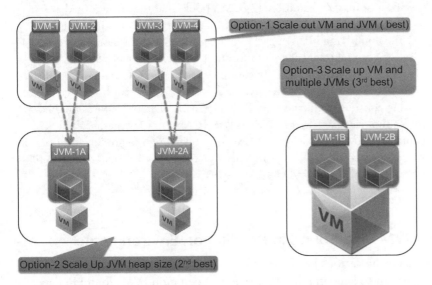

Figure 1-7   Horizontal Versus Vertical JVM Scalability Choices

The sections that follow detail the pros and cons of these three options.

Option 1

With Option 1, JVMs are introduced into the Java platform by creating a new VM and deploying a new JVM on it (hence, a scale-out VM and JVM model).

Option 1 Pros

This option provides the best scalability because the VM and the JVM are scheduled out as one unit by the ESXi scheduler. It is really the VM that is scheduled by the ESXi, but because there is only one JVM on this VM, the net effect is that the VM and the JVM are scheduled as one unit.

This option also offers the best flexibility to shut down any VM and JVM in isolation without impacting the rest of the Java platform. This is no doubt in relative terms, however, because most Java platforms are horizontally scalable, and in most cases there are enough instances to service traffic, even though JVM instances are being shut down. The relative comparison in terms of more instances having better scalability is based on having 100 JVMs and VMs versus having 150 JVMs and VMs for the exact same system, if for a specific instance you where comparing and contrasting platform design and were trying to choose between 100 JVM systems versus 150 JVMs, with both cases of 100 and 150 JVMs having the same net RAM. Clearly, the system with 150 JVMs will have the better flexibility and scalability. In the 150 JVM scenario, because you have more JVMs, it is likely that the size of the JVM is smaller compared to a system that has 100 JVMs. In this case, if a JVM from the 150 JVM platform encounters a problem, likely the impact is smaller because the JVM holds less data than in the 100 JVM scenario. So, the scale-out robustness of the 150 JVMs will prove to be more prudent.

If the system has been refined, the horizontal scalability advantages assumed previously apply. *Refined* here means that VM and JVM best practices have been applied based on a 64-bit JVM architecture having a reasonable-size JVM with an approximate minimum of 4GB heap space, and not fragmented around a legacy 32-bit JVM limit of 1GB heap space. (Some legacy 32-bit JVMs could withstand greater than 1GB, but for practical use, 32-bit JVMs have a legacy 1GB limit.)

Option 1 Cons

This option is expensive because it leads to having more operating system copies, and licensing becomes expensive quite quickly. Administering such a system is more expensive because there are more VMs and JVMs to keep track of.

No technical reason requires you to place one JVM on one VM. The only exception is in the case of systems that are in-memory databases (like category 2) that require high throughput memory from the local NUMA node. In those cases, the VMs are sized to fit within the NUMA node and will have only one JVM on them. Also note that the JVMs in in-memory databases tend to be quite large, sometimes as big as 128GB, as opposed to category 1 JVM sizes (typically 1 to 4GB heap size). In cases such as option 1, however, which are essentially in category 1 (as defined earlier in this chapter), you have many opportunities to consolidate the JVMs and eliminate wasteful JVMs and VM instances.

This is a common pattern among legacy 32-bit JVMs, where the 1GB limit of the 32-bit JVM would have forced Java platform engineers to install more JVM instances to deal with increases in traffic. The downside here is that you are paying for additional CPU/licenses. If you consolidate JVMs by migrating to 64-bit JVMs and increasing the heap at the same time, you will save by having fewer JVMs servicing the same amount of traffic. Of course, the JVM size will likely increase from, for example, 1GB to 4GB.

Option 2

Option 2 involves scaling up the JVM heap size by consolidating fragmented smaller JVMs and also as a result consolidate VMs.

Option 2 Pros

The pros for using Option 2 are as follows:

- Reduced administration cost due to the lower number of JVMs and VMs

- Reduced licensing cost due to fewer operating system copies

- Improved response times as more transactions are (most likely) now executed within the same heap spaces, as opposed to requiring marshaling across the network to other JVMs

- Reduced hardware cost

NOTE

If you look at option 2 in Figure 1-7, it shows that two JVMs (JVM-1A and JVM-2A) were consolidated from the four JVMs (JVM-1, 2, 3, and 4) of option 1. In this process, the four VMs were also consolidated into two VMs, as shown in the figure. For example, if JVM-1, 2, 3, and 4 were all of 2GB heap size, each running on VMs of 2vCPU, this implies the total RAM serviced to the heap, and in turn to the application, is 8GB across all the JVMs. The total vCPUs across all the VMs is eight vCPUs. Now when consolidating down to two VMs and two JVMs, the JVMs in option 2 (JVM-1A and JVM-2A) are each of 4GB heap, for a total of 8GB, and the VMs are two vCPUs each. This implies a total of four vCPUs across both VMs, a savings of four vCPUs, because originally in option 1 there were four VMs of two vCPUs each.

It is possible to scale down vCPUs while still maintaining an equal amount of RAM (Java heap space) because with larger JVM heap spaces, GC can scale vertically fairly well without having to excessively consume CPU. This is largely workload behavior dependent, and some workloads may indeed exhibit increased CPU usage when JVMs are scaled up. However, most category 1 workloads have exhibited a behavior of releasing the unneeded vCPU when consolidated into a larger JVM heap. 64-bit JVMs are highly capable runtime containers, and although there is an initial cost of launching one, they do enable you to crunch through a massive number of transactions that are within much larger heap spaces. When you are thinking about creating a new JVM, you want to ask the same questions as if you were about to create a new VM. If someone needs a new VM, a vSphere administrator always asks why it is needed. Because the JVM is a highly capable machine (just as the VM is a highly capable compute resource), vSphere administrators and DevOps engineers should always scrutinize whether the creation of a new JVM is necessary (as opposed to leveraging existing JVM instances and perhaps increasing the heap space, within reason, to facilitate more traffic).

Option 2 Cons

The cons for using Option 2 are as follows:

- Because of the larger-size JVMs, you risk losing more data (when compared with the case of smaller JVMs in option 1) if a JVM crashes without proper redundancy or persistence of transactions in place.

- Due to consolidation, you might have fewer high-availability (HA) JVM instances.

- Consolidation is limited to line of business. You do not want to mix applications from different lines of business into the same JVM; a crash of the JVM would impact both lines of business if you were to mix two into one JVM.

- Larger JVMs may require some more GC tuning.

Option 3

If option 1 and option 2 are not possible, consider option 3. In this case, you are placing multiple JVMs on a larger VM. Now JVM-1B and JVM-2B could be JVMs that are consolidated copies, like the ones in option 2, or nonconsolidated copies like in option 1. In either case, you can stack these JVMs on a larger VM, or multiple large VMs for that matter.

Option 3 Pros

The pros for using Option 3 are as follows:

- If the current platform is similar to that in option 1, it might be an advantage, because of logistical reasons, to keep the current number of JVMs intact in the deployment, but then consider building larger VMs with multiple JVMs stacked on them.

- Reduced number of operating system licenses.

- Reduced number of VM instances.

- Reduced administration cost due to having fewer VMs.

- You can have dedicated JVMs for each line of business but can also deploy JVMs from multiple lines of business on the same VM. You should do this only if the cost of VM consolidation outweighs the danger of having multiple lines of business impacted during a VM crash.

- Large VMs makes it possible to have more vCPUs for JVMs. If a VM has two large JVMs on it from different lines of business, for example, and they peak at different times, it is likely that all the vCPUs are available to the busy JVM, and then similarly for the next JVM when its peak arrives.

Option 3 Cons

Larger VMs will most likely be required. Scheduling larger VMs may require more tuning than smaller VMs.

> **NOTE**
>
> Various performance studies have shown that the sweet-spot VM size is two vCPUs to four vCPUs for category 1 workloads. Category 2 workloads require more than four vCPUs; at a minimum, four vCPUs may be needed. Remember, though, that scheduling opportunity from an HA perspective may be diminished. However, category 2 workloads, as in-memory databases, are mostly fault tolerant, redundant, and disk persistent, and therefore might not rely as much on VMware HA or automatic Distributed Resource Scheduler (DRS).

Because this option is about trying to consolidate VMs, it is highly likely that JVMs from different lines of business may be deployed on the same VM. You must manage this correctly because inadvertent restart of a VM may potentially impact multiple lines of business.

You can attempt to consolidate JVMs in this case and also stack them up on the same VM; however, this forces the JVMs to be much larger to fully utilize the underlying memory. If you configure fewer larger VMs, it literally means that you have VMs with a lot more RAM from the underlying hardware, and to fully consume this you might need larger JVM heap spaces. Because of the larger-size JVMs, you risk losing more data if a JVM crashes without proper redundancy or persistence of transactions in place.

This option might require large vSphere hosts, and larger servers cost more.

Summary

This chapter introduced the concept of large-scale Java platforms and described how they generally fall into one of three categories:

- **Category 1**: Large number of JVMs
- **Category 2**: Smaller number of JVMs with large heap sizes
- **Category 3**: A combination of category 1 and 2

The chapter also examined the various theoretical and practical limits that exists within the JVM and outlined various workload types and commonly encountered JVM sizes. The chapter also discussed the NUMA and the various pros and cons of horizontal scalability, vertical scalability, JVM consolidation, and VM consolidation.

Chapter 2

Modern Scalable Data Platforms

Although you can modernize application architectures in various ways, the key trends are as follows:

- Modernizing application architectures around the flexibility offered by the Spring Framework
- Modernizing data

As for data modernization, many different approaches exist. This chapter focuses mainly on the increasing trending use of horizontally scalable in-memory databases to improve scalability and response times. VMware vFabric SQLFire is used here to illustrate the capabilities of an in-memory data management system that you can use to build a horizontally scalable but also disk-persistent data fabric.

> **NOTE**
>
> Discussing such workloads will also help Java platform engineers to hone their Java platform tuning abilities. These types of in-memory database workloads consist largely of category 2 workloads. Depending on which topology you choose, however, you might also have to deal with category 3 workloads. Understanding how to tune such systems will enable you to handle the hardest tuning tasks that you may encounter. Before delving into deep tuning, though, it is best to first understand the functionality of such types of workloads.

vFabric SQLFire is an in-memory distributed data management platform that can be spread across many virtual machines (VMs), Java Virtual Machines (JVMs), and vFabric SQLFire servers to manage application data. Using dynamic replication and partitioning, vFabric SQLFire offers the following features in the platform: data durability, trigger-based event notification, parallel execution, high throughput, low latency, high scalability, continuous availability, and WAN distribution.

Figure 2-1 shows vFabric SQLFire as the middle tier data layer that orchestrates data delivery to enterprise data-consuming applications. As demand from consuming applications increases, the middle tier data layer expands to appropriately meet seasonal workloads. Further, vFabric SQLFire is a full data management system capable of managing transactions and data consistency, and therefore enterprise data-consuming applications can rely on vFabric SQLFire as the system of record.

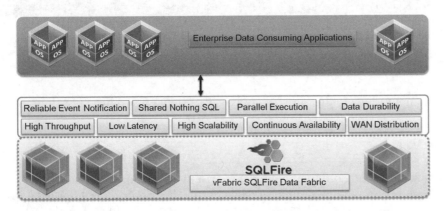

Figure 2-1 Enterprise Data Management with vFabric SQLFire

For additional persistence, data can be written behind to a backup store (such as a relational database) or other disk stores for archival purposes. vFabric SQLFire provides full persistence durability using its own native shared-nothing persistence mechanism. Figure 2-2 illustrates how vFabric SQLFire can write and read synchronously/asynchronously to external datastores.

vFabric SQLFire is based on the VMware vFabric GemFire distributed data management product and the Apache Derby project. As shown in Figure 2-3, the Apache Derby project is used for its relational database management system (RDBMS) components, Java Database Connectivity (JDBC) driver, query engine, and network server. The partitioning technology of GemFire is used to implement horizontal partitioning features of vFabric SQLFire.

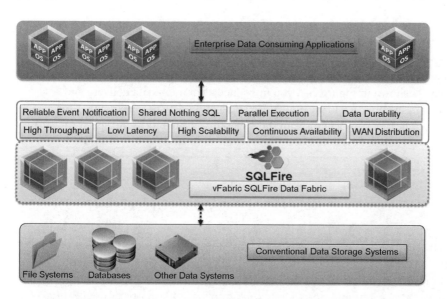

Figure 2-2 vFabric SQLFire Architecture with Capability to Write to Traditional Storage Systems

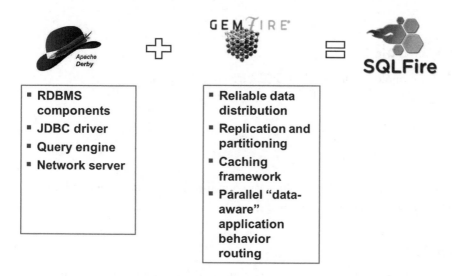

Figure 2-3 vFabric SQLFire Internal Architecture

vFabric SQLFire specifically enhances the Apache Derby components, such as the query engine, the SQL interface, data persistence, and data eviction; and it adds additional components like SQL commands, stored procedures, system tables, functions, persistence disk stores, listeners, and locators, to operate a highly distributed and fault-tolerant data management cluster.

Best Practice 1: Common Distributed Data Platform

When data delivery is required to be at the highest speed possible (in terms of milliseconds and microseconds), setting up vFabric SQLFire as an enterprise data fabric system is the correct approach. As shown in Figure 2-2, you introduce a common data delivery and consumption layer in memory for many enterprise application data requirements. This allows enterprise applications to benefit from the scalability, availability, and speed of execution features of vFabric SQLFire.

NOTE

Although vFabric SQLFire is a highly capable data platform for moving data at large transaction volumes (thousands of transactions per second), it has also been used for low-end volume (tens to hundreds of transactions per second) to achieve a rapid improvement on enterprise application response time and database resiliency. vFabric SQLFire compliance with SQL-92 makes the reconfiguration of custom enterprise applications to use vFabric SQLFire relatively noninvasive.

SQLFire Topologies

The three main setup topologies for vFabric SQLFire are as follows:

- Client/server
- Peer-to-peer
- Multisite

Each of these topologies can be used standalone or combined to form an extended full-featured distributed data management system.

Client/Server Topology

A client/server topology consists of two tiers: a *client tier* and a *server tier*, as shown in Figure 2-4.

The client tier communicates with the server tier to search for or update data objects from the server tier.

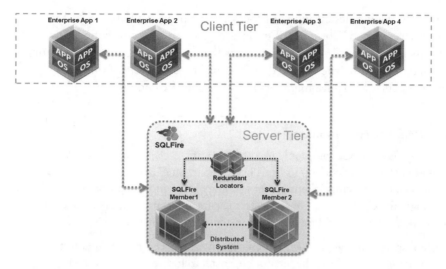

Figure 2-4   vFabric SQLFire Client/Server Topology

> **NOTE**
>
> The client/server topology is a category 3 type of workload, where hundreds to thousands of Java clients (enterprise applications running inside application servers) consume data from a vFabric SQLFire cluster made of a dozen or so SQLFire JVMs.

The server tier is made of many vFabric SQLFire members, each running its own JVM process that provides network distribution, in-memory, and disk-persisted data management functionality. Further, even though each vFabric SQLFire member runs within its own JVM process space, vFabric SQLFire members do have network connectivity with each other, and therefore form a single data management cluster that is presented to the client tier.

The clients are usually enterprise applications distributed within the organization and are outside the vFabric SQLFire cluster but need data access to and from the vFabric SQLFire cluster. The client uses a client driver that is a lightweight JDBC thin driver for Java applications, or ADO.NET for .NET applications. Thin clients do not host or persist cluster data, and they do not directly participate in distributed queries that execute in the cluster. Customers often have tens to hundreds of enterprise data-consuming applications accessing data managed within the vFabric SQLFire cluster, but the clients themselves are not part of the vFabric SQLFire cluster.

Clients use two or more fault-tolerant locator processes that provide vFabric SQLFire member location services. The vFabric SQLFire locator process tells new connecting peers and thin clients how to connect to existing peers that are already running. Locators perform both connection load balancing and dynamic load conditioning of thin client connections to available vFabric SQLFire members in a client/server deployment.

Best Practice 2: Client/Server Topology

Client/server topology is the most commonly used for enterprise-class applications. When tens to thousands of enterprise client applications need to consume data from the vFabric SQLFire data management system, a client/server topology is the most appropriate. In client/server topology, the clients have full access to the data and can manipulate the data without needing to be part of the vFabric SQLFire in-memory data management system.

In this topology, and specifically in production deployments, set `-mcast-port=0` to turn off multicast discovery and instead use the locator approach to locate vFabric SQLFire members.

Always make vFabric SQLFire locator processes highly available by having separate instances running on separate physical machines within the vFabric SQLFire system. Supply `-locators` on the command line with a comma-separated list of all possible locators.

Use client/server topology when any of the following are requirements of an enterprise-class application:

- **Dynamic server discovery:** The vFabric SQLFire server locator utility dynamically tracks server processes and directs clients to new servers, giving clients indirection from explicit cluster membership information. Clients need to know only how to connect to the locator services. They do not need to know where data servers are running or how many data servers are available at a given time.

- **Server load balancing:** The vFabric SQLFire server locator tracks current load information for all servers, directing new client connections to the servers with the least load. vFabric SQLFire provides a default load probe for your servers. To customize the algorithm by which server load is calculated, you can implement your own customized plug-in.

- **Server connection conditioning:** Client connections can be configured to be leased transparently and can potentially be moved to different servers, which allows overall server utilization to be rebalanced after new servers are started. This helps speed conditioning in situations such as adding servers or recovery from server crashes and other downtime.

Peer-to-Peer Topology

In the peer-to-peer topology, as shown in Figure 2-5, two or more intercommunicating vFabric SQLFire servers form a distributed system. The data is distributed according to the data table's configured redundancy rules.

NOTE

Peer-to-peer topology is a category 2 type of workload, with a dozen or so SQLFire JVMs communicating with each other.

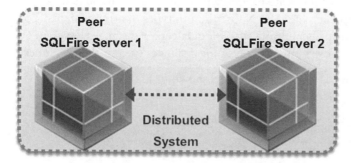

Figure 2-5   Peer-to-Peer GemFire Distributed System

Best Practice 3: Peer-to-Peer Multihomed Machines

- An intercommunicating set of vFabric SQLFire servers that do not have clients accessing them, or only a very few (for example, session-state data, web content, back office, or back-end type of processing providing a single-hop access pattern to data).

- Applications requiring a few peer clients (as opposed to hundreds in client/server topology) can be good candidates for peer-to-peer topology. Deploying many peers increases the buffering and socket overhead for every member.

- More convenient from an administration and management perspective. With an embedded cluster, there is no need to manage any external processes to deploy vFabric SQLFire peers. For example, if you embed vFabric SQLFire in a cluster of Java application servers, each application server and the associated vFabric SQLFire peer share the same process heap.

- If running on multihomed machines, you can specify a nondefault network adapter for communication. In nonmulticast peer-to-peer situations, communication uses the bind-address property. This address must map to the same subnet for all vFabric SQLFire servers within the distributed system.

Redundancy Zones

In vFabric SQLFire, you can set up various redundancy zones so that replicas (or redundant copies) are not placed on the same physical hardware. You can set the `redundancy-zone` boot property of each vFabric SQLFire member to a specific redundancy zone name. It is common practice for these redundancy-zone names to resemble those of the underlying physical hardware, so that no redundant vFabric SQLFire members are placed on the same physical hardware/server machine as their original partition member.

Global Multisite Topology

In vFabric SQLFire, you can set up a multisite topology that can span multiple data centers, for active-active, disaster recovery, and WAN distribution types of arrangements. You can set up a single data fabric that spans multiple sites for data center distances less than 60 miles, and use a vFabric SQLFire WAN gateway setup for distances greater than 60 miles.

A special case of multisite topology is global multisite, as shown in Figure 2-6.

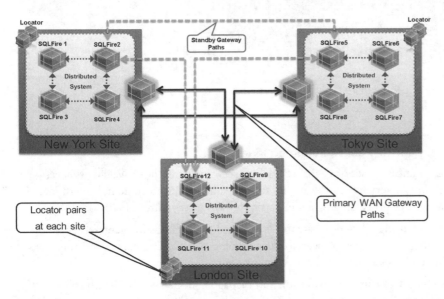

Figure 2-6   vFabric SQLFire Global Multisite Topology

There are three globally distributed (New York, Tokyo, and London) sites, each with a local distributed system. Within each site, a gateway is configured to provide data distribution between sites in case of a failure event, or for consistent global views of data around the world. Gateways work as fault-tolerant pairs. The primary member of each pairing handles data replication across to the other site. The primary is backed by a redundant standby gateway process that automatically becomes the primary gateway if the original primary gateway fails. As per regular client/server topology, each site has two or more locator processes that provide local site membership discovery services.

Best Practice 4: Multisite

- Each distributed system in a multisite configuration operates independently of other connected systems. Tables that are configured for replication between sites must be created using identical table names and column definitions. In addition, gateway senders and receivers must be configured to assign logical gateway connections to physical network connections in each system. For each table that is configured to use a gateway sender, data manipulation language (DML) events are automatically forwarded to the gateway sender for distribution to other sites. The events are placed in a gateway queue and distributed asynchronously to remote sites. Inserts/updates and deletes are sent across to the other sites, except when the delete is part of an expiration or eviction. However, queries, data definition language (DDL), transactions, and expirations are not distributed to the other remote sites.

- Each vFabric SQLFire distributed system that participates in WAN replication must use one or more locators for member discovery. WAN replication is not supported with multicast discovery.

- WAN deployments increase the messaging demands on a vFabric SQLFire system. To avoid connection starvation related to WAN messaging, always set `conserve-sockets=false` for vFabric SQLFire members that participate in a WAN deployment.

- WAN-enabled tables must be present in each distributed system that you want to connect.

- You can configure both partitioned tables and replicated tables to use a gateway sender. However, you must create replicated tables in the same server groups as the gateway senders that you specify in the `CREATE TABLE` statement.

- You must start the entire WAN system (that is, the global multisite system) before you populate tables with data, or you must populate the tables in a newly added site before enabling the WAN listener to accept WAN traffic. This is required so that the WAN sites can remain in sync from the very beginning. Failing to do this causes exceptions during data update operations.

- Normally you should use the conflation feature when using a gateway hub so that only the latest updates are passed over to the remote site. With conflation, earlier entry updates in the queue are dropped in favor of updates sent later in the queue. Enable conflation for optimal performance. You can set the `ENABLEBATCHCONFLATION` attribute to `true` within the definition of the listener. Only for applications that depend on seeing every update (for example, if any remote gateway has a table trigger or `AsyncEventListener` that needs to know about every state change) should you disable conflation.

- In a multisite installation using gateways, messages can back up in the gateway queues if the link between sites is not tuned for optimum throughput. If a receiving queue overflows because of inadequate buffer sizes, it can become out of sync with the sender, and the receiver is unaware of the condition. The gateway's `socket-buffer-size` attribute should match among intercommunicating gateways with the global multisite topology.

- Avoid overflowing to disk when possible by adjusting the `MAXQUEUEMEMORY` attribute to accommodate needed memory. This is the maximum amount of memory in megabytes (MB) that the queue can consume before overflowing to disk. The default is 100MB. If you are more concerned with reliability rather than high speed, an overflow to disk is recommended. Further tuning of `MAXQUEUEMEMORY` includes tuning `BATCHSIZE` and `BATCHINTERVAL` in concert until the appropriate service level agreement (SLA) is met, where `BATCHSIZE` is the maximum number of messages that a batch can contain (the default is 100 messages), and `BATCHINTERVAL` is the maximum number of milliseconds that can elapse between sending batches (the default is 1000 milliseconds).

SQLFire Features

This section covers critical SQLFire features that make it an in-memory-oriented and disk-persistent data management system. The SQLFire features include the following:

- **Server groups:** This enables you to logically group SQLFire members (JVMs) to give it a better scalability weight (that is, deploy more compute resource to a certain section of the SQLFire data fabric). A server group specifies the SQLFire members that will host data for a table. You use a server group to logically group SQLFire datastores for managing a table's data. Any number of SQLFire members that host data can participate in one or more server groups. You specify named server groups when you start a SQLFire datastore.

NOTE

The terms *data fabric* and *data cluster* are used interchangeably in this book.

- **Partitioning:** This is the capability to segment the data of a particular table into smaller manageable chunks within a distributed system (really just a mechanism to split the data across multiple JVMs). Traditional relational database administrators

(DBAs) would be familiar with this mechanism as applied on tables that get beyond a certain manageable and performing size, which would split out the tables into multiple tables and so on. In a similar manner, SQLFire uses a portioning mechanism to do similar splitting of the data, although instead of splitting it strictly across disk space as in an RDBMS, SQLFire splits across multiple SQLFire member JVMs (but, of course, with the ability to write to disk with additional persistence guarantees). You specify the partitioning strategy of a table in the PARTITION BY clause of the CREATE TABLE statement. The available strategies include hash partitioning on each row's primary key value, hash partitioning on column values other than the primary key, range partitioning, and list partitioning. SQLFire maps each row of a partitioned table to a logical *bucket*. The mapping of rows to buckets is based on the partitioning strategy that you specify. For example, with hash partitioning on the primary key, SQLFire determines the logical bucket by hashing the primary key of the table. Each bucket is assigned to one or more members, depending on the number of copies that you configure for the table. Configuring a partitioned table with one or more redundant copies of data ensures that partitioned data remains available even if a member is lost. When members are lost or removed, the buckets are reassigned to new members based on load. Losing a member in the cluster never results in reassigning rows to buckets. You can specify the total number of buckets to use with the BUCKETS clause of the CREATE TABLE statement. The default number of buckets is 113.

- **Redundancy:** This is the capability of nominating how many copies of the data you want SQLFire to manage for you. In production systems, a minimum of redundancy of one is usually expected. Redundancy is an in-memory additional copy of the partitioned data.

- **Colocation:** For example, if two tables are always joined to formulate a business query, colocation is used to have the primary and foreign key section of the data located within the same partition so that queries are executed within one SQLFire member JVM that contains all the data needed.

- **Disk persistence:** You can specify the data to be copied to the disk for additional resiliency.

- **Transactions:** Capability to control data consistency by optimistically locking data at in-memory commit time. This is one of the key features that makes SQLFire a database.

- **Cache plug-in:** Capability to execute custom business logic in the scenario that there is a cache-miss.

- **Listeners:** In vFabric SQLFire, you can implement any number of listeners that can be triggered based on certain SQL DML operations that an application executes.

- **Writers:** A vFabric SQLFire writer is an event handler that synchronously handles changes to a table before those changes take place. The main use of a cache writer is to perform input validation.

- **Asynchronous listeners:** An `AsyncEventListener` instance is serviced by its own dedicated thread in which a callback method is invoked. Events that correspond to DML operations are placed in an internal queue, and the dedicated thread dispatches a batch of events at a time to the user-implemented callback class.

- **DBSynchronizer:** `DBSynchronizer` is a built-in `AsyncEventListener` implementation that you can use to asynchronously persist data to a third-party JDBC 4.0-compliant RDBMS.

- **DDLUtils:** vFabric SQLFire provides a command-line interface and DDLUtils that can help you generate the target schema and data load files based on many supported RDBMS source schemas

Server Groups

A server group specifies the vFabric SQLFire members that host data for a table. You use a server group to logically group vFabric SQLFire datastores for managing a table's data. Any number of vFabric SQLFire members that host data can participate in one or more server groups. You specify named server groups when you start a vFabric SQLFire datastore. By default, all servers that host data are added to the *default* server group. Different logical database schemas are often managed in different server groups. For example, an order management system might manage all customers and their orders in an Orders schema deployed to one server group.

The same system might manage shipping and logistics data in a different server group. A single peer or server can participate in multiple server groups, typically as a way to colocate related data or to control the number of redundant copies in replicated tables. With support for dynamic group membership, the number of processes hosting data for a server group can change dynamically. However, this dynamic aspect of server group membership is abstracted away from the application developer, who can look at a server group as a single logical server.

Server groups determine only those peers and servers where a table's data is managed. Tables are always accessible for any peer member of the distributed system, and from thin clients that connect to a single server. When you invoke server-side procedures, you can parallelize the execution of the procedure on all members in the server group. These data-aware procedures also execute on any peer clients that belong to the server groups. Without associating tables to specific member IP addresses, the capacity of a server group can be dynamically increased or decreased without any impact to existing servers or client applications. vFabric SQLFire can automatically rebalance the tables in the server group to the newly added members. Figure 2-7 illustrates vFabric SQLFire server groups.

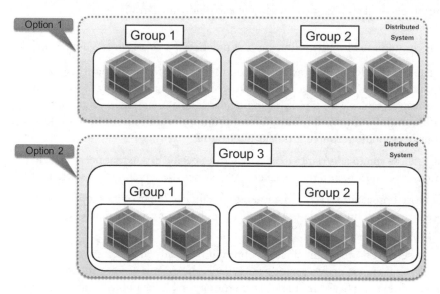

Figure 2-7   vFabric SQLFire Server Groups

Best Practice 5: Use Server Groups

■ You can assign your servers to logical groups that your clients can specify in their connection configurations. For example, if a subset of servers hosts the data for a particular table, you might use groups to ensure that clients interested only in access to that table connect only to those servers. Or you might use a group to direct all database-centric traffic to the subset of servers that are directly connected to a back-end database. Servers can belong to multiple groups. Clients specify only the group to use and are isolated from having to know which servers belong to which groups.

■ Option 1 in Figure 2-7 shows how a vFabric SQLFire data management system is divided into Group 1 and Group 2.

■ Option 2 in Figure 2-7 shows how a third group, Group 3, contains Group 1 and Group 2. A group such as Group 3 often allows for reference data to be shared across all members of the data fabric (all members within Group 1 and Group 2), and Group 1 and Group 2 have different data partitions. An example of this is to hold stock trade data within Group 1, pricing data within Group 2, and reference data in Group 3.

- Server groups are often aligned with various business functions (for example, risk management contained in one group and inventory management contained within another group). This allows you to service the various lines of business at various service qualities by being able to add and remove capacity to each individual group.

For example, it is common to have the following best practices for server group usage:

- Reference data can be allocated to reside in Group 1, because this is primarily replicated table data that does not change often and therefore might need only few compute resources. However, tables with rapidly changing data and a total size large enough to require partitioning (for example, trades, positions, and pricing data) can be managed by a more powerful compute resource group as in Group 2.
- Server groups allow you to add/remove capacity to the specific group that needs it. When adding capacity, you must issue a rebalance command once the servers are all started.
- For specific stored procedures, you can choose to parallelize the execution of server-side stored procedures on all the members of a server group or just on the members of a specific server group.
- Always specify server groups within a table definition to specify in which groups the table exists. If you do not specify a server group name, the default server group is used, which includes all vFabric SQLFire members in the system. This implies that tables are partitioned or replicated across all members of the default server group. If the data in a replicated table changes frequently, the cost of maintaining a copy on each server in the default group can be prohibitive. In this case, you should consider a smaller group that houses this kind of data on specific sets of members/hosts, encapsulated in a dedicated group. Replicated tables should be used only to satisfy many-to-many relationships among data elements. Partitioned tables also get replicated in a RAID-like fashion by setting the desired redundancy level.
- The convenience of the server group construct helps to set the heap percentage for eviction policy across a specific group, thus controlling resource consumption.
- You can also apply `AsynchEventListener` to a specific server group.

Partitioning

For custom enterprise applications backed by RDBMS schema tables that are highly accessible during the course of a regular business day, a partitioning strategy improves performance to more easily meet SLA requirements. These types of frequently accessed tables are often referred to as *hot tables* because of their high rate of data insert, update, delete, and read operations. In addition to the high rate of data change, it is common for these hot tables to become unmanageable within a single node because of their size. In such cases, you can use a vFabric SQLFire horizontal partitioning strategy to split the data volume into smaller, more manageable data partitions.

With vFabric SQLFire horizontal partitioning, an entire row is stored in the same hash indexed bucket. Buckets are the containers for data that determine its storage site, redundant sites, and the unit of migration for rebalancing. You can hash partition a table based on its primary key or on an internally generated unique row ID if the table has no primary key. Other partitioning strategies can be specified in the PARTITION BY clause in a CREATE TABLE statement. Strategies supported by vFabric SQLFire include hash partitioning on columns other than the primary key, range partitioning, and list partitioning.

Figure 2-8 shows an example Flights table partitioned by FLIGHT_ID (primary key for Flights table) into three buckets, where the first bucket for rows 1 to 3 resides on vFabric SQLFire Server 1, the second bucket for rows 4 to 6 resides on vFabric SQLFire Server 2, and the third bucket for rows 7 to 9 resides on vFabric SQLFire Server 3. vFabric SQLFire directs that all access to flights data by the FLIGHT_ID primary key for rows 1 to 3 are executed on vFabric SQLFire Server 1, and similarly for the other rows. vFabric SQLFire automatically manages all partitioning through this bucketing system as long as the designer has provided the correct PARTITION BY COLUMN(FLIGHT_ID) clause in the table definition.

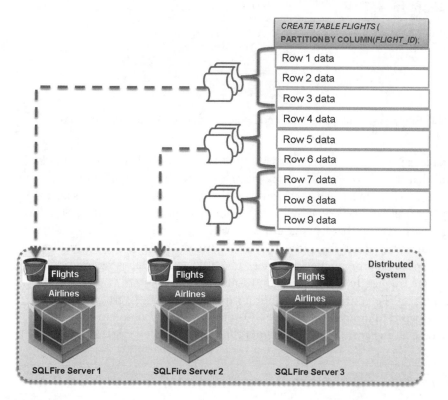

Figure 2-8 Partitioning the Flights Table Using the vFabric SQLFire Bucket System

In Figure 2-9, the preceding discussion is extended to look at a snapshot of an example flights schema. The schema shown is typical of the master-detail design pattern seen in most RDBMS schemas. Figure 2-9 shows a flights schema with FLIGHTS, FLIGHTAVAILABILITY, and AIRLINES tables. FLIGHTS and FLIGHTAVAILABILITY have a one-to-many relationship. AIRLINES, however, has a many-to-many relationship to FLIGHTS and FLIGHTAVAILABILITY.

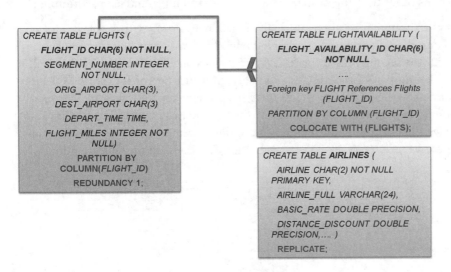

Figure 2-9   Flights Schema with Master-Detail and Lookup-Table Types of Relationships

The Flights table is partitioned by its primary key FLIGHT_ID and has a REDUNDANCY of 1. This means that there is one backup copy of each FLIGHT on a redundant vFabric SQLFire server somewhere in the cluster. However, the FLIGHTAVILABILITY is partitioned by FLIGHT_ID and COLOCATE with FLIGHTS, and that means that vFabric SQLFire manages the data partitions so that when there is a qualifying join between the FLIGHTS and FLIGHTAVILABILITY tables, the query executes within the same vFabric SQLFire member/memory space, optimizing performance. The AIRLINES table is reference data that does not change frequently and has a many-to-many relationship to FLIGHTS and FLIGHTAVAILABILITY. To configure this relationship in vFabric SQLFire, you can use the REPLICATE keyword to indicate to vFabric SQLFire to place a complete copy of the AIRLINES table on every vFabric SQLFire member in the distributed system.

Best Practice 6: Horizontal Partitioning

- Horizontal partitioning can greatly enhance scalability and performance of enterprise applications.

- Most commonly, `Partition By` is applied on the primary key of a table.

- vFabric SQLFire horizontal partitioning places an entire row in the same hash indexed bucket, and therefore all data operations against rows in the bucket are executed within the same memory space.

- Test your partitioning scheme often to confirm balance for all vFabric SQLFire members.

Redundancy

In vFabric SQLFire, you can specify how many redundant copies of specific data to keep. vFabric SQLFire manages the synchronization of all data changes across the primary copy and all backup copies. When a server fails, vFabric SQLFire automatically reroutes any operations that were trying to read or write from the failed member to the surviving members. In Figure 2-10, the redundancy clause is used as REDUNDANCY 1 to indicate to vFabric SQLFire that one redundant copy should be copied to another member somewhere in the cluster.

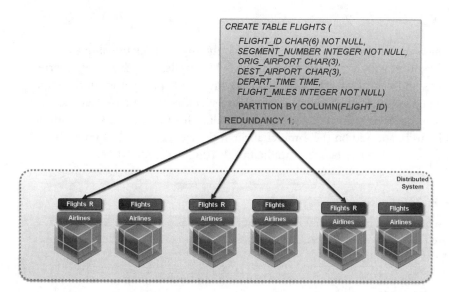

Figure 2-10 Using Redundancy on the `Flights` Table

Best Practice 7: Redundancy

- When you use the REDUNDANCY 1 specification in a vFabric SQLFire table definition, vFabric SQLFire manages a redundant copy of the data in memory. In the event
of a vFabric SQLFire member failure, vFabric SQLFire promotes the backup server to
primary and routes all accesses to that new primary, thus allowing for continuous fault-
tolerant operation of enterprise applications.

- Because vFabric SQLFire is a memory-oriented data management system, having a
certain level of redundancy is a recommended approach. However, the redundancy level
must be balanced against the advantages and disadvantages of increased redundancy.
Increased redundancy provides a more robust system at the cost of performance. Additional redundant copies cause increased network and memory usage because vFabric
SQLFire always keeps redundant copies in sync.

- In production systems, REDUNDANCY 1 is adequate, particularly when combined
with disk asynchronous PERSISTENCE. This combination of REDUNDANCY 1 and
asynchronous PERSISTENCE on disk allows for a good combination of performance,
scalability, and reliability for most production systems that rely heavily on vFabric
SQLFire as a data management system.

- Size your system so that if a failure occurs the remaining nodes have enough capacity to
take on new data and new clients' capacity.

Colocation

As shown previously in the schema in Figure 2-9, a parent-to-child relationship exists
between FLIGHTS and FLIGHTAVAILABILITY tables. This implies that SQL join queries
across the FLIGHTS and FLIGHTAVAILABILITY tables must be kept together in the same
memory space. The vFabric SQLFire COLOCATE clause specifies that the two tables are
colocated; that is, it forces partitions having the same values for the foreign key relationship in both tables to be located on the same vFabric SQLFire member. In Figure 2-11,
the COLOCATE WITH (FLIGHTS) clause is applied to FLIGHTAVAILABILITY.

Best Practice 8: Colocation

- Using the schema in Figure 2-9, if you have queries as per the following Select statement, where there is a join across FLIGHT and FLIGHTAVAILABILITY tables, use the
COLOCATE WITH clause:

```
Select * from Flights f, FlightAvailability fa where
f.flight_id = fa.flight_id
```

- The join condition must be on the `flight_id` because that was the partition by column of the `FLIGHTS` and `FLIGHTAVAILABILITY` tables. In this case, you would use `COLOCATE WITH (FLIGHTS)`, as shown in Figure 2-11.

- Tables referenced in the `COLOCATE WITH` clause must exist at the time you create the partitioned table. When two tables are partitioned and colocated, it forces partitions having the same values for their foreign key relationships in both tables to be located on the same vFabric SQLFire member.

- For two partitioned tables to be colocated, the `SERVER GROUP` clauses in both `CREATE TABLE` statements must be identical.

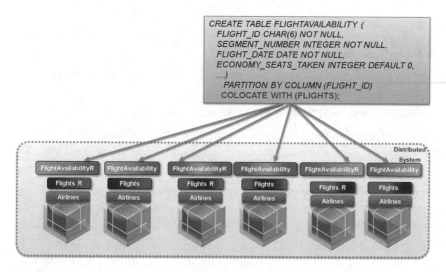

Figure 2-11   Using vFabric SQLFire `COLOCATE` on the `FLIGHTS` and `FLIGHTAVAILABILITY` Tables

Disk Persistence

To provide additional data reliability, vFabric SQLFire can persist table data to disk as a backup to the in-memory copy or can overflow table data to disk. The two disk store options, overflow and persistence, can be used individually or together. Overflow uses disk stores as an extension of in-memory table management for both partitioned and replicated tables. Persistence stores a complete copy of all table data managed in each peer. Figure 2-12 shows how primary and redundant vFabric SQLFire members can persist to an external disk storage.

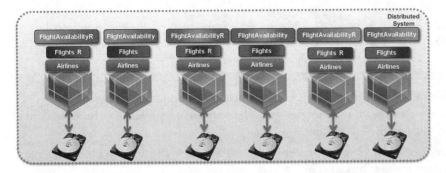

Figure 2-12   vFabric SQLFire Disk Persistence for Additional Data Reliability

---

Best Practice 9: Disk Persistence

- Gateway sender, `AsyncEventListener`, and `DBSynchronizer` queues are always overflowed and can be persisted.

- For best performance, locate each disk store on a separate physical disk.

- Use disk persistence for gateway sender queues because those always have overflow enabled and the ability to persist these queues provides additional high-availability protection.

- Tables can be overflowed, persisted, or both. For efficiency, place table data that is overflowed on one disk store with a dedicated physical disk. Place table data that is persisted, or persisted and overflowed, on another disk store with a different physical disk.

- When calculating your disk requirements, consider your table modification patterns and compaction strategy. vFabric SQLFire creates each oplog file at the specified `MAXLOGSIZE`. Obsolete DML operations are removed from the oplogs only during compaction, so you need enough space to store all operations that are done between compactions. For tables with a mix of updates and deletes, if you use automatic compaction, a good upper bound for the required disk space is as follows:

  $(1 / (1 - (\text{Compaction\_threshold} / 100)))$ * *Data size*

  where *data size* is the total size of all the table data you store in the disk store.

  Therefore, for the default `COMPACTIONTHRESHOLD` of 50, the disk space is roughly twice your data size. The compaction thread could lag behind other operations, causing disk use to rise above the threshold temporarily. If you disable automatic compaction, the amount of disk required depends on how many obsolete operations accumulate between manual compactions.

- When you start your system, start all the members that have persistent tables in parallel. Create and use startup scripts for consistency and completeness.

- Shut down your system using the `sqlf shut-down-all` command. This is an ordered shutdown that fully flushes and safely stores your disk stores.

- Decide on a file compaction policy and, if needed, develop procedures to monitor your files and execute regular compaction.

- Decide on a backup strategy for your disk stores and follow it. You can back up by copying the files while the system is offline, or you can back up an online system using the `sqlf` backup command. If you drop or alter any persistent table while your disk store is offline, consider synchronizing the tables in your disk stores.

- If you bring the entire data fabric down, compact the disk stores while the system is shut down to maximize start up performance.

Transactions

In vFabric SQLFire, any one or more SQL statements comprise a logical unit of work that has transaction semantics; that is, the unit of work can be committed or rolled back in its entirety. The vFabric SQLFire implementation of distributed transaction coordination allows for linear scalability without compromising atomicity, consistency, isolation, and durability, which are the ACID properties. Because vFabric SQLFire members that participate in a transaction hold their own transaction state, queries on the database always see committed data, and they do not need to acquire locks. Therefore, reads and writes can run in parallel in the READ_COMMITTED isolation level.

In the case of transactional writes, vFabric SQLFire locks each copy of a row that is being updated on each member. This alleviates the need for a distributed lock manager, and it allows for greater scalability. Also, vFabric SQLFire uses special read locks for REPEATABLE_READ and foreign key checks to ensure that those rows do not change for the duration of a transaction. vFabric SQLFire locks generally fail eagerly (fail-fast) with a conflict exception if a lock cannot be obtained because of concurrent writes from other active transactions. An exception to this fail-fast behavior occurs when the vFabric SQLFire member that initiates the transaction also hosts data for the transaction. In this case, vFabric SQLFire batches the transaction on the local member for performance reasons, and conflicts might not be detected on other nodes until just before commit time when vFabric SQLFire flushes the batched data.

When data is managed in partitioned tables, each row is implicitly owned by a single member for nontransactional operations. However, with distributed transactions, all copies of a row are treated as being equivalent, and updates are routed to all copies in parallel. This makes the transactional behavior for partitioned tables similar to the behavior for replicated tables. The transaction manager works closely with the vFabric SQLFire membership management system to make sure that, irrespective of failures or adding/ removing members, changes to all rows are either applied to all available copies at commit time, or they are applied to none.

For example, as shown in Figure 2-13, a transaction is initiated to execute updateFlights. All statements within this method are treated as one logical unit and are applied in parallel to all other replicas in the system. In the example, vFabric SQLFire Server 1 acts as the "row-owning member" that coordinates the execution of the transaction as one logical unit of work.

> **NOTE**
> Figure 2-13 through Figure 2-16 refer to multiple steps of a single transaction.

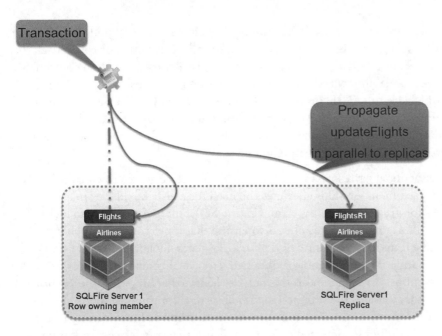

Figure 2-13   Update Flight Transaction

Figure 2-14 shows a continuation of the updateFlights transaction from Figure 2-13. The vFabric SQLFire member that has the updateFlights transaction is the row-owning member that distributed the update commands in parallel to all the replicas. In turn, this member will wait for all ACKs (acknowledgments) before proceeding to commit. The ACK is to indicate that the update was received and that the transaction can prepare to enter the on commit state.

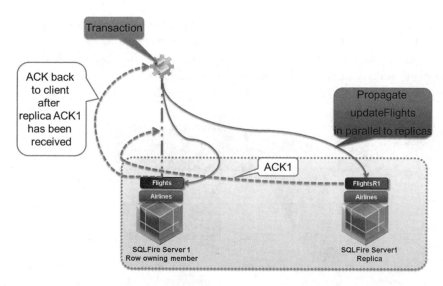

Figure 2-14   Update Flight Transaction Showing Row-Owning vFabric SQLFire Member Waiting to Receive ACKs Before Proceeding to Commit

Figure 2-15 shows the potential of a second transaction being initiated, as Transaction 2. Transaction 2 may be contending for the same data as the initial transaction of updateFlights, and therefore to avoid data corruption, vFabric SQLFire will roll back the entire logical unit of Transaction 2 to allow the original updateFlights transaction to proceed.

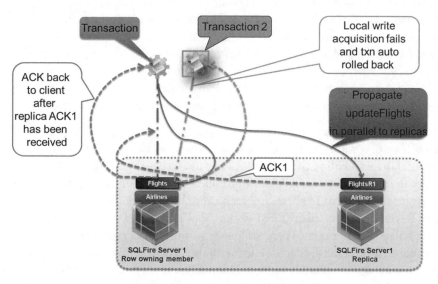

Figure 2-15   Update Flight Transaction Safely Guarded from a Second Contending Transaction

In Figure 2-16, the `updateFlights` transaction proceeds to the commit state, and just as it is about to exit the commit state it issues a lock to the appropriate data replicas to propagate the changes in a data consistent manner. The vFabric SQLFire Server 1 is the "row-owning member" because it acts as the transaction coordinator during commit by acquiring a local write lock and distributing all changes to the replicas.

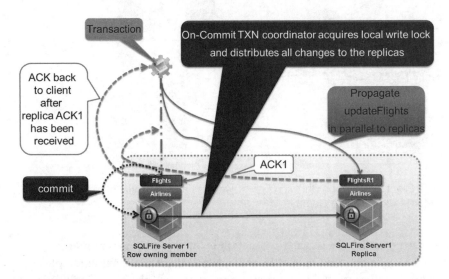

Figure 2-16   Update Flight Transaction Proceeding to Commit Changes

vFabric SQLFire has no centralized transaction coordinator. Instead, the member on which a transaction was started acts as the coordinator for the duration of the transaction. If the application updates one or more rows, the transaction coordinator determines which owning members are involved and acquires local "write" locks on all of the copies of the rows. At commit time, all changes are applied to the local datastore and any redundant copies. If another concurrent transaction attempts to change one of the rows, the local write acquisition fails for the row, and that transaction is automatically rolled back.

If no persistent table is involved, there is no need to issue a two-phase commit to redundant members. In this case, commits are efficient, single-phase operations. Unlike traditional distributed databases, vFabric SQLFire does not use write-ahead logging for transaction recovery in case the commit fails during replication or redundant updates to one or more members. The most likely failure scenario is one where the member is unhealthy and gets forced out of the distributed system, guaranteeing the consistency of the data. When the failed member comes back online, it automatically recovers the replicated/redundant data set and establishes coherency with the other members. If all copies of some data go down before the commit is issued, this condition is detected using the group membership system, and the transaction is rolled back automatically on all members.

Best Practice 10: Transactions

- vFabric SQLFire implements *optimistic* transactions. The transaction model is highly optimized for colocated data, where all of the rows updated by a transaction are owned by a single member.

- Keep the transaction duration and the number of rows involved in the transaction as low as possible. vFabric SQLFire acquires locks eagerly, and long-lasting transactions increase the probability of conflicts and transaction failures

- Understand all the transaction isolation levels offered by vFabric SQLFire. The vFabric SQLFire isolation levels are as follows:

    - **NONE:** By default, connections in vFabric SQLFire do not engage in transactions, unlike in other databases. However, this default behavior does not mean that there is no isolation and that connections have access to uncommitted state from other in-process transactions. Without a transaction (transaction isolation set to NONE), vFabric SQLFire ensures first in, first out (FIFO) consistency for table updates. Writes performed by a single thread are seen by all other processes in the order in which they were issued, but writes from different processes may be seen in a different order by other processes. When a table is partitioned across members of the distributed system, vFabric SQLFire uniformly distributes the data set across members that host the table so that no single member becomes a bottleneck for scalability. vFabric SQLFire assigns ownership of a particular row (identified by a primary key) to a single member at any given time. When an owning member fails, the ownership of the row is transferred to an alternate member in a consistent manner so that all peer servers have a consistent view of the new owner.

    - **READ_UNCOMMITTED:** vFabric SQLFire internally upgrades this isolation to READ_COMMITTED.

    - **READ_COMMITTED:** vFabric SQLFire does not allow ongoing transactional as well as nontransactional (isolation level NONE) operations to read uncommitted (dirty) data. vFabric SQLFire accomplishes this by maintaining transactional changes in a separate transaction state that is applied to the actual datastore for the table only at commit time.

    - **REPEATABLE_READ:** vFabric SQLFire supports this isolation level according to the ANSI SQL standard. A transaction that reads the same row more than once always sees the same column values for the row. REPEATABLE_READ also guarantees that the underlying committed row in a table never changes after the first read in a transaction, until the transaction completes. vFabric SQLFire applies read and write locks to copies of selected data so that reads are repeatable for the duration of a transaction. vFabric SQLFire does not use range locks, and phantom reads are still possible with this isolation level.

- vFabric SQLFire always clones the existing row, applies the update (changes one or more fields), and then atomically replaces the row with the updated row. This isolates all concurrent threads reading or writing that row from access to any partial row updates. *If transactions are running in your system, plan your rebalancing operation carefully. Rebalancing might move data between members, which could cause a running transaction to fail with a* `TransactionDataRebalancedException`. *Use adequate exception handling and transaction retry logic in the application.*

- vFabric SQLFire VSD provides statistics for transaction commits, rollbacks, and failures that enable you to monitor vFabric SQLFire transactions.

Cache Plug-In

When an incoming query request for a uniquely identified row cannot be satisfied by the distributed system, a loader can be invoked to retrieve the data from an external source. vFabric SQLFire locks the associated row and prevents concurrent readers that are trying to fetch the same row from overloading the back-end database.

In Figure 2-17, a `RowLoader` is registered on each of the vFabric SQLFire servers in the distributed system. The `RowLoader` implements the `getRow()` method that is invoked when a cache miss occurs. `RowLoader.getRow`, in turn, has the necessary business logic to retrieve the needed data from an RDBMS or from an external system.

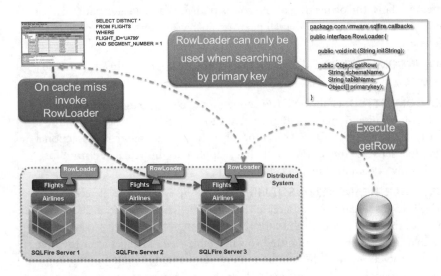

Figure 2-17   Using `RowLoader` to Handle a Cache Miss

Best Practice 11: RowLoader

- When a loader is configured for a table, performing a `select` statement against the table internally fetches and inserts data into a vFabric SQLFire table. Because of this behavior, it is possible to receive a constraint violation when you query a table that is configured with a loader (for example, if the loader attempts to insert data from a back-end database that violates a table constraint in vFabric SQLFire).

- When implementing a `RowLoader`, adhere to the `RowLoader` interface.

- The `RowLoader` interface is made of the following:

  - `init(String initStr)` method: Used to obtain parameters that are defined when you register your implementation with a table. vFabric SQLFire calls your implementation's `init()` method when the `SYS.ATTACH_LOADER` procedure is used to register the `RowLoader` with a table. All parameters are passed in the single `String` object.

  - `getRow(String schemaName, String tableName, Object[ ] primarykey)` method: vFabric SQLFire calls this method implementation to provide the schema name, table name, and an array of objects that are the primary key values (in the order presented by the table definition) each time the loader is invoked to fetch data from the external source.

    Your implementation of the `getRow` method must return one of the following:

    - An object array with one element with the value for each column, including the primary key, in the order defined by the vFabric SQLFire table definition.

    - `null`, if there is no element found.

    - An instance of `java.sql.ResultSet`, possibly the result of a query against another database. Only the first row is used. The result columns should match the vFabric SQLFire table.

    - An empty `java.sql.ResultSet` if no element is found.

- After compiling your `RowLoader` implementation and adding it to the classpath, register the `RowLoader` with a table by executing the built-in `SYS.ATTACH_LOADER` procedure.

Listeners

In vFabric SQLFire, you can implement any number of listeners that can be triggered based on certain SQL DML operation that an application executes. The listeners are triggered as post insert/update/delete operations, as *after-events*. In Figure 2-18, three listeners have been registered to listen for SQL DML changes.

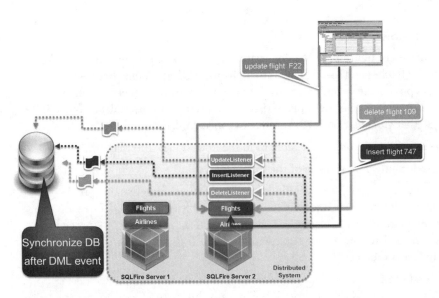

Figure 2-18   vFabric SQLFire SQL DML Listeners

The listeners are as follows:

- An `UpdateListener` is depicted in the green text box of Figure 2-19. This listener is triggered whenever there is an update to the `Flights` table. The `Flights` table is from the schema that was introduced previously in Figure 2-9. Any update using SQL DML in vFabric SQLFire against the `Flights` table triggers the execution of the `UpdateListener` as an after-event. This implies that the data changes in the vFabric SQLFire `Flights` table first, and then the `UpdateListener` callback is executed synchronously to synchronize the data changes to the back end traditional RDBMS/DB. In Figure 2-18, the update DML event is triggered by "update flight F22" depicted in the green callout box against a solid green arrow. This solid green arrow shows that the vFabric SQLFire member is changed first, and then the dotted green arrow triggers the `UpdateListener` as an after-event synchronously. When the `UpdateListener` is triggered, the execution involves a call to the listener callback handler, which then sends the changes to the database over the green dotted line with a small document fragment to depict that a change has been sent to the database.

- An `InsertListener` and `DeleteListener` are also registered on the `Flights` table, as depicted in Figure 2-18. The activation of these listeners is similar to the `UdpateListener` described earlier.

In Figure 2-19, if `UpdateListener` blocks for some reason while the change is already applied to the vFabric SQLFire member holding the specific `Flights` partition, the listener throws an exception and does not complete.

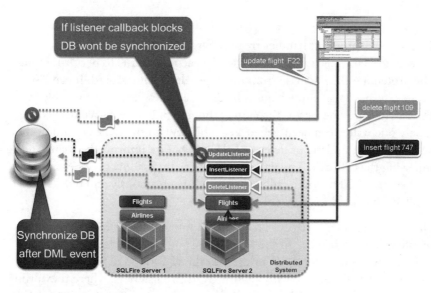

Figure 2-19 UpdateListener Callback Handler Blocking

Best Practice 12: Listeners

- A listener enables other systems to receive after-event notifications of changes to a table (insert, update and delete). They can be very useful in integrating enterprise-wide systems that depend on data changes within the data fabric.

- You might want to execute DML without having to trigger the listeners. You can override configured listeners on a per connection basis using the property skip-listeners. Setting this property does not affect WAN distribution. DML events are always sent across WAN setup/gateway sender.

- You can use the SYS.ADD_LISTENER built-in procedures to attach one or more listeners to a table.

- Any number of listeners can be defined for the same table. This can helpful in providing several customized insert/update/delete listeners to meet different business requirements. If only one listener were allowed, the event handling code would require complex if/else context switching or large CASE statements, making the code difficult to maintain. Listeners are an implementation of the EventCallback interface (https://www.vmware.com/support/developer/vfabric-sqlfire/102-api/com/vmware/sqlfire/callbacks/EventCallback.html).

- If an exception is thrown in a listener, the update succeeds, but the exception is propagated back to the originating node.

Writers

A vFabric SQLFire writer is an event handler that synchronously handles changes to a table before those changes take place. The main use of a cache writer is to perform input validation, thereby protecting the database from improper data being stored. It can also be used to update an external data source before the data becomes visible in the table in vFabric SQLFire. A writer provides write-through caching with your external data source. Unlike listeners, only one writer can be attached to a table. When the table is about to be modified because of an insert, update, or delete, vFabric SQLFire informs the writer of the pending operation using the callback. The writer can choose to disallow the operation by throwing an SQLException. The writer callback is called synchronously and blocks the operation if the callback blocks.

In Figure 2-20, an InsertWriter is registered on the Flights table. An "Insert flight 747" triggers the callback event handler of the InsertWriter to synchronize with the external database first, and then performs an insert into the vFabric SQLFire Flights data partition. This is the key difference with vFabric SQLFire listeners, where they propagate changes to external systems after the DML has been applied to the vFabric SQLFire data partition. One other key difference is that you can register multiple listeners, but only one writer.

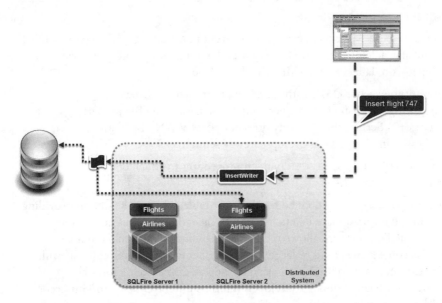

Figure 2-20   An InsertWriter on the Flights Table

In Figure 2-21, the `InsertWriter` event handler throws an exception after attempting to write to the external database. In this case, the entire data change is rolled back from the database and is not applied to the vFabric SQLFire `Flights` data partition.

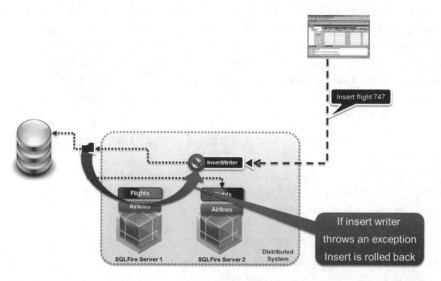

Figure 2-21   `InsertWriter` Throws an Exception That Causes a Full Rollback

---

Best Practice 13: Writers

- A writer enables other systems to receive before-event notifications of changes to a table (insert, update and delete). In keeping an external DB synchronized with vFabric SQLFire, changes are applied to vFabric SQLFire post validation with an external system that the writer handler would do.

- You can use the `SYS.ATTACH_WRITER` built-in procedure to attach a writer.

Note that only one writer can be registered against a table.

- vFabric SQLFire installs a sample writer implementation in <your install directory for sqlfire>/vFabric_SQLFire_10x/examples/EventCallbackWriterImpl.javam. This writer implementation can be used to perform writes to any JDBC data source, if the appropriate driver is available in the classpath.

- The type of the event can be found as `TYPE.BEFORE_INSERT`, `TYPE.BEFORE_UPDATE`, and `TYPE.BEFORE_DELETE`.

Asynchronous Listeners

The previous discussion focused on listeners and writers, which essentially are synchronous callback handlers. If synchronous handlers are not possible for an enterprise application because of their potential to block, or perhaps there is an unreliable consuming client, asynchronous listeners can be a prudent alternative. An `AsyncEventListener` instance is serviced by its own dedicated thread in which a callback method is invoked. Events that correspond to DML operations are placed in an internal queue, and the dedicated thread dispatches a batch of events at a time to the user-implemented callback class. The frequency of dispatching events is governed by the configuration of the `AsyncEventListener` in vFabric SQLFire.

In Figure 2-22, a `TestAsynchEventListener` is registered on the `Flights` table to be called back when a DML event happens. The DML events are enqueued into an event queue and then later dequeued from the event queue based on the configured cycle. When the event is dequeued, it in turn calls the registered `TestAsyncEventListener.processEvents()` method.

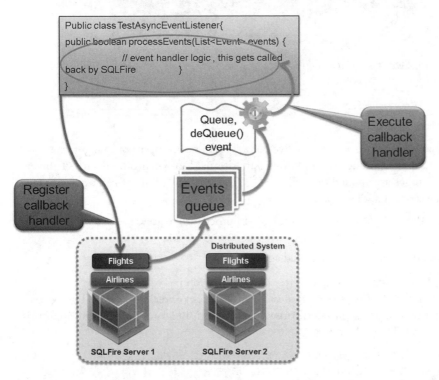

Figure 2-22   An Example `TestAsynchEventListener` Showing a Registration and Execution Cycle Through an Event Queue

Best Practice 14: Asynchronous Listeners

- An `AsyncEventListener` instance is serviced by its own dedicated thread in which a callback method is invoked.

- Events that correspond to DML operations are placed in an internal queue, and the dedicated thread dispatches one batch of events at a time to the user-implemented callback class. This can be very beneficial in integrating systems across the enterprise that might have varied reliability and response-time SLAs.

- Certain data consistency problems can occur if multiple threads update data that is queued to an `AsyncEventListener` implementation. This implies that there is no order of events guarantee.

NOTE

vFabric SQLFire preserves the order of DML statements applied to the distributed system (and queued to `AsyncEventListeners` or remote WAN sites) only for a single thread of execution. Updates from multiple threads are preserved in FIFO order. Otherwise, vFabric SQLFire provides no "total ordering" guarantees.

Data inconsistency can occur if multiple threads concurrently update the same rows of a replicated table, or if threads concurrently update related rows from replicated tables in a parent-child relationship. Concurrently updating the same row in a replicated table can result in some replicas having different values from other replicas. Concurrently deleting a row in a parent table and inserting a row in a child table can result in orphaned rows.

When DML operations are queued to an `AsyncEventListener` or remote WAN site, similar inconsistency problems can occur with concurrent table access. For example, if two separate threads concurrently update rows on a parent table and child table, respectively, the order in which vFabric SQLFire queues those updates to an `AsyncEventListener` or WAN gateway might not match the order in which the tables were updated in the main distributed system. This can cause a foreign key constraint violation in a back-end database (for example, when using `DBSynchronizer`) or in a remote WAN system that does not occur when the tables are initially updated. These types of out-of-order updates do not occur when multiple threads concurrently update the same key of a partitioned table. However, an application should always use a transaction for any operation that updates multiple rows.

- All `AsyncEventListener` implementations should check for the possibility that an existing database connection might have been closed due to an earlier exception. For example, check for `Connection.isClosed()` in a catch block and re-create the connection as needed before performing further operations. The `DBSynchronizer` implementation in vFabric SQLFire automatically performs this type of check before reusing a connection.

- An `AsyncEventListener` implementation must be installed on one or more members of the vFabric SQLFire system. You can install `AsyncEventListeners` only on datastores (peers configured with the property `host-data` set to `true`).

- You can install a listener on more than one member to provide high availability and guarantee delivery for events, in case a vFabric SQLFire member with an active `AsyncEventListener` shuts down. At any given time, only one member has an active thread for dispatching events. The threads on other members remain on standby for redundancy.

- For high availability and reliable delivery of events, configure the event queue to be both persistent and redundant.

DBSynchronizer

`DBSynchronizer` is a built-in `AsyncEventListener` implementation that you can use to asynchronously persist data to a third-party JDBC 4.0-compliant RDBMS. You install `DBSynchronizer` as an `AsyncEventListener` on multiple datastores. The DML statements executed on vFabric SQLFire are passed on to the `DBSynchronizer` and the configured JDBC RDBMS. `DBSynchronizer` should be installed only on datastores (configured with `host-data` property set to `true`). Each instance of `DBSynchronizer` maintains an internal queue to batch up the DML statements and is serviced by its own dedicated thread. This thread picks up DML statements from the queue, and applies them to the external database using prepared statements as illustrated in Figure 2-23.

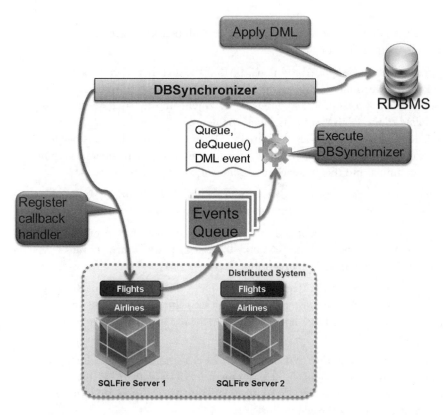

Figure 2-23   Using DBSynchronizer to Keep an External RDBMS in Sync

---

Best Practice 15: DBSynchronizer

- Configure the DBSynchronizer queue for both persistence and redundancy for high availability and reliable delivery of events. Installing DBSynchronizer on more than one datastore provides high availability. At any given time, only one member has a DBSynchronizer thread active for executing DML on the external database. The threads on other members are on standby (redundant) to guarantee execution of DML if the member with the active DBSynchronizer thread fails.

NOTE

By default, any pending DML operations residing in the internal queue of the DBSynchronizer are lost if the active member shuts down. You can avoid losing operations by configuring the internal queue of DBSynchronizer to be persistent.

- Install no more than one standby DBSynchronizer (redundancy of at most one) for performance and memory reasons.

- A DML operation may be reapplied to the RDBMS if the member with the active DBSynchronizer thread fails. If the member with the active DBSynchronizer fails while sending a batch of operations, some DML statements in the batch might already have been applied to the RDBMS. On failover, the new DBSynchronizer thread resends the failed batch and reapplies the initial DML operations. When this occurs, the RDBMS can get out of sync depending on the nature of the DML operation, how it modifies table columns, and the presence or absence of column constraints.

- If the table has any constraint (primary key, unique) defined, the following types of DML operations do not cause out-of-sync problems when reapplied during failover:

    - A create operation that is reapplied to a table with a primary key. A primary key constraint violation occurs and a SQLException is thrown, but DBSynchronizer ignores the exception.

    - A create or update operation that causes a unique constraint violation. Reapplying a create or update operation causes a duplicate value, violating the unique constraint. DBSynchronizer ignores the SQLException that is thrown in this situation.

    - A create or update operation that causes a check constraint violation. Reapplying create or an update (for example, incrementing or decrementing a column value) can cause a check constraint to be violated. DBSynchronizer ignores the SQLException that is thrown in this situation.

    - If DBSynchronizer encounters an exception while updating or committing to the database, the batch is retained and the DBSynchronizer thread continues to try to apply the batch until it is successful.

    - If DML operations are executed concurrently on a vFabric SQLFire system that has a foreign key relationship based on parent and child table, a foreign key violation may occur while applying DML operations to the external database. This can occur even if the vFabric SQLFire system successfully executed the DML. Although inserts into the parent and child table occur in order in the vFabric SQLFire system, the inserts can reach DBSynchronizer in reverse order. To avoid this behavior, perform updates to parent and child tables in a single application thread.

SQLF Commands and DDLUtils

vFabric SQLFire provides a command-line interface and DDLUtils that can help you generate the target schema and data load files based on many supported RDBMS source schemas. Figure 2-24 lists supported RDBMs that DDLUtils can migrate.

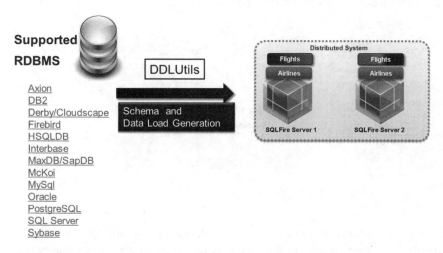

Figure 2-24   DDLUtils for Generating Target Schema and Data Files

Active-Active Architectures and Modern Data Platforms

Figure 2-25 shows four active-active sides within two datacenters. In Datacenter-1, there are the Active-1A and Active-1B sides, and in Datacenter-2, there are the Active-2A and Active-2B sides. Each of the Active-1A, 1B, 2A, and 2B sides has all the layers that make up a typical enterprise application; in this case, we are using SpringTrader as a reference application. Further, enterprise application instances would be spread across both Active-1A and 1B for Datcenter-1 and similarly for Datcenter-2. If Active-1A fails, application instances in Active-1B will continue to service traffic regardless of when Active-1A will come back online. This implies that Active-1B must be prepared to take on the full peak load of Active-1A. Now, of course, sometimes that it is not feasible, and hence some of the additional traffic can be diverted to Datacenter-2, especially if Datacenter-2 is within less than 60 miles geographic distance. SLA requirements will dictate which approach to take, balancing between hardware cost and location versus impact to SLA and response times. You can also have a variant to this where Datacenter-1 and 2 are within 60 miles and Datacenter-3 can be over a WAN.

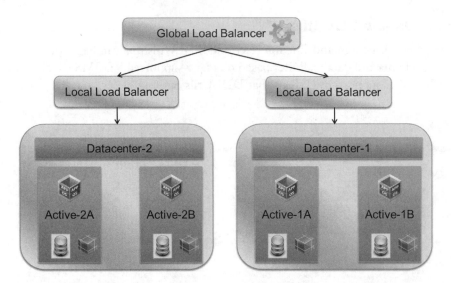

Figure 2-25   Multicluster and Multi-Datacenter Active-Active Architecture

As shown in Figure 2-26, a combination of global load balancer (GLB) and local load balancers (LLBs) are used to ascertain fast application response times that are not negatively impacted by geography. The GLB works by directing user traffic to the local geography LLB. (For example, the London traffic will be directed to the London LLB, the New York users will be directed to the New York LLB, and the Tokyo traffic will be directed to the Tokyo LLB.) The GLB keeps a heartbeat connection between all the LLBs and determines the best routing decision.

The LLB configuration pools for each geographic site have entries for each of the Spring-Trader application services. Figure 2-26 shows three LLB configurations.

The Tokyo LLB pool configuration is essentially a configuration of four SpringTrader application services configured in a load-balancer pool arrangement. The LLB pool has four entries to send traffic to. In turn, the four entries are logically separated by Active-1A and Active-1B; this is to indicate that the Active-1A application services are VMs residing in the same vSphere host and that the other Active-1B SpringTrader application services VMs live on another vSphere host. This pattern of LLB configuration is repeated in a similar manner across New York and London sites. Note that the traffic is load balanced to the SpringTrader application services; however, from each application service to the SQLFire data fabric the communication is via the locator, and the load-balancer architecture is not involved in the call. It would be redundant to intercept the call between the SpringTrader application services and the SQLFire data members with a load-balancer configuration; instead, the vFabric SQLFire locator process fulfills the role of load balancing and load moderation across the data fabric.

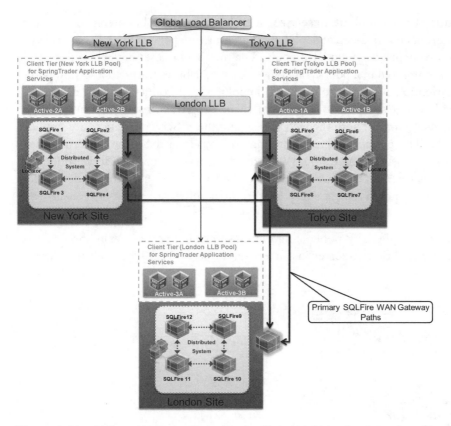

Figure 2-26 GLB and LLBs for SpringTrader Global Multisite Configuration

Furthermore, the details of the web server pool have been omitted to provide clarity about the remaining portion of the configuration. If you choose to add a separate configuration pool for web servers, the web servers would essentially distribute traffic from the LLB down to the application services LLB pool, ideally on a least-connection type of distribution algorithm. In basic terms, this would mean that the front-end pool (in this case, the local LLB web server pool) receives traffic from the GLB and that the web server pool directs traffic to the application services local LLB. After the traffic has been distributed down to a specific SpringTrader application service, it is important to maintain session stickiness. Note that it is advisable to avoid having only an LLB web server pool (which would then mean that each pool web server member points to only a specific SpringTrader application service); this provides a false fault-tolerant service level. The SpringTrader application service, essentially an instance of vFabric tc Server, could be down, but because the service level test is to the LLB web server member, it could return a false positive. It is best to follow the two-LLB pool approach, one pool for the web servers and a second pool for the SpringTrader application services at each local geographic site governed by the local LLB. From an active-active deployment architecture perspective, the enterprise application layer contains two main LLB pools. The first pool is a set of vFabric web server instances configured in a pool arrangement that distributes traffic to a second pool. The typical distribution algorithm to the second pool is a least-connection type of distribution algorithm. The second pool is made of vFabric tc Server instances running in a stateless arrangement; in fact, both the web servers and the tc Server instances are stateless in their own right. There is no need for additional web server or tc Server clustering; the LLB will take care of distributing traffic. While the distribution from web server pool to the tc Server pool is based on the least-connection algorithm, once a SpringTrader session is initiated the session should remain sticky for the entire activity of a user-session/browser lifecycle.

Figure 2-27 expands on the LLB pool configuration shown in Figure 2-26 by showing two LLB pools, one for vFabric web server instances and the second pool for vFabric tc Server instances.

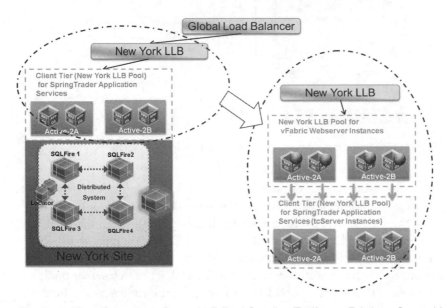

Figure 2-27   vFabric Web Server LLB Pool Sending Traffic to vFabric tc Server LLB Pool

Chapter Summary

This chapter examined vFabric SQLFire features that you can use to modernize various aspects of enterprise data. When enterprise data scalability and performance seems to be an issue that can no longer be solved with just hardware adjustments and reconfiguration of existing applications, it is probably time to rearchitect the data layer, focusing on in-memory data management systems.

Chapter 3

Tuning Large-Scale Java Platforms

There are two main garbage collection (GC) policies: throughput/parallel GC and concurrent mark sweep (CMS). Discussion of others is omitted because they do not currently apply to latency-sensitive workloads such as those found in category 2 and 3.

> **NOTE**
>
> When tuning category 2 or any response-time sensitive/latency-sensitive Java platforms, using the combination of throughput/parallel GC in young generation and CMS in old generation often yields the most prudent memory throughput and response-time combination.

The throughput/parallel GC policy is called the throughput GC because it focuses on improved memory throughput as opposed to better response time. It is also synonymously called the parallel GC because it uses multiple worker threads (configured with `-XX:ParallelGCThreads=<nThreads>`) to collect garbage. The throughput/parallel GC is essentially a stop-the-world type of collector, and therefore the application is paused when GC activity occurs. To minimize this effect and create a more scalable system, multiple parallel GC threads can be configured to help parallelize the minor GC activity.

Although the throughput GC uses multiple worker threads to collect garbage in the young generation, when those threads run they pause application threads, which could be problematic for latency-sensitive workloads. The combination of `-XX:ParallelGCThreads=<nThreads>` and `-Xmn` (young generation size) tuning are two key tuning options to consider adjusting up or down. The GC activity might not be as frequent in old generation, but when GC activity takes place in old generation the application experiences a garbage collection time that is significantly longer than that of the younger generation GC time. This is especially true if the parallel/throughput collector is used in old generation. To mitigate this pause problem in old generation, it is possible to use the concurrent mark sweep (CMS) GC in old generation while young generation is still being collected by the throughput/parallel collector.

CMS refers to concurrent mark sweep. When the GC threads run, they do not pause the application threads because they are running concurrently alongside the application threads. In CMS, there are multiple phases, so it is also sometimes referred to as the *multipass collector*, or mostly concurrent because it does have two short pauses that are usually insignificant. The phases are as follows:

1. Initial mark

2. Marking and precleaning

3. Remark

4. Sweeping

Although the CMS collector is named as the concurrent collector, it is sometimes more accurately referred to as the "mostly concurrent collector" because there are two short pausing phases, first in the initial mark and then later in the remark phase. These pauses are of no significance to the overall cycle of CMS and therefore are mostly ignored from a practical concurrency versus amount of pause perspective.

The CMS phases operate as follows:

- **Initial mark phase (short pausing):** The beginning of tenured generation collection within the overall phases of CMS. This initial marking phase of CMS is where all the objects directly reachable from roots are marked. This is done with all the mutator threads stopped.

- **Concurrent marking phase (no pause):** Threads stopped in the first initial mark phase are started again and all the objects reachable from the objects marked in the first phase are marked here.

- **Concurrent precleaning phase (no pause):** Looks at the objects in the heap that got updated by promotions from the young generation or got updated by mutator threads during the concurrent marking in the previous concurrent marking phase. The rescanning of objects concurrently in the pre-cleaning phase helps to reduce the work in the next "re-mark" pausing phase.

- **Re-mark phase (pausing):** This phase rescans any residual updated objects in the heap, retracing them from the object graph.

■ **Concurrent sweeping (nonpausing):** Start of sweeping of dead objects and where sweeping is a concurrent phase performed with all other threads running.

Figure 3-1 is a graphical representation of the configurations that use a combination of -XX:ParNewGC in young generation and CMS in old generation. Figure 3-1 shows the young generation in the blue box, sized by the -Xmn and configured to have -XX:ParNewGC and -XX:ParallelGCThreads. The minor GC threads run as dotted blue arrows, between application threads depicted as green arrows. There are multiple worker threads conducting garbage cleaning in young generation due to the -XX:ParallelGCThreads configuration. Each time these worker threads run to collect garbage, they pause the green arrow application threads; however, having multiple worker threads does help to alleviate the problem. Naturally, the size of the young generation plays a role in this because the duration of the minor GC increases, but it is not as often because the size of the young generation increases. The smaller the young generation, the more often minor GC is of shorter duration.

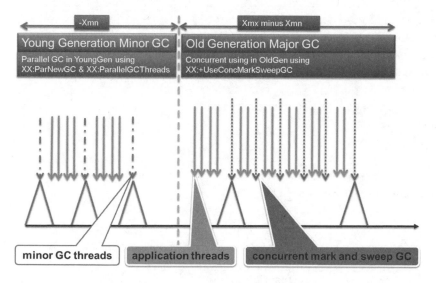

Figure 3-1 Parallel GC in Young Generation and CMS in Old Generation

In the old generation, which cannot be directly sized, but instead is implicitly sized by being the difference between -Xmx and -Xmn, the GC policy is configured with -XX:+UseConcMarkSweepGC. This GC runs concurrently alongside application threads without pausing them, as depicted by the red arrow that denotes CMS activity.

Refer to Example 3-1 and Example 3-2 (JVM options described in Table 3-1) for an actual demonstration with complete JVM options that use the combination of ParNewGC and CMS.

Example 3-1   JVM Configuration Using ParNewGC and CMS, 64GB Heap

```
java -Xms64g -Xmx64g -Xmn21g -Xss1024k
-XX:+UseConcMarkSweepGC
-XX:+UseParNewGC -XX:CMSInitiatingOccupancyFraction=75
-XX:+UseCMSInitiatingOccupancyOnly
-XX:+ScavengeBeforeFullGC
-XX:TargetSurvivorRatio=80 -XX:SurvivorRatio=8
-XX:+UseBiasedLocking
-XX:MaxTenuringThreshold=15
-XX:ParallelGCThreads=4
-XX:+OptimizeStringConcat -XX:+UseCompressedStrings
-XX:+UseStringCache -XX:+DisableExplicitGC
```

Example 3-2   JVM Configuration Using ParNewGC and CMS, 30GB Heap

```
java -Xms30g -Xmx30g -Xmn9g -Xss1024k
-XX:+UseConcMarkSweepGC
-XX:+UseParNewGC -XX:CMSInitiatingOccupancyFraction=75
-XX:+UseCMSInitiatingOccupancyOnly
-XX:+ScavengeBeforeFullGC
-XX:TargetSurvivorRatio=80 -XX:SurvivorRatio=8
-XX:+UseBiasedLocking
-XX:MaxTenuringThreshold=15
-XX:ParallelGCThreads=2
-XX:+UseCompressedOops -XX:+OptimizeStringConcat -XX:+UseCompressedStrings
-XX:+UseStringCache -XX:+DisableExplicitGC
```

Table 3-1   JVM Configuration Options Used for Parallel Young Generation and CMS in Old Generation

JVM Option	Description
-Xmn21g	Establishes fixed-size young generation. In this setting, 21GB is being allocated to the young generation.
-XX:+UseConcMarkSweepGC	Enables the use of the concurrent collector to collect the old generation and does most of the collection concurrently with the execution of the application. The application is paused for short periods during the collection. A parallel version of the young generation copying collector is used with the concurrent collector; see -XX:ParNewGC.

JVM Option	Description
`-XX:+UseParNewGC`	Enables the usage of the modified parallel throughput collector in the young generation, with the ability to specify multiple worker GC threads. The parallel collection threads are configured with `-XX:ParallelGCThreads=4`, for example. This is used with CMS only. By default, this is enabled in Java 6u13, and probably any Java 6 when the machine has multiple processor cores.
`-XX:CMSInitiatingOccupancy` `Fraction=75`	Sets the percentage of the heap that must be full before the JVM starts a concurrent collection in the tenured generation. The default is approximately 92 in Java 6, but that can lead to significant problems. Setting this lower allows CMS to run more often (all the time sometimes), but it often clears more quickly to avoid fragmentation.
`-XX:+UseCMSInitiating` `OccupancyOnly`	Enables the feature that all concurrent CMS cycles should start based on `-XX:CMSInitiatingOccupancyFraction=75`.
`-XX:+ScavengeBeforeFullGC`	Enables the feature that forces a young generation collection before starting a new CMS cycle or before a full GC is attempted.
`-XX:TargetSurvivorRatio=80`	Sets the desired percentage of survivor space used after scavenge.
`-XX:SurvivorRatio=8`	Establishes the ratio of Eden/survivor space size.
`-XX:+UseBiasedLocking`	Enables a technique for improving the performance of uncontended synchronization. An object is "biased" toward the thread that first acquires its monitor using a `monitorenter` bytecode or synchronized method invocation; subsequent monitor-related operations performed by that thread are relatively much faster on multiprocessor machines. Some applications with significant amounts of uncontended synchronization can attain significant speedups with this flag enabled. Some applications with certain patterns of locking can see slowdowns, although attempts have been made to minimize the negative impact.

JVM Option	Description
`-XX:MaxTenuringThreshold=15`	Determines the maximum age that a young object is allowed to live in the young generation after each minor GC, before it is tenured to the old generation. The tenure of an object is incremented by 1 when the object survives a minor GC and is copied to survivor spaces. The maximum for the HotSpot JVM J6 is 15. A smaller value causes premature promotions to the old generation that can lead to more frequent old generation activity that can hurt response times.
`-XX:ParallelGCThreads=4`	Sets the number of GC worker threads in the young generation. The default value varies with the JVM platform.
	This value should not be higher than 50% of the cores available to the JVM.
	There is an assumption that a single JVM is running on one VM and that no other JVM is contending for the cores available to the VM on which the JVM runs.
	For example, in Option 2 shown in Figure 2-14, the vSphere cluster has 16 VMs and therefore 16 vFabric SQLFire members. Each VM is configured to have 68GB RAM and 8 vCPUs. One vFabric SQLFire member JVM VM runs on one 8-core socket within the vSphere host. This implies that 8 cores are available to service the 8 vCPUs allocated to the VM, because `-XX:ParallelGCThreads=4`. Four vCPUs are consumed by the `ParallelGCThreads`, and the remaining four are available to service application threads, concurrent old generation activity, off-the-heap activity, and any other workloads that might be running on the VM, such as a monitoring agent.
	One minor caveat here is that in the very short pausing phases of the initial mark (aside from the other concurrent phases) it is single threaded but finishes rather quickly, and then the re-mark is multithreaded. The initial mark being single threaded does not use any of the `-XX:ParallelGCThreads` allocated, but the re-mark phase being multithreaded uses some of the parallel threads allocated. Because re-mark is a very short phase, it uses negligible parallel thread cycles.

JVM Option	Description
	There is enough variance from workload to workload that these assumptions should be verified for your own application with a load test.
`-XX:+UseCompressedOops`	Enables the use of compressed pointers (object references represented as 32-bit offsets instead of 64-bit pointers) for optimized 64-bit performance with Java heap sizes less than 32GB.
`-XX:+OptimizeStringConcat`	Optimizes string concatenation operations where possible. (Introduced in Java 6 Update 20.)
`-XX:+UseCompressedStrings`	*Use with caution!* Use a `byte[]` for strings that can be represented as pure ASCII. (Introduced in Java 6 Update 21 Performance Release.) In certain versions of Java 6, this option may have been deprecated.
`-XX:+UseStringCache`	Enables caching of commonly allocated strings.
`-XX:+DisableExplicitGC`	Disables all calls to `System.gc()` that might still be embedded erroneously in the application code.
`-XX:+AlwaysPreTouch`	Use of this is optional. It is not used in the example, but from time to time it can be an optimization worth considering. `PreTouch` the Java heap during JVM initialization. Every page of the heap is thus demand-zeroed during initialization rather than incrementally during application execution. Setting this option will increase startup time, but may improve runtime performance of the JVM.
`-XX:+UseNUMA`	*Do not use!* This JVM option should not be used because it is not compatible with the CMS garbage collector. vFabric SQLFire Server JVMs deployed on VMs running on the vSphere ESXi 5 hypervisor do not need this flag because VMware provides many Non-Uniform Memory Access (NUMA) optimizations that have been proven to provide great locality for vFabric SQLFire types of workloads. This flag is not compatible with CMS GC policy.

GC tuning presented so far is usually adequate for most workloads, with some caveats in terms of adjusting -Xmn, ParallelGCThreads, SurvivorRatio, and stack size -Xss. The following section presents more detail for a potential GC tuning approach that can help guide your decisions to further tune GC cycles in young and old generations. There are many possible approaches, but the GC approach discussed in the next section is quite prudent.

GC Tuning Approach

Many other approaches can be applied, and JVM tuning can take many weeks of discussion on theory and practice. This section describes what is applicable to JVM tuning for latency-sensitive workloads.

Figure 3-2 outlines a three-step tuning approach:

Step A.   **Young generation tuning:** This involves measuring frequency and duration of minor GC and then adjusting -Xmn and -XX:ParallelGCThreads to meet application response time service level agreements (SLA).

Step B.   **Old generation tuning:** This involves measuring the frequency and duration of the CMS GC cycles and adjusting -Xmx and -XX:CMSInitiatingOccupancyFraction to meet SLA application workload response-time requirements.

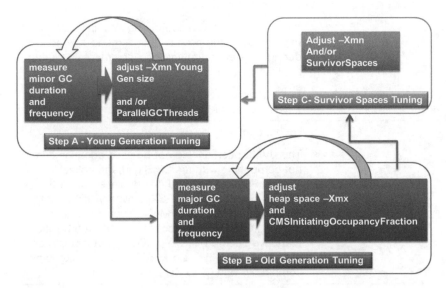

Figure 3-2   GC Tuning Approach for Parallel GC in the Young Generation and CMS in the Old Generation

Step C. **Survivor spaces tuning:** This is a refinement step in tuning the survivor spaces to either delay promotion from young generation by increasing survivor spaces size or to reduce minor GC duration and speed up the onset of promotion from young generation to old generation by reducing survivor spaces sizes.

Step A: Young Generation Tuning

In this step (step A from Figure 3-2) the frequency (how often GC runs) and duration (how long GC runs for) of the minor GC are first measured, then compared with the GC pause and response-time requirements, to determine whether the GC cycle must be tuned. Understanding the internals of the young generation is critical to fine-tuning the minor GC cycle, and therefore the diagram from Figure 3-1 appears in Figure 3-3 with a slight modification to further detail the young generation cycle. The main objective of this tuning is to measure the frequency and duration of minor GC and determine whether sufficient time is made available for application threads to run in between minor GC activity. In Figure 3-3, the application threads are shown as green arrows running between the minor GC activity.

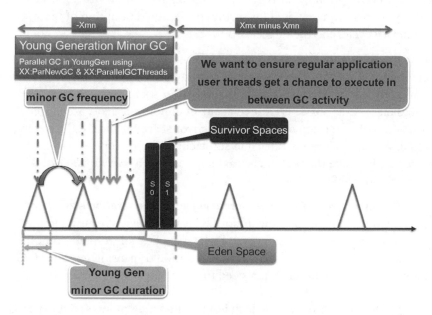

Figure 3-3   Measuring Minor GC Duration and Frequency in the Young Generation

The young generation is sized by -Xmn, as shown in Figure 3-3, and configured with the -XX:ParNewGC, as indicated previously, along with having multiple worker threads to help with the GC cycles configured with -XX:ParallelGCThreads=<nThreads>. The young generation also contains two survivor spaces (dark blue boxes), indicated as S0 and S1 on the diagram. These spaces are sized as *SurvivorSpaceSize* = -Xmn / (-XX:SurvivorRatio + 2). The other space of significance, and one of the most important spaces within young generation, is the Eden space (orange box on Figure 3-3). Eden space is implicitly sized as the difference between -Xmn and the *SurvivorSpaceSize* * 2. A more complete tuning discussion of survivor spaces is given with step C of this tuning approach, but in brief, starting with a survivor ratio of 8 makes *SurvivorSpaceSize* 10% of -Xmn. Therefore, S0 is 10% of -Xmn, and S1 is also 10%. The Eden space size is 80% of -Xmn if *SurvivorRatio* is set to 8.

Assuming at this point that the frequency and duration of minor GC have been measured, coupled with the discussion of each parameter that plays a role in the young generation tuning, the next section describes the impact of adjusting some of these parameters.

Impact of Adjusting -Xmn

The single most critical JVM option by far is -Xmn, the young generation size. Consider the impact of reducing or increasing -Xmn. This section presents a description of the young generation internal cycle, and the impact of adjusting it:

- **Understanding the young generation GC cycle:** All objects are created in the Eden space. When minor GC occurs, the Eden space is completely cleaned, and all objects that survive are moved to the first survivor space S0. After some time, when another minor GC takes place, Eden space is cleaned again, and more survivors are moved to the survivor space, with some copying between survivor space S0 and S1. Therefore, it is critical to have ample space for Eden and sufficient space for survivor space. As mentioned previously, make the preliminary assumption that a *SurvivorRatio* of 8 is adequate for *SurvivorSpaceSize*.

- **Understanding the impact of reducing or increasing young generation size -Xmn:** If you determine that the duration of the minor GC is too long and pausing longer than the application threads can tolerate (seen by long application response times), it is appropriate to reduce the value of -Xmn. A long duration or pausing in minor GC is an indication of young generation being sized too large for your application.

In Example 3-1, -Xmn is about 33% of -Xmx, which is a good starting point, and it depends on the scale of the heap. In smaller-scale JVM heap sizes less than 8GB, 33% might make sense, but as you get to larger sizes (for example, 33% of 64GB implies -Xmn is 21GB, which is a significant amount of space), the 33% rule might make less sense.

If response-time requirements are met, you do not have to adjust the assumption of -Xmn = 33% of -Xmx. However, if the duration of the pause is too long, you should adjust-Xmn down and observe the impact on the response time of the application. As you reduce -Xmn, you usually reduce the pause time of minor GC, and at the same time increase the frequency of minor GC. This is because a reduction in -Xmn implies a reduced Eden space size, which causes minor GC to run more frequently. This might not be a bad compromise as enough application threads are spread across the full lifecycle of the young generation more uniformly and with less abrupt long pauses, leading to smoother application thread execution across many shorter pauses.

However, if minor GC runs too frequently, meaning that the application threads are hardly getting a chance to execute, or rarely execute, you have sized the -Xmn too low. Increasing -Xmn causes the duration of the pause to increase. You can iteratively adjust -Xmn first downward to the point where you start to see too many frequent minor GCs and then adjust -Xmn slightly higher in the next iteration so that you find the best compromise. If after many iterations you are satisfied with the frequency of the minor GC, but yet the duration is slightly problematic, you can adjust -XX:ParallelGCThreads by increasing them to allow for more parallel GCs to take place by more worker threads.

When setting -XX:ParallelGCThreads, start the size for this at 50% of the available number of underlying vCPU or CPU cores. If you find that there are ample CPU cycles and you would like to further improve performance and speed up GC, increase the number of ParallelGCThreads one increment at a time. Increasing ParallelGCThreads has direct correlation to consuming more CPU cycles. In Example 3-1, one JVM is configured to run on one VM that resides on one socket that has eight underlying CPU cores, and therefore 50% of the CPU compute resource is allocated to potentially be consumed by -XX:ParallelGCThreads. The other 50% on the socket remains for regular application transactions; that is, four vCPUs are consumed by the ParallelGCThreads, and the remaining four are available to service application threads, concurrent old generation activity, off-the-heap activity, and any other workload that might be running on the VM, such as a monitoring agent.

One minor caveat here is that in the very short pausing phases of the initial mark (aside from the other concurrent phases) it is single threaded but finishes rather quickly, and then the re-mark is multithreaded. The initial mark being single threaded does not use any of the -XX:ParallelGCThreads allocated, but the re-mark phase being multithreaded uses some of the parallel threads allocated. Because re-mark is a very short phase, it uses negligible parallel thread cycles.

You can tune -XX:ParallelGCThreads to below 50% allocation to give more threads back to your applications. If you attempt this and it does not hurt overall response time, it might be prudent to reduce -XX:ParallelGCThreads. Conversely, if you have exhausted young generation size tuning, -Xmn, and have ample CPU cycles, consider increasing beyond the 50% mark progressively in one thread increments. Load test and measure response times for the application.

When considering reducing -XX:ParallelGCThreads, the minimum should be two. Any lower than this can negatively impact the behavior of the parallel collector. When sizing large-scale JVMs for vFabric SQLFire types of workloads (for example, 8GB and greater), it requires at least a 4-vCPU VM configuration, because two vCPUs are taken by -XX:ParallelGCThreads, and the other two vCPUs are taken by the application threads. This configuration rule is shown for both the JVM configuration in Example 3-2 (a 4-vCPU VM has two *ParallelGCThreads*) and Example 3-1 (an 8-vCPU virtual machine has four *ParallelGCThreads* allocated). This is 50% of the available vCPUs in both cases.

Furthermore, when using CMS type of configuration, you should always use VM with four vCPUs or more.

> **NOTE**
>
> As previously described, assume a starting survivor ratio of 8 and defer any survivor space tuning until step C.

Figure 3-4 demonstrates the impact of reducing -Xmn as described in the preceding discussion about understanding the impact of reducing or increasing young generation size -Xmn. The diagram shows the original frequency of minor GC as solid blue triangles having larger duration/pause, but then when -Xmn is reduced, the frequency of minor GC is increased, as depicted by the dashed triangles.

Figure 3-5 demonstrates the impact of increasing -Xmn, which has the benefit of reducing the frequency of minor GC but the drawback of increasing its duration or pause. You can use the iterative approach to balance how far to increase -Xmn versus how much to decrease it. The effective range for large-scale JVMs ranges from a few gigabytes, but is never more than approximately 33% of -Xmx.

You can mitigate the increase in minor GC duration by increasing the -XX:ParallelGCThreads. When increasing -XX:ParallelGCThreads, it is a common best practice to start at 50% of available CPU cores dedicated to the vFabric SQLFire member JVM residing on a VM and then progressively adjust upward. This should be done in concert with measuring the core CPU utilization to determine whether ample CPU is left to allocate even more parallel GC threads.

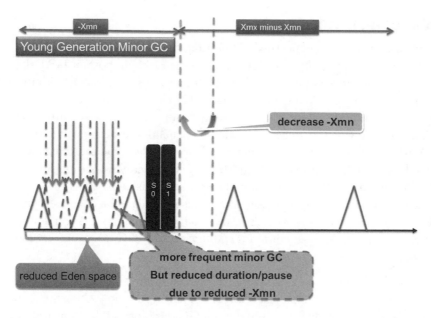

Figure 3-4   Impact of Reducing –Xmn

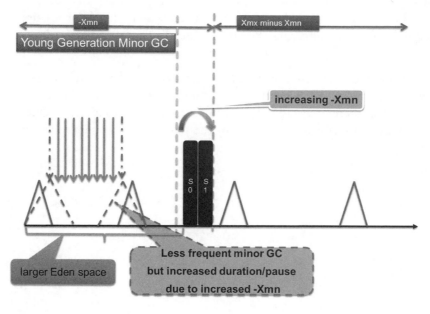

Figure 3-5   Impact of Increasing –Xmn

Step B: Old Generation Tuning

This step (step B from Figure 3-2) is concerned with tuning the old generation after measuring the frequency and duration of major/full GC. The single most important JVM option that influences old generation tuning is often the total heap size, -Xmx, and adjusting this up or down has a bearing on old generation full GC behavior. If you increase -Xmx, you will cause the duration of full GC to take longer, but occur less frequently, and vice versa. The decision as to when to adjust -Xmx directly depends on the adjustments we made in step A, where we adjusted -Xmn. When you increase -Xmn, you cause the old generation space to be reduced, because the old generation is implicitly sized (not directly through a direct JVM option) as -Xmx *minus* -Xmn. The tuning decision to offset the increased -Xmn size is to proportionally increase -Xmx to accommodate the change. If you increased -Xmn by 5% of -Xmx, then -Xmx needs to be also increased by 5%. If you don't, the impact of increasing -Xmn on old generation is an increased full GC frequency because now the old generation space has been reduced.

The inverse argument also holds in the case where -Xmn is reduced; -Xmx has to be proportionally reduced as well. If you don't adjust -Xmx as a result of reducing -Xmn, the old generation space is proportionally larger and the full GC duration will be longer in this case.

In Figure 3-6, the impact of decreasing young generation size -Xmn has the effect of increasing the full GC duration on the old generation. The increase in the old generation full GC duration can be offset by decreasing -Xmx proportionally to the amount -Xmn was reduced by.

Figure 3-7 shows the impact of increasing the young generation size -Xmn on the old generation. When you increase the young generation size, it implicitly causes the old generation size to become smaller, therefore causing the frequency of full GC to increase. One way to offset this is to proportionally increase -Xmx by the amount -Xmn was increased by.

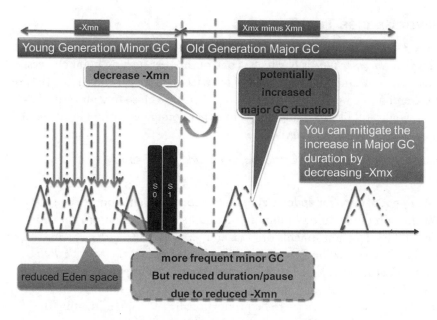

Figure 3-6   Impact of Decreasing the Young Generation on the Old Generation

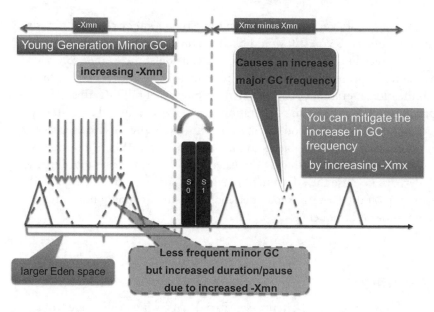

Figure 3-7   Impact on the Old Generation of Increasing the Young Generation

Step C: Survivor Spaces Tuning

Step C from Figure 3-2 attempts to refine the survivor spaces. The assumption thus far in the discussion is that *SurvivorRatio* is 8, which is one of the best starting point choices. When *SurvivorRatio* is 8, this implies that the survivor space sizes for S0 and S1 are 10% of -Xmn each. If at the end of the iterative step A and step B you are close to your response-time objectives but would still like to refine things in either young generation or old generation, you can attempt to adjust the survivor spaces sizes.

Before tuning the *SurvivorRatio*, note that the *SurvivorSpaceSize* = -Xmn / (*SurvivorRatio* +2).

- **Refinement impact of survivor space sizing on the young generation:** If you still have a problem with the duration of minor GC in the young generation, but you have exhausted the sizing adjustments of -Xmn and -XX:ParallelGCThreads, you can potentially increase the *SurvivorSpaceSize* by decreasing the *SurvivorRatio*. You can try setting the *SurvivorRatio* to 6 instead of 8, which implies that the survivor spaces will be 12.5% of -Xmn for each of S0 and S1. The resulting increase in *SurvivorSpaceSize* causes Eden space to be proportionally reduced, mitigating the long duration/pause problem. Conversely, if minor GC is too frequent, you can choose to increase the Eden space size by increasing *SurvivorRatio* to not more than 15, which reduces the *SurvivorSpaceSize*.

- **Refinement impact of survivor space sizing on the old generation:** If, after iteratively following step A and step B you still would like to refine the old generation but have exhausted all the preceding recommendations, you can adjust the *SurvivorSpaceSize* to delay the tenure or promotion of surviving objects from S0 and S1 to the old generation. If in the old generation you have a high frequency of full GC, this indicates excessive promotion from the young generation. If -Xmn was adjusted as in step A and you need only a refinement, you can increase the size of the survivor spaces to delay the promotion of surviving objects to the old generation. When you increase the survivor space size, you are reducing the Eden space, which causes more frequent minor GC. Perhaps because the adjustment of survivor spaces is in the range of 5% to 10% depending on the *SurvivorRatio*, this small adjustment should not cause a large spike in minor GC frequency.

Chapter Summary

This chapter explored how to best tune latency-sensitive JVMs, which can range from 4GB to 128GB and more. We explored how a combination of the CMS and ParNewGC GC can work cooperatively to yield the best response-time numbers and hence minimize the negative impacts of latency.

Chapter 4

Designing and Sizing Large-Scale Java Platforms

This chapter explores various approaches to designing and sizing large-scale Java platforms. The three key topics discussed include the following:

- How to design and size a new environment

- How to design and size a new large-scale Java platform when migrating an existing physical deployment to a virtualized one

- How to design and size large-scale Java platforms for latency-sensitive in-memory databases such as vFabric SQLFire

Designing and Sizing a New Environment for a Virtualized Large-Scale Java Platform

When deploying completely new environments, it is important to conduct an extensive performance test so that any potential bottlenecks are exposed early in the lifecycle of the project. The three-step process is as follows:

Step 1. Establish the load profile.

Step 2. Establish the benchmark.

Step 3. Size the production environment.

The first step is to establish the workload profile; if this is a completely new application, an initial test is conducted at step 2 to establish the benchmark. If the application already exists, and you are simply trying to load test the Java platform to determine compute resource requirements in a virtualized environment, then in step 1 you will need to obtain the service level agreement (SLA) requirements and test against these in step 2.

Step1: Establishing Your Current Production Load Profile

When estimating the load profile, measure some, if not all, of the properties listed in Table 4-1 to establish your Java application's production load. The load profile should also have a good transactional mix of common functionality that your users execute when using the application.

Table 4-1   Load Profile Properties

Load Profile Properties	Description
Modeling functionality access patterns	By studying the user access behavior of the business application, you can model performance load driver design based on this. It is important to model the load driver functionality very closely to the way the users access the application. Most applications will have a certain mix of access to read functions, write functions, CPU bound, memory bound, network, and then storage/disk bound access patterns. Any slight variation on the percentage of access between these can alter the benchmark numbers. It is therefore imperative (by studying access patterns through inspecting logs and monitoring system information) to review these with application developers and applications operations teams to reach an agreement on whether the load driver design and implementation is accurate.

Load Profile Properties	Description
Concurrent users	Based on how you track user access to your application, you can use that information to establish peak and average user profiles. Some methods of establishing the number of users are a combination of inspecting login-logout functionality, or if that does not exist, some user access logs in combination with URL cookie tracking (or a commercial monitoring tool).
	Concurrent users is a common term used to express the load applied during a test. This metric measures how many users are active at any one time.
	This is different from requests per second (RPS), because potentially one user can generate a high number of requests, whereas other users may generate a relatively low number. When establishing your load test, the delay between the requests is the *think time*. Average think time can vary depending on your application.
Requests per second (RPS)	RPS is the measurement of how many requests are being sent to the target server. It includes requests for HTML pages, CSS style sheets, XML documents, JavaScript libraries, images, and Flash/multimedia files.
	In addition to these requests, there are requests for dynamic pages: JavaServer Pages (JSP) and others, that are server-bound requests—requests from the web server that are handled by the application server. You can establish the request mix (how many static requests versus dynamic requests) by studying the redirect rules and the access logs of your web server. Dynamic requests are important because they turn into Java threads being consumed from the Java application server, and in turn, if they access the database, then database connections are checked out from the Java Database Connectivity (JDBC) connection pool configured at the Java application server.
Average response times	This can be measured as the time to first/last byte received from your application requests. If you have production response time SLA monitoring in place, you can use reports from those tools. If not, you can establish this via benchmark during the load test.
Peak response time	Measures the round-trip time for request/response cycle.

Step 2: Establish a Benchmark

The objective of step 2, as shown in Figure 4-1, is to establish a benchmark and conduct vertical scalability (scale-up test) and horizontal scalability (scale-out) tests.

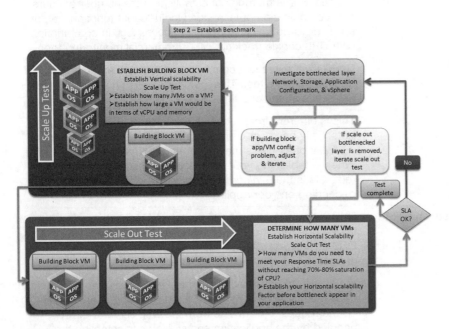

Figure 4-1   Establishing Building Block VM and Scaling Out

Step 2a: Establish a Benchmark for Vertical Scalability Test

In the vertical scalability test, try to establish how large a virtual machine (VM) can be and the number of Java Virtual Machines (JVMs) that can be stacked on top of the VM before you reach the desired SLA and maintain tolerable CPU and memory saturation levels. The resulting VM configurations with the various JVMs from this test form the building block VM for the scale-out test. It is imperative that the deployment is representative of the actual application mix for the intended production deployment. For example, if your application uses another two applications, these must be present to appropriately profile the performance. It is also important to know that as much as possible should be conducted within the first JVM before you decide to create a second JVM on top of the building block VM. Sometimes this is not possible for reasons related to application architecture, but sometimes applications are made of at minimum two JVMs per VM for various business functionality reasons. However, most commonly JVMs in a scale-out arrangement are independent entities, and whether one JVM carries the execution of the functionality or two JVMs is a matter of your design and how comfortable the engineers involved are with tuning larger JVM heap sizes. By the time you finish reading this book, let's hope that larger JVMs will not be an issue and you can easily apply them to your Java platform.

The reason why we would want to prevent having to create a second JVM on top of a VM is because of the overhead that the second JVM would add due to its additional garbage collection (GC) cycle. Although VMs can handle multiple JVMs on a VM, the second JVM really comes at an overhead and a cost that can be prevented by trying to carry more transactions within one JVM. If you are able to do more within the first JVM that is currently on the building block VM, you will find GC algorithms have become much better in being able to vertically scale up without consuming proportionally more CPU with increased heap size. The act of adding more JVMs on top of a VM is sometimes referred to as *JVM stacking*, meaning multiple JVMs being deployed on one VM. Instead of this, it is always best to have a scale-out approach, where if you decide that you need a second JVM, instead of placing that JVM on top of the existing VM, consider creating a second VM and place the second JVM on the second VM. For further information about the pros and cons of the JVM scale-out versus scale-up (JVM stacking on a VM), see the section "Horizontal Scaling Versus Vertical Scaling of JVMs and VMs," in Chapter 1, "Introduction to Large-Scale Java Platforms."

> **NOTE**
>
> In the preceding discussion, we simplify the scenario to a single JVM versus two JVMs being stacked on a VM. This is intentional to simplify the comparisons. However, the comparisons, and the pros and cons of JVM stacking versus scaling out with VMs, can apply to *n* number of JVMs and VMs.

The building block VM is a key output of the scale-up test. For example, you may have established that for a JVM of 4GB heap, and a VM with 5GB memory reservation and two vCPUs (assuming one vCPU is equal to one pCPU/core), 300 concurrent user sessions were achieved. This implies that you can save this building block VM along with its configuration as a golden copy that is certified to achieve 300 concurrent user sessions. Future VM deployments when scaling out should use this building block VM template to deploy from.

> **NOTE**
>
> Here we ignore the effects of hyperthreading, and we will address this during scale out, step 2b. Hyperthreading should be enabled, but we don't factor it into the calculation just yet. Hyperthreading effects usually appear during a near-saturated test, where all the

physical cores are busy and a need to leverage the hyperthread is used. For production systems, we do not size the hyperthread into the capacity (although it is available in case it is needed, just in case the system is close to the maximum ceiling of the CPU capacity). However, in benchmarking we may sometimes try to see how far we can drive the virtual setup versus the physical setup. In those cases, we would typically calculate vCPU <= 1.25 pCPU, where pCPU is physical CPU cores. Finally, what we do in benchmarking does not always translate to a best practice for production systems, specifically in this case of running systems so close to the CPU capacity.

To calculate the various memory segment requirements of a JVM deployed on a VM, it is important to understand the requirements of each memory section that exists within a JVM, as shown in Figure 4-2. In this figure, the total memory for the VM is made of guest OS memory and the memory required by the JVM (that is, JVM memory). The JVM memory is essentially made of the Java heap and the off-heap section. In many cases, not much is known about the off-heap section, and it gets missed in calculations. This section cannot be ignored; it must be accounted for. Formula 4-1 shows how to calculate the memory requirements of this VM.

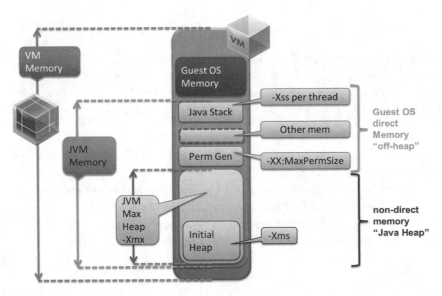

Figure 4-2   Memory Segments Depicted on One HotSpot JVM Deployed on One VM

The total memory reservation required for a VM and JVM configuration shown in Figure 4-2 is shown in Formula 4-1.

> **VM Memory = Guest OS Memory + JVM Memory**
>
> *JVM Memory =*
>
>   JVM Max Heap (-Xmx value) +
>   JVM Perm Size (-XX:MaxPermSize) +
>   NumberOfConcurrentThreads * (-Xss) + "other Mem"

Formula 4-1   VM Memory Reservation

The following is a sizing example that you can you can refer to and adjust according to your workload needs. It is an example of how to apply Formula 4-1:

Assume that through load testing a JVM max heap (-Xmx) of 4096m has been determined as necessary. Proceed to size as follows:

- Set -Xmx4096m and set -Xms4096m.

- Set -XX:MaxPermSize=256m. This value is a common number and depends on the memory footprint of the class-level information within your Java application code base.

- The other segment of NumberOfConcurrentThreads * (-Xss) depends mostly on the NumberOfConcurrentThreads the JVM will process, and the -Xss value you select. A common range of -Xss is 128K to 256K. If, for example, NumberOfConcurrentThreads is 100, then 100 * 192K => 19200K (assuming you set -Xss to 192K).

> **NOTE**
>
> The stack -Xss is application dependent; that is, if the stack is not sized correctly, you will get a StackOverflow error. The StackOverflow error will appear in the application server logs. The default value is sometimes quite large, but you can size it down to help save on memory consumption.

- Assume that the OS has a requirement of about 500MB to run as per the OS spec.

- Total JVM memory (Java process memory) = 4096m (-Xmx) + 256m (-XX:MaxPermSize) + 100 * 192K (NumberOfConcurrentThreads * -Xss) + Other Mem.

  - Therefore, JVM memory is approximately 4096MB + 256MB + 19.2MB + Other Mem = 4371MB + Other Mem.

- Other Mem is usually not significant. However, it can be quite large if the application uses a lot of New I/O (NIO) buffers and socket buffers. Otherwise, assuming about 5% of the total JVM process memory (that is, 4% to 5% of 4371 => Assume 217MB) should be enough, although proper load testing should be used to verify.

- This implies that JVM process memory is 4371MB + 217MB = 4588MB.

- To determine the VM memory, assume that you are using Linux with only this single Java process and no other significant process running. The total configured memory for the VM translates to VM memory = 4588MB + 500MB = 5088MB.

- Finally, you should set the VM memory as the memory reservation. You can choose to set the memory reservation as 5088MB.

Figure 4-3 illustrates these numbers and where the memory sections are located within the VM and the JVM.

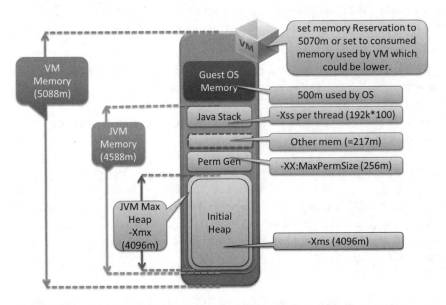

Figure 4-3   JVM with 4GB Heap on a 2-vCPU VM with a 5GB Reservation

Step 2b: Establish a Benchmark for Horizontal Scalability Test

In this step, the output from step 2a: Establish a Benchmark for Vertical Scalability Test, the building block VM is used to horizontally scale out multiple VMs. These VMs are built from the building block VM template deployed on a single vSphere host. Because in step 2A the capacity of a VM was certified within the building block VM template, next we want to establish how much traffic can be driven across one vSphere host. Since, for example, from step 2A you know that the building block VM is of 5GB memory reservation and two vCPUs, it is now a matter of selecting the appropriately sized vSphere host and working backward to figure out how many VMs you can deploy on the host. Essentially, it becomes a matter of dividing the total RAM and physical CPU of the vSphere host by the building block VM. If the JVMs you are sizing are of category 1 (many JVMs but of smaller size) and if you restrict the JVM heap to 4GB, you will create far too many JVMs and VMs reaching CPU contention before one can fully consume the amount of physical RAM available on a typical vSphere host. Hence, selecting the right size vSphere host with just enough memory is critical to the horizontal scalability test.

Let's take a look at a few examples to help understand how critical it is to choose the right amount of RAM within a vSphere host.

Example 1

For example, let's take a vSphere host that has two sockets of eight cores on each socket and 128GB of RAM. Based on a memory calculation, let's assume a building block VM of 4GB heap and 5GB total VM memory reservation. By applying Formula 1-2 from Chapter 1 here without dividing by the number of sockets as shown in the original formula (ignoring NUMA for a minute), $128 - ((128GB*0.98) +1GB) => 124.44GB$ is available for VM memory configurations on the vSphere host in total.

> **NOTE**
>
> The 0.98 multiplier assumes two VMs would be configured to start with, just to commence the first iteration of the calculation, and then if you add more VMs you have to accommodate about 1% memory overhead for each VM that vSphere will utilize. It turns out that two VMs (that is, one VM per NUMA node/socket) is the configuration with the least amount of overhead that can leverage all the compute resources available. This needs to be weighed against other practicality factors, however, such as the application deployment topology and how many JVMs and VMs are needed. Refer to Table 1-1 in Chapter 1, which details the pros and cons. In addition, the 2-VM configuration would lead to very large VMs, the kind more appropriate for category 2 Java platform workloads (in-memory databases), but may not necessarily be the best configuration for category 1, where there are potentially line of business (LOB) requirements that demand more JVMs and VMs to offer better isolation of functionality.

Now if the 124.44GB is divided by the 4.5GB as required by a building block JVM (the building block VM memory reservation is 5GB because 0.5GB is allocated for guest OS; therefore, the actual JVM process is only using 4.5GB), it implies 124.44GB/45GB => 27.65 building block JVMs can be safely configured on the vSphere host of this example. Naturally, this is from a memory perspective, and these 27.65 JVMs are to be deployed equally across two large VMs. In some cases, this might be an adequate configuration; however, you can easily see that on a vSphere host in the example of two 8-core sockets we have a total of 16 CPU cores, this implies a ratio of 16 CPU cores / 27.65 JVMs => 0.57 physical CPU cores per JVM, which is slightly aggressive. Although, as mentioned earlier, it is heavily dependent on how aggressive the workload is, and in some cases it may be sufficient. In most ideal cases, we want to see a starting JVM to vCPU ratio of about one JVM per two vCPUs (assuming one vCPU is equal to one CPU core). So, if we take this assumption, then 2 sockets of 8 cores on each socket, for a total of 16 CPU cores on the vSphere host, we should only have 8 JVMs and VMs on this vSphere host to keep the 1-JVM to 2-vCPU ratio intact (assuming multiple JVMs to be deployed on 2 VMs). With this assumption, to fully consume the 128GB (124.44GB when accounting for VM and ESXi overhead) of RAM available, each JVM will have an allocation of (124.44 – 2GB) / 8 => 15.3GB). The 2GB in the formula is to account for OS memory consumption in the VM and because we have two VMs (OS memory requirements could be as low as 0.5GB; it depends what else is running on the VM that consumes more guest OS memory). This, in turn, implies that the Java heap size will be approximately at minimum (15.3 – 1GB) * 0.75 to a maximum of (15.3 – 1GB) * 0.9 (that is, a minimum of approximately 11 to 13GB). The minimum multiplier of 0.75 accounts for off-the-heap overhead, and the 0.9 multiplier is the maximum calculation accounting for a much smaller off-the-heap overhead. Usually, though, if you have a JVM sized with a heap of 4GB (-Xmx4g), you would want the memory allocation for the entire Java process to be about 10% to 25% more than the heap, and then add 0.5 to 1GB for the guest OS.

> **NOTE**
>
> The preceding example didn't factor in the effects of hyperthreading. If we did, we could add an additional 25% of vCPUs, making the total number of vCPUs with hyperthreading enabled as 1.25 * pCPUs, where pCPUs is the number of physical cores. (This example has a 16-CPU core vSphere host; that is, 16 pCPUs.) Hence, the total hyperthreaded vCPUs would be 16 * 1.25 => 20vCPUs. So, to fully commit the vSphere host, you can add at least 2 more JVMs, for a total of 10. Of course, if you choose to put 10 JVMs, the previously mentioned memory calculation of 15.3GB would adjust downward to => (124.44 – 2) / 10 number of hyperthreaded JVMs. (10) => 12.2GB would be allocated to the JVM, from a maximum perspective. This in turn translates to approximately (12.2 * 0.75) => 9.18GB for Java heap space. (That is, the -Xmx JVM command options can be set to this.) The 0.75

multiplier assumes the heap is about 75% of the total Java process, allowing about 25% for the off-the-heap section of the Java process, which is ample space.

Typically, during sizing we don't account for the effects of hyperthreading, although it is recommended that you leave hyperthreading enabled. During load testing and when trying to establish a benchmark, or if trying to overcommit the vSphere host, you can account for the hyperthreading adjustments; however, for production systems you would not want to size for a saturated situation, but rather a conservative assumption of 1 vCPU = 1 pCPU non-hyperthreaded, even though hyperthreading is enabled. Leave hyperthreading as your buffer ceiling just in case a saturated situation materializes accidentally in production. In load testing, you might attempt to determine the break point of a vSphere host, which implies accounting for hyperthreading. However, sizing production takes a more conservative approach of not trying to account for the adjustment in CPU cycles that hyperthreading introduces.

At this juncture (assuming eight JVMs selected to be deployed on the vSphere host, with two VMs), you can either stay with the vSphere host of 128GB, with 16 physical cores, and be forced to size the heap much larger than what you are comfortable with (for instance, 11 to 13GB), or you can decide that you will purchase less RAM on the vSphere host and adjust heap to a more comfortable territory.

NOTE

Smaller vSphere hosts may lead to the need to have larger vSphere clusters because you need more hosts. The sweet spot of vSphere cluster sizes is around 8 to 16, but there is nothing magical about this number. It is likely that category 1 workloads will have a larger number of vSphere hosts, with less RAM, to permit plenty of opportunity for Distributed Resource Scheduler (DRS) to load balance VM movement. In contrast, category 2 in-memory database workloads within vSphere clusters would have a smaller number of hosts (four to eight hosts, usually with very large 144 to 512GB RAM configurations). Naturally, in category 2, these decisions are really driven by the size of the data, and again you could have a larger number of hosts in a cluster, larger than eight, but you are most likely to have about eight. This keeps the cluster in closer distribution proximity, minimizing the effects of latency and being able to crunch more within larger JVMs that are typical of in-memory database type of workloads often found in category 2 workloads. Like any design decision, there are pros and cons, and the more vSphere hosts, the better redundancy. Of course, you must balance this against cost and realistic performance capabilities for category 2 workloads.

Example 2

If you instead decide to purchase a vSphere host with 48GB RAM, you can adjust all the RAM numbers downward by applying Formula 1-2. Let's double-check this by applying Formula 1-2 here without dividing by the number of sockets as shown in the original formula (ignoring NUMA for a minute): ((48GB * 0.98) – 1GB) => 46GB is available for JVM memory configurations across the vSphere host in total. If you account for running two copies of the guest OS, due to the two VMs to be deployed on this vSphere host, the net available RAM to the JVMs is effectively => 46 – 1 => 45GB. If this is then divided by the 4.5GB required by a building block VM (note that the building block VM memory reservation is 5GB because 0.5GB is allocated for guest OS, therefore the actual JVM process is only using 4.5GB.), it implies 45GB / 4.5GB => 10.2 building block JVMs. This means the ratio of JVMs is 16 cores / 10 JVMs => 1.6 cores per JVM, which is pretty close to our desired best practices ratio of each JVM having 2 vCPUs. To be in line with the 1-JVM to 2-vCPU ratio rule, this vSphere host should really have only eight JVMs on it. From here, the adjustment downward or upward of the number of VMs will depend on your actual performance metrics against the utilized CPU and memory. You have the luxury to decide whether you want the eight JVMs distributed on eight VMs, or eight JVMs on two VMs, or eight JVMs on four VMs. In each case, there are pros and cons, as discussed earlier in Chapter 1 (see Table 1-1). However, for the most part, these are all valid configurations that will still maintain a healthy 1-JVM to 2-vCPU ratio regardless of whether you choose eight VMs, four VMs, or two VMs.

> **NOTE**
>
> The preceding calculation uses a multiplier of 0.98 to allow for 2% VM overhead; this assumes about 1% memory overhead for every VM, in line with Formula 1-2; hence, the more VMs you add, the more likely memory overhead will be needed.

> **NOTE**
>
> If during the scale-out test saturation is reached, investigate all the layers (network, application configuration, and vSphere) and determine where the bottleneck is. Remove the bottleneck and repeat the test by adjusting the number of VMs. Alternatively, if you find that the original building block VM has a misconfiguration at the VM or application configuration level, adjust and repeat the vertical load test to determine a new building block VM. For example, if you had originally chosen a 4-vCPU VM as your building block, and you scaled out based on this, driving max load against the Java platform, you may find that the 4-vCPU

building block as a scale-out VM causes the entire Java platform to drive excessive load against the database tier. In this case, you should revise the building block VM downward to a more reasonable configuration such as 2-vCPU VM.

Use the VM from the scale-up test as a repeatable building block for the scale-out test. This helps in two ways. First, it allows for a well-defined and known configuration to be repeated, eliminating configuration guesswork. Second, it means that all the nodes in your application cluster are identical, which simplifies load-balancer logic. The load balancer can thus distribute load equally without having to know the configuration of the individual VMs. For example, if your VM is a 2-vCPU VM, all the VMs in the application cluster are 2-vCPU VMs and can potentially handle the same workload. If the VMs have different configurations, the load balancer requires a special configuration to accommodate the different VM configurations in the application cluster. In the following scale-out test, you are actually testing the capacity of a single vSphere host to see how many building block JVMs or VMs can be afforded.

At this point, you have selected a vSphere host from Example 2 above after various discussions with your architects and performance engineers. This is a vSphere host made of two eight-core sockets and 48GB of RAM, and you have decided to place eight JVMs and eight VMs on it. Naturally, the fewer VMs, the fewer OS copies you need to size and provide memory to. So, you can get away with just having two big VMs deployed on the vSphere host. Because we assumed approximately 300 concurrent user transactions were achievable across one building block 2-vCPU VM and a 5GB memory reservation (essentially a 4.5GB RAM building block JVM is contained on the 5GB building block VM), on this vSphere host you can safely assume, approximately, that eight building block JVMs (two VMs, as suggested in Example 2) will be able to achieve 8 * 300 => 2400 concurrent user transactions.

The essence of step 1 and 2 has been to get to a number that you can certify for a JVM or VM and a vSphere host in terms of your SLA and then from this determine how big the vSphere cluster should be to service the entire anticipated traffic for the application. During the step 2 tests, it is really just one vSphere host being tested (with no DRS/VMotion being applied). Step 3 is a process of sizing the entire vSphere cluster and then turning on DRS and watching the entire cluster behave under stress.

It is also important in this step to test various failure scenarios and monitor how the Java platform behaves when there are forced JVM and VM restarts or high-availability (HA) failover events.

Table 4-2 describes some key considerations when sizing the benchmarking environment.

Table 4-2   Key Considerations for Sizing the Benchmark Environment

Consideration	Description
Establish vertical scalability.	This test establishes the building block VM. This VM is used as a repeatable VM for the scale-out test. Each VM in the application cluster of the scale-out test will be based on this building block VM: ■ Determine the vCPU and memory size of the VM to meet the desired SLA. ■ Establish how many JVMs can be stacked on this VM.
Establish horizontal scalability.	The horizontal scalability load test takes the building block VM from the vertical scalability load test and uses it to scale out the load-testing environment: ■ If saturation occurs before reaching the desired SLA, investigate whether this is due to any of the network, application layer, vSphere, or storage layers. ■ When the system can maintain the desired SLA under a production level of traffic, you have found your desired configuration. This system configuration is usually the configuration you will start with in production as most migration to virtualization projects start with a completely new environment. This environment is then verified through the described load testing in the preproduction phase.

Consideration	Description
Establish appropriate thread ratios (HTTP threads:Java threads:DB connections).	■ This is the ratio of HTTP threads to Java threads to database connections.
	■ Establish the initial setup by assuming that each layer requires a 1:1:1 ratio of HTTP threads:Java threads:DB connections, and then based on the response time and throughput numbers, adjust each of these properties until you have met your SLA objectives.
	■ Using an example of 100 concurrent requests, the ratio would initially be 100 HTTP threads to 100 Java threads to 100 DB connections
	For example, if you have 100 HTTP requests initially submitted to the web server, assume that all of these will have an interaction with Java threads and in turn DB connections. As you perform the benchmark testing, you will find that not all HTTP threads are submitted to the Java application server, and in turn, not all Java application server threads will each require a DB connection. The ratio for 100 requests may translate to 100 HTTP threads:25 Java threads:10 DB connections. This depends on the enterprise Java application behavior; benchmarking helps to establish this ratio. You can get closer to the correct ratio by observing the number of database connections active in the pool (by means of Java Management Extensions [JMX]) or by taking a thread stack dump of the application server under heavy load and seeing how many request threads are waiting on database connections.

Consideration	Description
Establish appropriate number of HTTP threads for web server and application server request threads.	■ HTTP threads (web server). Whether you are using the Apache web server or Internet Information Services (IIS) as your web server, you must configure enough HTTP worker threads to handle the requests per second that your application incurs.
	■ With Apache, the number of client threads is configured via the `MaxClients` attribute. See the Apache tuning guides if you want to tune more extensively, but most default values are an adequate starting point. Take into account the scale-out number of Apache instances when sizing for `MaxClients`. For example, if you have 1000 concurrent requests and 4 Apache web server VM nodes, each node only needs a `MaxClients` value of 250. In IIS, set `MaxConnections` similarly. See the vendor documentation for settings.
	■ The web server is the front end for all HTTP requests that get routed to it from the load balancer, whether the requests are for *static content* or *dynamic content*. Some applications are configured such that static content such as HTML pages and images are completely handled by the web server, and these requests are never seen by the Java application server. In this kind of configuration, when a web server detects a request for dynamic content, such as a request for JavaServer Pages (JSP) or servlet, these requests are directed to the Java application server where a Java application server thread is checked out from the Java application server's pool to service the request. Benchmarking helps establish the total transactional mix and guides you in adjusting the thread ratios up or down accordingly.

Consideration	Description
Establish the appropriate ratio of application server threads to database connections by configuring the application server JDBC pool.	■ Adjust the number of available DB connections in the application server's connection pool settings and count the number of potential concurrent Java threads that might need a DB connection. For simplicity, you can assume a 1:1 ratio, and add some room to reduce potential contention or a race for DB connections.
	■ Deadlock can occur if the application requires more than 1 concurrent connection per thread and the database connection pool is not large enough for the number of threads. Suppose that each of the application threads requires 2 concurrent database connections and that the number of threads is equal to the maximum connection pool size. Deadlock can occur when both of the following are true:
	■ Each thread has its first database connection, and all are in use.
	■ Each thread is waiting for a second database connection, and none becomes available because all threads are blocked.
	■ To prevent the deadlock in this case, increase the maximum connections value for the database connection pool by at least 1. This allows at least 1 of the waiting threads to obtain a second database connection and avoids a deadlock scenario.
	■ See the application server documentation for any additional JDBC pool tuning you can do in terms of start size of the connection pool minimum/maximum, growth rate, idle connections, recycle and timeout parameters, and so on.

Step 3: Size the Production Environment

During this step, you try to determine the size of the vSphere cluster that will support the SLA for the application. Figure 4-4 shows a vSphere cluster with eight vSphere hosts, two VMs of eight vCPUs each deployed on each vSphere host. Each VM is configured to have approximately 23GB memory reservation, and in turn each of these VMs has four JVMs on them. From step 2, we determined that a vSphere host was able to support 2400 concurrent user transactions; it is safe to assume that eight vSphere hosts can handle 8 * 2400 => 19200 concurrent user transactions. Of course, linear extrapolation is only accurate to a certain point before a bottleneck starts to appear. Therefore, before going live, it is wise to have the entire vSphere cluster tested to ascertain its capacity. During this test, you also want to ensure that DRS is turned on and observe VMotion impact on your applications.

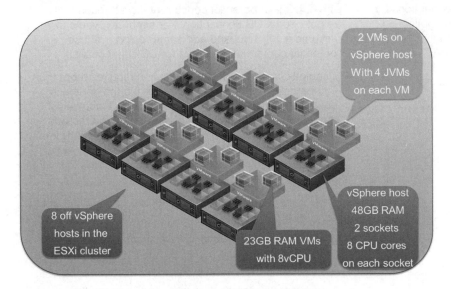

Figure 4-4   vSphere Cluster Design

Sizing vFabric SQLFire Java Platforms: Category 2 Workloads

Designing and sizing is a three step-process:

Step A.   Determine entity groups.

Step B.   Determine the memory size of the data fabric.

Step C.   Establish building block VM and JVM size and how many SQLFire members are needed.

After these steps have been concluded, a load test should be used to verify the calculation and sizing assumptions.

NOTE

Entity groups are logical design constructs that percolate the query usage patterns within the application and the schema. It is kind of a grouping of various queries and trying to relate them to a handful of tables that are always accessed. Another perspective is that entity groups are a way of categorizing the access patterns (SQL queries) within the application to determine how the database schema is being used. With this information, you can establish an appropriate indexing/partitioning strategy. The general exercise is to determine the root primary keys that link all the queries or set of queries, and then use such top-level common primary keys as the partition-by key.

Step A: Determine Entity Groups

The process of determining entity groups helps with establishing your partitioning strategy and then iteratively determining how much data to keep in memory within the vFabric SQLFire data fabric. This method of establishing entity groups for your schema is a helpful design-time technique for large schemas or multiple schemas servicing different lines of business and data access patterns. Customers often refer to the vFabric SQLFire data fabric as the daily transactional data, 1 to 10 days' worth of data, or longer in some cases depending on the use case being implemented. After this size is determined, you can determine the appropriate entity groups. The process of selecting what portion of the daily transactional data to keep and entity group selection is an iterative process.

Step A can be further detailed as substeps A1, A2, A3, and A4, as outlined in Figure 4-5.

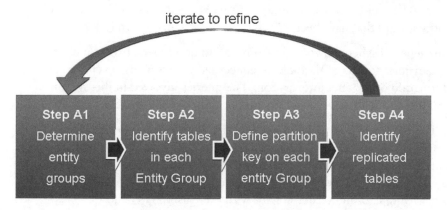

Figure 4-5 Step A Substeps for Designing Entity Groups

Figure 4-6 shows an example of a product and order management schema. This schema is used to identify its various entity groups by inspecting the usage patterns.

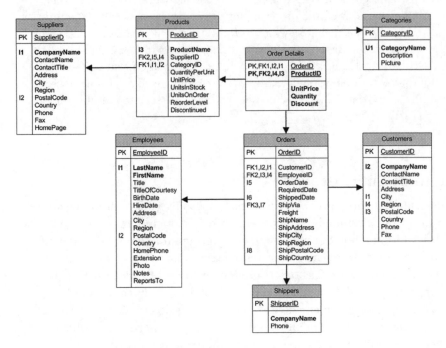

Figure 4-6   A Product Order Management Schema

In Figure 4-7, steps A1 to A4 (steps from Figure 4-5) are applied iteratively, and therefore there are two entity groups that have been selected for the schema shown in Figure 4-6.

Based on the experience of schema owners and application developers, two groups are selected because a majority of the SQL joins are concerned with looking up either customer order information or product information. The queries involved in this system can fall into these two broad categories, which leads to the choice of the two entity groups.

The first group, Entity Group-1 for Customers, Orders, Shippers, and Order Details tables is partitioned by the `CustomerID` because that is the best key that all the queries of the associated enterprise application use. In addition, because the queries often join the Customer table with Orders, Shippers, and Order Details, it is highly recommended to colocate the Orders, Shippers, and Order Details with the Customers table.

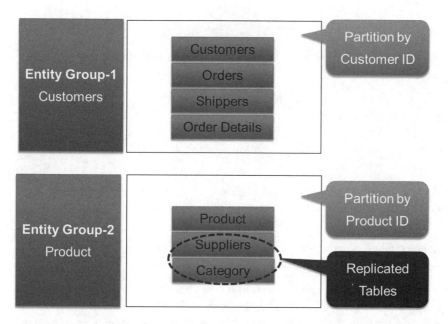

Figure 4-7   Selecting Entity Groups and Partition by ID for the Product Order Management Schema

The second entity group is Entity Group-2 for Product, Suppliers, and Category. In this case, the Product table is partitioned by `ProductID` because it is the natural primary key for that table and therefore all queries against it can be appropriately matched within the specific partition in vFabric SQLFire. In addition, the Suppliers and Category tables, which are "code tables / lookup tables" that do not change rapidly and have a many-to-many relation with products, should be replicated across all the vFabric SQLFire members in the data fabric.

NOTE

Refer to the previous discussion on vFabric SQLFire partitioning, co-location, and replication. Partitioning is used for rapidly changing data, and co-location is to help qualify joins within the same partition for parent-child type of queries, like Order and Order Details. Replication is for data that rarely changes but is needed in almost every query due to a many-to-many relationship (in this case associated with a Product).

> **NOTE**
>
> - Entity groups are a logical abstraction that drives your partitioning, colocation, and replication strategy.
>
> - It is important to understand the SQL access patterns of data from the application. Obtain a listing of the most commonly used SQL queries and understand how they are logically grouped, and map that back to your schema and decide which queries dictate which tables are to be included in an entity group, and therefore which partition key is to be nominated.
>
> - Understand which data changes rapidly, has large scale, and therefore must be partitioned by a certain key. Also understand parent-child relationships between tables and based on this, colocate the appropriate tables.
>
> - Understand which tables do not change much, like lookup/static/metadata tables and so forth, and decide on those to be replicated instead of partitioned.
>
> - Choosing a portion of your transactional data to live in vFabric SQLFire data fabric is the correct approach. Understand how much data you want to keep and that you are willing to deliver at extreme speeds, versus other data that has less-stringent response-time requirements. For example, you might have 1TB on disk of an RDBMS traditional DB, but only 50GB as daily transactional data or hot data, which is data that rapidly changes and has stringent response-time requirements that are dictated by enterprise data-consuming applications.
>
> - Test your partitioning scheme under load so that connections are evenly spread across the system and so that "hot spots" do not develop in the system.

Step B: Determine the Memory Size of the Data Fabric

This step summarizes all the sizing formulas associated with determining how much RAM is needed to house the "raw daily transactional data set" within the vFabric SQLFire data fabric.

The formulas are summarized for the general case and then used in an actual sizing example, for both the entire data fabric within a vSphere cluster, and also the sizing ratios for the JVM and associated VM construct.

Step A (determine entity groups) presented a process that gives an idea of the "raw daily transactional data set" and type of data kept within the data fabric. The next formulas highlight what the actual size is within the data fabric for this raw daily transactional data set that is to be managed in the data fabric. Factors that impact the raw daily transactional data set are explained in the following formulas, and are in the following general categories:

- The total size of the raw data (that is, the raw daily transactional data set nominated to be managed within all partitioned and replicated tables)

- The memory size of the colocated data

- The memory size of all the redundant copies

- The number of concurrent threads and socket buffers accessing data and the associated memory footprint

- General GC overhead and overhead associated with using CMS (concurrent mark sweep) type of Java garbage collector that is most appropriate for latency-sensitive workloads such as those in vFabric SQLFire

- General overhead due to the number of indexes and other vFabric SQLFire constructs

In Formula 4-2, the total memory requirement for the vFabric SQLFire data fabric is captured as *TotalMemoryPerSQLFireSystemWithHeadRoom*, which in turn is calculated from *TotalMemoryPerSQLFireSystem* with 50% headroom. The headroom is sometimes needed because of the nature of memory-hungry latency-sensitive systems that typically require a GC policy with CMS, because CMS is a multiphase, noncompacting GC policy that requires substantial headroom to deliver better response time. Also, the *TotalMemoryPer-SQLFireSystem* is calculated from the daily transaction raw data size for the entire data fabric that you have selected to be managed in vFabric SQLFire, plus the vFabric SQLFire overheads discussed in the following formulas.

TotalMemoryPerSQLFireSystemWithHeadRoom = TotalMemoryPerSQLFireSystem * 1.5

Formula 4-2 Total Memory for the Entire vFabric SQLFire System with Approximately 50% Overhead Allowance

In Formula 4-3, the *TotalMemoryPerSQLFireSystem* is calculated from *TotalOfAllMemoryForAllTables*, *TotalOfAllMemoryForIndicesInAllTables*, and *TotalMemoryForSocketsAndThreads*. Each of these components is further expanded by the following formulas. For example, *TotalOfAllMemoryForAllTables* is described in Formula 4-4.

TotalMemoryPerSQLFireSystem =

TotalOfAllMemoryForAllTables +
TotalOfAllMemoryForIndicesInAllTables +
TotalMemoryForSocketsAndThreads

Formula 4-3   Total Memory for the Entire vFabric SQLFire System

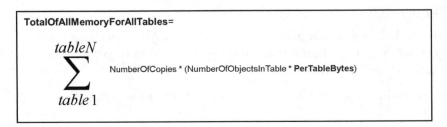

TotalOfAllMemoryForAllTables=

$$\sum_{table\,1}^{tableN} NumberOfCopies * (NumberOfObjectsInTable * \textbf{PerTableBytes})$$

Formula 4-4   Sum of All Memory Across All Tables

In this formula, the terms are as follows:

- NumberOfCopies = Number of primary and redundant copies of the data across vFabric SQLFire members in the system.

- NumberOfObjectsInTable = Number of rows in each table partition.

- PerTableBytes in Formula 4-4 is expanded in Formula 4-5 and in Table 4-3:

- PerTableBytes = TableEntryBytes + IfPartitionedTable * PartitionedTableBytes +

  - IfPersist * PersistBytes +

  - IfStatistics * StaticticsBytes + IfLRU * LRUEvictionBytes +

  - KeyBytes + ObjectBytes + IfEntryExpiration * ExpirationBytes

The PerTableBytes variables and overhead values are documented in Table 4-3.

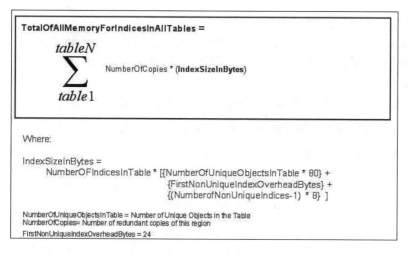

Where:

IndexSizeInBytes =
    NumberOFIndicesInTable * [{NumberOfUniqueObjectsInTable * 80} +
                             {FirstNonUniqueIndexOverheadBytes} +
                             {(NumberofNonUniqueIndices-1) * 8}]

NumberOfUniqueObjectsInTable = Number of Unique Objects in the Table
NumberOfCopies= Number of redundant copies of this region
FirstNonUniqueIndexOverheadBytes = 24

Formula 4-5   Total of All Memory Across Indexes in All Tables

Table 4-3   PerTableBytes Variables for vFabric SQLFire Overhead

Variable	Value
TableEntryBytes	64
IfPartitionedTable	1 if present, otherwise 0
PartitionedTableBytes	4
IfPersist	1 if present, otherwise 0
PersistBytes	40
IfStatistics	1 if present, otherwise 0
StaticticsBytes	16
IfLRU	1 if present, otherwise 0
LRUEvictionBytes	24
KeyBytes	0 bytes, unless the entry overflows to disk; in that case, primary key fields size + 8
ObjectBytes	550 this is an average approximation; enter the real ObjectBytes for your system
IfEntryExpiration	1 if present, otherwise 0
ExpirationBytes	96

In Formula 4-5, the terms are as follows:

- IndexSizeInBytes = NumberOfIndicesInTable * [{NumberOfUniqueObjectsInTable * 80} + {FirstNonUniqueIndexOverheadBytes} + {(NumberofNonUniqueIndices-1) * 8}].

- NumberOfUniqueObjectsInTable = Number of unique objects in the table.

- NumberOfRedundantCopies = Number of redundant copies of this table.

- FirstNonUniqueIndexOverheadBytes = 24.

Formula 4-6 illustrates the total memory consumed by various sockets and threads of the client/server topology.

TotalMemoryForSocketsAndThreads =
TotalMemoryForSockets + TotalMemoryForThreadOverhead

TotalMemoryForThreadOverhead = MaxClientThreads * ThreadStackSize

TotalMemoryForSockets = TotaNumbrOfSockets * SocketBufferSizeBytes

TotalNumberOfSockets = NumberOfServers * NumberOfThreadsOnServer
    + AppThreads
    + MaxClientThreads
    + MaxClientThreads * 2 * NumberofServers *
        IfHostPartitionedTableAndConserveSocketsIsFalse

Formula 4-6   Total Memory for Sockets and Threads

The variables in Formula 4-6 are as follows:

- **MaxClientThreads:** The sum of all threads from all clients accessing the data fabric. So, for example, if you have 10 application server instances, such as vFabric tc Server instances, each with an application that accesses data from the data fabric, the number of `MaxClientThreads` will be 10 * Max Threads Configured on each tc Server.

- **SocketBufferSizeInBytes:** This is configured in SQLFire as the socket-buffer-size property, and the default is 32768

- And **TotalNumberOfSockets** is made of the following:

  - **NumberOfServers:** This is the number of SQLFire members within the data fabric (that is, the number of JVMs).

- **AppThreads:** This is the number of application threads, and can be equal to the number of `MaxThreads` configured with the application server that the SQLFire members are running in. So, if there are eight SQLFire member JVMs within the data fabric, and each of these JVMs is managed within tc Server, the AppThreads will be 8 * `MaxThreads` of each tc Server instance. If each tc Server has, say, 256 `MaxThreads` configured in it, AppThreads is 8 * 256 => 2048.

- **MaxClientThreads:** As described earlier.

- **IfHostPartitionedTableAndConserveSocketsIsFalse:** If the host is partitioned and conserve socket property is set to false, this portion of the equation allows for an adjustment to double the MaxClientThreads and NumberOfServers as sockets (that is, MaxClientThreads * 2 * NumberOfServers * TRUE); otherwise, if conserve sockets is not set, MaxClientThreads * 2 * NumberOfServers * FALSE => 0.

Step C: Establish Building Block VM and JVM Size and How Many vFabric SQLFire Members Are Needed

This section shows how to calculate how many vFabric SQLFire members are feasible to have and the total RAM for the server machine / vSphere host that the designer is likely to select. The assumption in Formula 4-7 is that the VM holding the vFabric SQLFire member has 32GB of memory reservation. This is because within the HotSpot JVM the `-XX:+UseCompressedOops` value is applied to a limit of up to 32GB. You can choose smaller JVM heap space than this, or larger. If you do consider larger JVM heap spaces, the designer must be cognizant of the Non-Uniform Memory Access (NUMA) architecture of the server machine to understand how much memory there is within each local NUMA node. After the designer knows the size of local NUMA nodes, this helps to avoid sizing a JVM and VM to be greater than this local NUMA memory to avoid NUMA node remote memory interleave. NUMA node interleave causes performance problems in the amount of memory throughput because you always want to have the VM process fetch memory from the local NUMA node.

NumberOfSQLFireServers=NumberOfVMsInSystem=
NumberOfJVMsInSystem= TotalMemoryPerSQLFireSystemWithHeadRoom / 32GB

Formula 4-7   Number of vFabric SQLFire Members in a Data Fabric (Number of VMs and JVMs)

NOTE

Formula 4-8 highlights how much data redistribution the system and the specified SLAs can tolerate in the event of a machine failure.

```
ApproxServerMachineRAM=
TotalMemoryPerSQLFireSystemWithHeadRoom *
                (DataRedistributionTolerancePercentage/  (NumberOfRedundantCopies +1) )
```

Formula 4-8   Approximate RAM Size on Server Machine / vSphere Host

Formula 4-9 highlights one more sizing consideration if you are trying to understand how much data you can transmit through the WAN gateway process offered by vFabric SQLFire. It is best to describe this with an example. If the TCP window size is 64KB, and you are communicating between New York and Japan, the round-trip latency is approximately 6500 miles * 2 / 186,000 miles/second = 0.069 seconds, which implies a maximum throughput of 64,000 * 8 / 0.069 = 7.4Mbps. Therefore, regardless of the network link, do not expect anything higher than 7.4Mbps.

NOTE

Adjusting the TCP window size higher can help, but it can cause an increase in memory buffer usage. One way to alleviate this is to implement a WAN accelerator device at both ends of the site to help provide larger TCP windows and to implement TCP selective acknowledgments.

```
Maximum throughput can be determined as:

MaximumThroughput (bits/second) =  TCP-Windows-Size In Bits / Round Trip Latency in Seconds
```

Formula 4-9   WAN Practical Throughput Due to Geographic Distance

The following section completes the sizing discussion with the details of the internal memory sections of the HotSpot JVM and the practical limitations of how large a JVM can be in terms of RAM and the NUMA impact.

Understanding the Internal Memory Sections of HotSpot JVM

Figure 4-8 shows one vFabric SQLFire member running in one HotSpot JVM deployed on one VM. The various memory segments are captured in Formula 4-10.

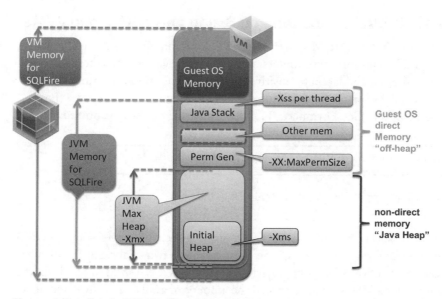

Figure 4-8   vFabric SQLFire Virtual Machine Memory Segments Depicted on One HotSpot JVM Deployed on One VM

VM Memory for SQLFire = Guest OS Memory + JVM Memory for SQLFire

JVM Memory for SQLFire =

> JVM Max Heap (-Xmx value) +
> JVM Perm Size (-XX:MaxPermSize) +
> NumberOfConcurrentThreads * (-Xss) + "other Mem"

Formula 4-10   VM Memory for vFabric SQLFire Running on One HotSpot JVM and One VM

NOTE

JVM Perm Size is where class information is held, and Other Mem is where New I/O (NIO) buffers, just-in-time (JIT) code cache, class loaders, socket buffers (receive/send), Java Native Interface (JNI), and GC internal information are held. These are outside the heap in an area commonly referred to as the "off-the-heap" area. It is important to account for these because they can account for a portion of the total JVM process memory in addition to the -Xmx heap value.

Understanding NUMA Implications on Sizing Large VMs and JVMs

Non-Uniform Memory Access (NUMA) architecture is common on servers with multi-processor sockets, and it is important to understand this memory access architecture when sizing memory-bound and latency-sensitive systems. In the simplest terms, the total amount of memory available on a server machine / vSphere host is divided among the number of processor sockets. See Formula 4-11, where this rule has been captured.

> *NUMA Local Memory = Total RAM on Server/Number of Sockets*

Formula 4-11   High Throughput Fast Access Local NUMA Memory

Figure 4-9 shows a two-socket (proc1 is socket1, and proc2 is socket2) server with a NUMA architecture of two NUMA memory nodes. The diagram shows two vFabric SQLFire VMs running within their respective NUMA boundaries because they were sized to fit within the NUMA node. Whenever a VM is sized to exceed the amount of available NUMA memory from the local NUMA node, the VM is forced to fetch memory from the remote NUMA node, as shown by the red arrows. This remote NUMA memory access comes at a performance cost of reduced speed of access and reduced memory throughput that will impact memory-bound (latency-sensitive) workloads like those implemented on vFabric SQLFire.

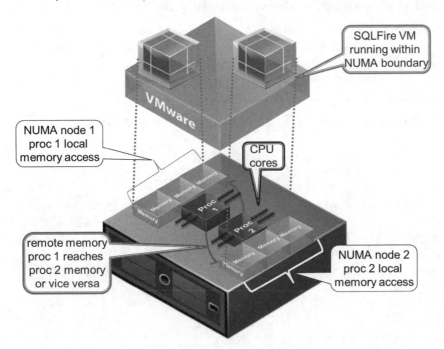

Figure 4-9   Two-Socket NUMA Server with Two vFabric SQLFire VMs (Configuration Option 1)

NOTE

The VMware vSphere ESXi scheduler has many NUMA optimizations that attempt to localize the execution of the process and fetch memory from the local NUMA node.

Sometimes, ample memory exists on the second NUMA node after the first NUMA node has been used by the vFabric SQLFire member VM. In this case, you might be able to place a second vFabric SQLFire server on the second NUMA node, as demonstrated in Figure 4-9. However, due to stringent redundancy rules, for example, you opt not to place a second vFabric SQLFire server on the same server machine/vSphere host. In this case, you can instead place other enterprise applications. These enterprise applications most likely are the ones consuming data from the vFabric SQLFire fabric, and therefore it makes sense to have them deployed on the same vSphere host. The idea is to utilize the full available memory capacity on the vSphere host. Figure 4-10 shows this type of approach, where one NUMA node has the application server instances of the client tier that consume data from distributed cache data member that resides in the second NUMA node.

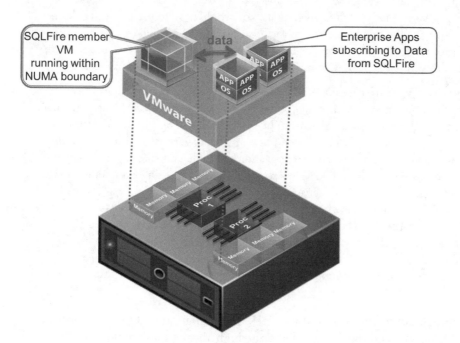

Figure 4-10 One vFabric SQLFire Member and Data-Consuming Enterprise Application Placed on the Same vSphere Host (Configuration Option 2)

NOTE

In vSphere 5+, the ability to configure vNUMA is available. This is the mechanism by which the hypervisor provides a configuration that enables you to expose the underlying NUMA architecture of the vSphere host to the guest OS running on the VM. This is so that NUMA-aware applications can take additional advantage of NUMA locality for better memory throughput and hence higher performance. In Java, for example, there is the -XX:+UseNUMA JVM option that will localize the execution to the local NUMA node. However, in the case of category 2 in-memory database Java platforms, this is where the JVMs are fairly large and NUMA awareness is critical; but also to get the required response time and minimize impact of latency, it is likely you will need to use the CMS GC. In fact, you will almost always use the combination of -XX:+ParNewGC and CMS GCs. If that is the case, then as of this writing, the -XX:+UseNUMA flag is not supported when using CMS GC. The good news is that you really don't need to use this -XX:+UseNUMA flag when running on vSphere; it turns out that if you use the sizing examples in this book and the default vSphere NUMA optimization, NUMA locality is most likely already well intact. If you suspect the VM has poor NUMA locality, inspect the N%L counter from esxtop. With good NUMA locality, this should be 100%. Hence, default vSphere NUMA locality is one advantage of VMware virtualized category 2 workloads as compared with category 2 workloads running on physical systems. On physical systems, you would have to use numactl to force a manual placement of the Java process onto the local NUMA node, and this process is not always straightforward. However, on virtualized systems, usage of numactl is not required because the entire VM is localized within the NUMA node as long as it is sized correctly.

In some cases, if two VMs are running on the same vSphere host, and these VMs have a high amount of chatter, and the VMs could potentially fit within one NUMA node from a size perspective, the default vSphere algorithm biases toward placing the two VMs on the same node. This type of biasing has been seen to cause poorer performance and scalability numbers. Now in some cases to prevent the activation of the default rule, a performance tuning applied to prevent this would be to leverage the advanced setting parameter */Numa/ LocalityWeightActionAffinity to 0*. This setting controls the weight that the CPU scheduler gives to inter-VM communication when making decisions about assigning VMs to NUMA nodes. For further information about the performance study pertaining to this conclusion, see topic 3 of the vFabric Reference Architecture, which you can download from http:// blogs.vmware.com/vfabric/2013/02/introducing-a-new-reference-architecture-that-will-speed-knowledge-development-of-modern-cloud-applications.html.

Figure 4-9 (Configuration Option 1) and Figure 4-10 (Configuration Option 2) provide the best NUMA locality, and therefore can allocate high-throughput memory to the vFabric SQLFire data fabric and the enterprise data-consuming applications. However, there are times when you want to consume the entire CPU capacity across all the sockets of the server machine for a particular vFabric SQLFire member configuration VM. Therefore, consider Configuration Option 3 shown in Figure 4-11.

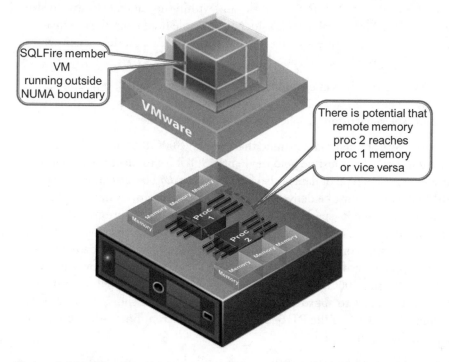

Figure 4-11 One vFabric SQLFire Member Virtual Machine Running Across Two NUMA Nodes (Configuration Option 3)

The vFabric SQLFire member VM in this case is configured to take up the majority of the RAM available on the server and across the two NUMA nodes, also configured to consume the majority of the CPU available across the two processor sockets available on the server. This could be a CPU-intensive application running on the vFabric SQLFire data fabric, requiring ample CPU, executing all within each individual vFabric SQLFire member of the data fabric. Although there is potential that the memory access might interleave between the two NUMA nodes, the benefits of in-memory data access might be adequate for your SLA, and an occasional interleave might not hurt overall response time. vSphere attempts to localize the execution of threads within the local NUMA node as much as possible. This implies that some threads and associated memory are allocated on the first socket and NUMA node, while other threads are allocated on the second socket and the second NUMA node. This process continues until some threads cannot be scheduled and therefore interleave in between nodes.

vFabric SQLFire Sizing Example

The preceding sections discussed all the critical sizing formulas and constraints that dictate sizing of an entire vFabric SQLFire data fabric, and within the data fabric how to size the individual vFabric SQLFire members. Consider an example here from the schema presented in Figure 4-6, and the three-step design and sizing process on this schema as depicted by Figure 4-5, steps A1, A2, A3, and A4.

Step 1 of the process followed the same steps as discussed in the section "Step A: Determine Entity Groups," where the two customer and product entity groups were identified with their associated tables, partitions, replicated, and colocated tables.

Then the step 2 rules were applied to determine that roughly 300GB of data represents the "raw daily transaction data" that must be held in vFabric SQLFire to meet the response time SLA requirements. This type of data is also known as *fast data* because it is the portion of the RDBMS data that must be delivered to enterprise applications quickly. This is data that otherwise has reached its speed and scalability limits in the traditional RDBMS and it must be housed in a vFabric SQLFire data fabric to continue to meet fast data SLAs of the specific enterprise data-consuming applications. With the 300GB raw daily transaction data set, after applying redundancy 1, which implies one redundant copy is made available, 300GB translates to 300GB * 2 = 600GB. Then when you apply all the other sizing formulas, the size translates to approximately 1.1TB. Figure 4-12 shows an illustration of how we are taking about 10% of the RDBMS to model as current hot/daily transaction data and treating it as in-memory data.

Next, step 3 rules of the design and sizing process are applied to determine how to distribute the 1.1TB of data across the vFabric SQLFire data members. Using a vSphere host machine that has 144GB of RAM, two processor sockets of eight cores each, approximately divide the 1.1TB equally among eight of these vSphere hosts.

At this point, there are two configuration options, Option 1 and Option 2, as shown in Figure 4-13 and Figure 4-14, respectively. In Option 1, there are 32 VMs, and therefore 32 vFabric SQLFire members/JVMs, and 8 vSphere hosts. The VMs in Option 1 yield a VM configuration of 34GB RAM and four vCPUs. This, in turn, yields to a more optimal JVM size that is less than the 32GB mark of the optimal operating range of -XX:+UseCompressedOops for the HotSpot JVM. This option provides the most efficient memory footprint by treating the JVM heap pointer addresses as 32-bit pointers when running within a 64-bit JVM. However, the downside of this design is that you have 32 vFabric SQLFire members/VMs to manage within the cluster, and that does need more administration attention. If managing a large number of vFabric SQLFire members is a concern, Option 2 shown in Figure 4-14, where there are 16 VMs, might be a more viable alternative.

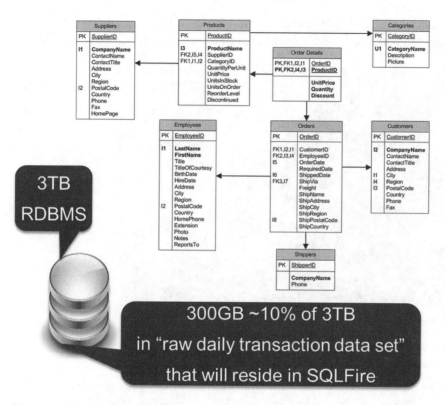

Figure 4-12 Product Order Management RDBMS Is 3TB, Raw Daily Transaction Data Is 300GB

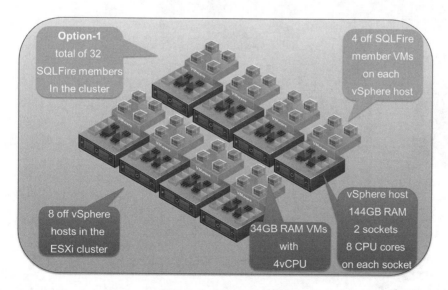

Figure 4-13 Option 1 vFabric SQLFire Data Cluster Within an ESXi Cluster with 32 VMs

Figure 4-14 shows Option 2, where the vSphere cluster has 16 VMs, and therefore 16 vFabric SQLFire members. Each VM is configured to have 68GB RAM and eight vCPUs.

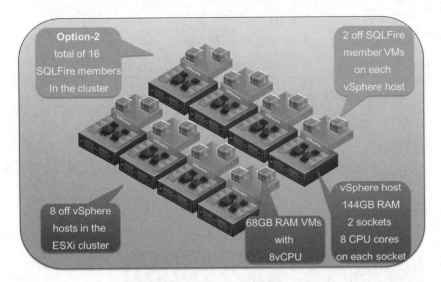

Figure 4-14   Option 2 vFabric SQLFire Data Cluster Within an ESXi Cluster

Figure 4-15 shows the JVM-to-VM relative memory sizing for Option 1 shown in Figure 4-13.

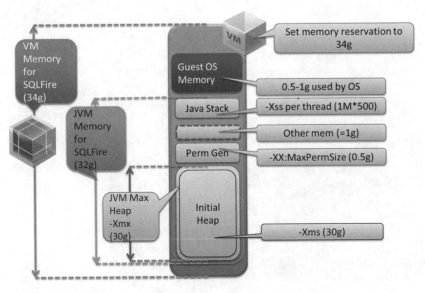

Figure 4-15   vFabric SQLFire Member Virtual Machine with 34GB RAM Reservation

The following values are used in Figure 4-15:

- The guest OS memory is approximately 0.5GB–1GB (depending on the operating system and other processes).

- -Xmx is the JVM maximum heap size set to 30GB.

- -Xss is the Java thread stack size. The default is dependent on the operating system and JVM, but in this case is set to 1MB.

- Perm Size is an area additional to the –Xmx (maximum heap) value and contains class-level information.

- Other Mem is additional memory required for NIO buffers, JIT code cache, class loaders, socket buffers (receive/send), JNI, and GC internal info.

- VM memory for vFabric SQLFire = Guest OS memory + JVM memory for vFabric SQLFire.

To set the sizes, follow these steps:

1. Set -Xmx30g, and set -Xms30g.

2. Set -XX:MaxPermSize=0.5g. This depends on the memory footprint of the class-level information within your Java application code base.

3. The other segment of NumberOfConcurrentThreads * (-Xss) depends largely on the NumberOfConcurrentThreads the JVM will process and on the -Xss value you have chosen.

> **NOTE**
>
> -Xss is dependent on the operating system and JVM. In most cases, the default is 256K on HotSpot JVM running on a Linux OS, and could be as high as 1MB on a Windows-based OS. If the stack is not sized correctly, you may get a StackOverflow error. If you see this exception, you should increase the size of the stack or investigate the cause. Memory-sensitive workloads that consume memory much greater than 256K (for example, in the range of 1 to 4MB) can benefit from having these larger -Xss values. The key here is that objects allocated within these larger stacks don't escape to other threads. As an example, we chose a 1MB thread stack size, 500 threads * 1MB => 500MB => 0.5GB.

4. Assume the operating system has a requirement of about 1GB.

5. Total JVM memory (Java process memory) = 30GB (-Xmx) + 0.5GB (-XX:MaxPermSize) + (500*1MB = NumberOfConcurrentThreads * -Xss) + Other Mem.

Therefore, JVM memory is approximately 31GB + Other Mem. Other Mem is usually not significant, but it can be quite large if the application uses many NIO buffers and socket buffers. This value can be approximated with ample space as about 5% of the heap (in this example, 3% * 30GB = 1GB), although proper load testing should be used to verify. The resulting JVM process memory in this example is 30GB + 1GB = 31GB.

6. To determine the VM memory, assume that you are using Linux with only this single Java process and no other significant processes. The total configured memory for the VM is as follows:

   VM memory for vFabric SQLFire server = 31GB + 1GB = 32GB

7. Set the VM memory as the memory reservation. You can choose to set the memory reservation at 32GB.

As shown in Figure 4-16, the GC configuration for this uses a combination of CMS in the old generation and parallel/throughput collector in the young generation.

```
java –Xms30g –Xmx30g –Xmn9g –Xss1024k –XX:+UseConcMarkSweepGC
–XX:+UseParNewGC –XX:CMSInitiatingOccupancyFraction=75

–XX:+UseCMSInitiatingOccupancyOnly –XX:+ScavengeBeforeFullGC

–XX:TargetSurvivorRatio=80 -XX:SurvivorRatio=8 -XX:+UseBiasedLocking

–XX:MaxTenuringThreshold=15 –XX:ParallelGCThreads=2

–XX:+UseCompressedOops –XX:+OptimizeStringConcat –XX:+UseCompressedStrings

–XX:+UseStringCache -XX:+DisableExplicitGC
```

Figure 4-16   JVM Configuration for a 30GB Heap vFabric SQLFire Member

In Figure 4-16, because we have a 4-vCPU VM size, with -XX:ParallelGCThreads=2, 50% of the available four vCPUs is allocated to the minor GC cycle.

Each of the vFabric SQLFire member VMs shown in Figure 4-17 (Option 2 in the vSphere cluster) has 16 VMs, and therefore 16 vFabric SQLFire members. Each VM is configured to have 68GB RAM and eight vCPUs. In Figure 4-17, the vFabric SQLFire member VM is shown with 68GB of reservation and eight vCPUs allocated. In this example, the total size of the Java process memory (that is, the vFabric SQLFire member) is 67GB. Adding roughly 1GB for the operating system makes the resulting VM RAM size 68GB. Within the Java process, the heap size was determined to be roughly 64GB.

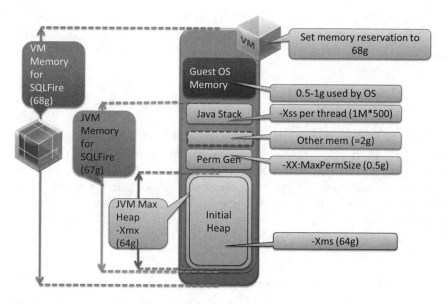

Figure 4-17   vFabric SQLFire Member VM with a 68GB RAM Reservation

The following values are used in Figure 4-17:

- The guest OS memory is approximately 0.5GB–1GB (depends on the operating system and other processes).

- –Xmx is the JVM maximum heap size set to 64GB.

- –Xss is the Java thread stack size. The default is dependent on the operating system and JVM, but in this case is set to 1MB.

- Perm Size is an area additional to the -Xmx (maximum heap) value and contains class-level information.

- Other Mem is additional memory required for NIO buffers, JIT code cache, class loaders, socket buffers (receive/send), JNI, and GC internal info.

- VM memory for vFabric SQLFire = Guest OS memory + JVM Memory for vFabric SQLFire.

To set the sizes, follow these steps:

1. Set -Xmx64g, and set -Xms64g.

2. Set -XX:MaxPermSize = 0.5g. This depends on the memory footprint of the class-level information within your Java application code base.

3. The other segment of NumberOfConcurrentThreads * (-Xss) depends largely on the NumberOfConcurrentThreads the JVM will process and on the -Xss value you have chosen.

> **NOTE**
>
> -Xss is dependent on the OS and on the JVM. In most cases, the default is 256K on HotSpot JVM running on a Linux OS, and could be as high as 1MB on a Windows-based OS. If the stack is not sized correctly, you may get a StackOverflow error. If you see this exception, you should increase the size of the stack or investigate the cause. Memory-sensitive workloads that consume memory much greater than 256K (for example, in the range of 1 to 4MB) can benefit from having these larger -Xss values. The key here is that objects allocated within these larger stacks don't escape to other threads. As an example, we chose a 1MB thread stack size, 500 threads * 1MB => 500MB => 0.5GB.

4. Assume the operating system has a requirement of about 1GB.

5. Total JVM memory (Java process memory) = 64GB (-Xmx) + 0.5GB (-XX:MaxPermSize) + (500 * 1MB = NumberOfConcurrentThreads * -Xss) + Other Mem.

   Therefore, JVM memory is approximately 65GB + Other Mem. Other Mem is usually not significant, but it can be quite large if the application uses many NIO buffers and socket buffers. This value can be approximated with ample space as about 5% of the heap (in this example, 3% * 64GB = 2GB), although proper load testing should be used to verify. The resulting JVM process memory in this example is 65GB + 2GB = 67GB.

6. To determine the VM memory, assume that you are using Linux with only this single Java process and no other significant processes. The total configured memory for the VM is as follows:

   VM memory for vFabric SQLFire server = 67GB + 1GB = 68GB

7. Set the VM memory as the memory reservation. You can choose to set the memory reservation at 68GB.

As shown in Figure 4-18, the GC configuration for this uses a combination of CMS in the old generation and parallel/throughput collector in the young generation.

```
java -Xms64g -Xmx64g -Xmn21g -Xss1024k -XX:+UseConcMarkSweepGC
-XX:+UseParNewGC -XX:CMSInitiatingOccupancyFraction=75

-XX:+UseCMSInitiatingOccupancyOnly -XX:+ScavengeBeforeFullGC

-XX:TargetSurvivorRatio=80 -XX:SurvivorRatio=8

-XX:+UseBiasedLocking -XX:MaxTenuringThreshold=15

-XX:ParallelGCThreads=4 -XX:+OptimizeStringConcat

-XX:+UseCompressedStrings -XX:+UseStringCache -XX:+DisableExplicitGC
```

Figure 4-18   JVM Configuration for a 64GB Heap vFabric SQLFire Member

In Figure 4-18, because we have an 8-vCPU VM, with -XX:ParallelGCThreads = 4, 50% of the available eight vCPUs is allocated to the minor GC cycle.

Chapter Summary

In this chapter, we explored how to best establish a Java platform size by conducting scale-up and scale-out tests to determine the building block VM and JVM. This building block VM and JVM then was used to establish the best size for a vSphere host. Once the size of a vSphere host was established, sizing a cluster to accommodate the traffic for your application was a relatively simple matter of linearly scaling. Now, of course, with linear scaling comes unforeseen bottlenecks that break the linearity and scalability of a system; this is why you should load test the entire vSphere cluster. The chapter concluded with an exploration of how to best size in-memory databases such as vFabric SQLFire, a category 2 and 3 type of workload.

Chapter 5

Performance Studies

This chapter looks at several performance studies that showcase performance capabilities of Java platforms.

SQLFire Versus RDBMS Performance Study

Several customers have asked what vFabric SQLFire can do for their custom Java applications and how they can modify the architecture of the application accordingly. These customers typically run custom Java applications against relational database management systems (RDBMS) that have reached the limits of scalability and response time with their current architecture. They want to make the changes only if they are not too invasive.

To answer these questions fairly, a customer scenario was simulated with no specific assumptions about specialized tuning. This is essentially what a software engineer might attempt when conducting an evaluation of vFabric SQLFire versus other RDBMS. First, a load test was run against Spring Travel with RDBMS as is. Then the Spring Travel schema was converted to run against vFabric SQLFire, also without tuning, and the results were plotted side by side, as shown in Figure 5-1.

To demonstrate how quickly this change could be made without assumptions about any code intrusion/change, it was simulated how a developer might download the Spring Travel application, run the DDLUtils conversion utility to generate the vFabric SQLFire schema and the data load file, and then quickly test to see the performance improvements.

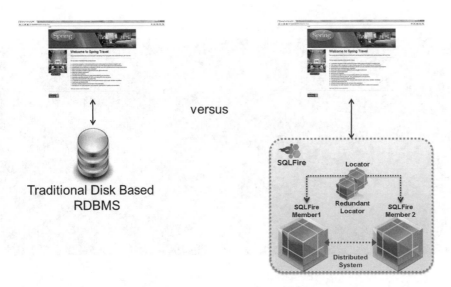

Figure 5-1   Spring Travel Application Running Against RDBMS Versus vFabric SQLFire

The conversion process took less than a day, and the total process, including downloading the Spring Travel application, installing vFabric SQLFire, running the schema and data conversion utility, and running the load test, took 3 days. The results were iterated for another week for verification.

> **NOTE**
>
> You can download the Spring Travel application from http://www.springsource.org/ download, and it is found under the booking-mvc project within a subdirectory of the Spring Web Flow project, identified as spring-webflow-2.3.0.RELEASE/projects/ spring-webflow-samples/booking-mvc. For VMware vFabric SQLFire, go to http://www.vmware.com/products/application-platform/vfabric-sqlfire/overview.html.

The other assumption to make this study as fair as possible is that the total compute resource in both scenarios is exactly the same. A total of 4GB of RAM and 8 vCPUs in one virtual machine (VM) was dedicated to the traditional RDBMS, and the same amount of compute resource dedicated to vFabric SQLFire. Although in the vFabric SQLFire case two vFabric SQLFire VMs were used, each of the VMs had 4 vCPUs and 2GB of RAM, for a total of 4GB RAM and 8 vCPUs. These compute resource requirements are the default for the RDBMS used. Therefore, to remain consistent with the objective of absolutely no tuning on any system, the default compute resource requirements were not altered. Based on this, vFabric SQLFire was given equal compute resources. Although distributed across two VMs, the net compute resources were the same across the configurations used for this comparison. This resembles what customer developers might simulate in a development environment on the first day of inspecting and evaluating vFabric SQLFire versus traditional RDBMS.

Performance Results

Table 5-1 plots the results, and the legend for the columns is as follows:

- **"Threads" column:** The number of concurrent Spring Travel application threads executed during the two load tests

- **"SQLF R/T (ms)" column:** The response time of Spring Travel application in milliseconds

- **"SQLF CPU %" column:** The percentage of CPU utilization at peak for the vFabric SQLFire VMs

- **"RDBMS R/T (ms)" column:** The Sprint Travel application response time in milliseconds when running against the traditional disk-based RDBMS

- **"RDBMS CPU %" column:** The CPU utilization percentage at peak on the RDBMS VM

The results are for the range of 18 to 7200 concurrent threads. Where Failed is indicated, it implies the Spring Travel application running against the traditional disk-based RDBMS failed to respond; it was essentially frozen, and therefore no data was collected.

Table 5-1 Spring Travel Results with RDBMS Versus vFabric SQLFire

Threads	SQLF R/T (ms)	SQLF CPU %	RDBMS R/T (ms)	RDBMS CPU %
18	14	9	25	1
200	8	32	23	19
1800	5	61	172	76
3600	6	77	Failed	Failed
7200	984	98	Failed	Failed

Spring Travel Response Time Versus Concurrent Threads Test Results

Figure 5-2 shows the results of response time along the vertical axis, and concurrent number of threads along the horizontal axis. The red line is for the configuration of Spring Travel application running against traditional disk-based RDBMS, and the blue line is for Spring Travel application running against vFabric SQLFire. This chart presents the response time behavior of the configurations with an increase in the number of Spring Travel application concurrent user threads. We see that as the number of concurrent threads increases along the horizontal axis, for the Spring Travel application against RDBMS configuration, the response time increases linearly (depicted by the red line on the chart). By contrast, the configuration of the Spring Travel application with vFabric SQLFire maintains a fairly low and flat line of response time (as indicated by the bottom line on the chart).

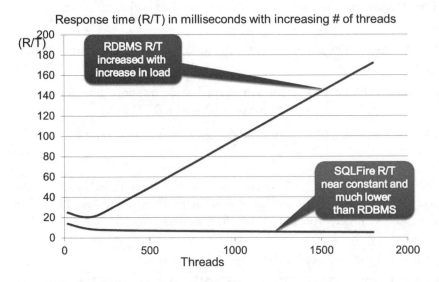

Figure 5-2   Spring Travel Response Time Versus Concurrent Threads

Scalability Test Results

In this test, and as shown in Figure 5-3, the goal is to demonstrate the extent of scalability of both configurations. In the case of the Spring Travel application server, after reaching 1850 concurrent threads, the system stopped responding after nearing a response time of 172ms, indicating that the scalability limit, as shown by the red line on Figure 5-3, had been reached. The Spring Travel configuration against vFabric SQLFire, as labeled in Figure 5-3, continued to function to the limit of 7200 concurrent threads and a response time of 984ms.

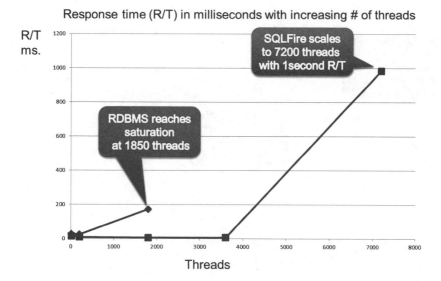

Figure 5-3 Spring Travel Response Time Versus Concurrent Threads: Scalability Test

> **NOTE**
>
> At approximately 3600 concurrent threads, vFabric SQLFire started to overflow to disk, and the response time increased. This is normal, and that kind of overflow can be contained by appropriately sizing the available RAM.

CPU Versus Concurrent Threads Test Results

Figure 5-4 plots the CPU utilization of the relevant VM, the RDBMS VM as a red line, and the vFabric SQLFire VMs as a blue line. This is the CPU utilization measured for the duration of the test in Figure 5-3. The red line shows that the Spring Travel application against RDBMS peaked at approximately 80% CPU and 1850 concurrent threads. It is at this point where it completely failed to respond. In contrast, as shown by the blue line, the vFabric SQLFire-based Spring Travel configuration continued to 98% CPU and 7200 concurrent threads and was still responsive, at approximately just under 1s application response time. You can also see that the red and blue lines crossed over at approximately 1000 concurrent threads, indicating that Spring Travel with vFabric SQLFire handled much higher loads at a more steady CPU utilization increase.

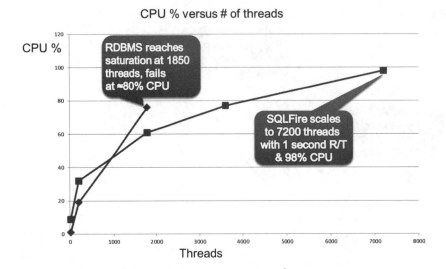

Figure 5-4   Spring Travel Application CPU Versus Concurrent Threads

Summary of Findings

The following findings are learned from this study:

- It was relatively straightforward to use the DDLUtils utility to convert the schema and the data of the RDBMS associated with the Spring Travel application.

- The installation of vFabric SQLFire was also straightforward.

- The test results show that Spring Travel using vFabric SQLFire scaled approximately 4x when compared to the Spring Travel application using an RDBMS.

- The response times of vFabric SQLFire were 5x to 30x faster with vFabric SQLFire. Further, the response times on vFabric SQLFire were more stable and constant with increased load.

- The configuration of Spring Travel with an RDBMS has a response time that increases linearly with increased load.

- The breakpoint for the Spring Travel application against an RDBMs was at 80% CPU utilization for about 1850 concurrent threads, when the Spring Travel application stopped responding. By contrast, the vFabric SQLFire version of Spring Travel continued to pace ahead at 98% CPU utilization and achieved 7200 concurrent threads.

The Olio Workload on tc Server and vSphere Performance Study

Several Java on vSphere performance studies are public. This is one I particularly like, and it was conducted by a colleague of mine at VMware, Harold Rosenberg, a senior performance engineer.

The full performance paper by Harold Rosenberg is a public document available at http://www.vmware.com/resources/techresources/10158.

In Figure 5-5, the left side of the diagram shows the geocoders that drive load toward the application VMs, along with an NFS file store where images are stored. The application places a lot of traffic onto the network, and it is geared toward demonstrating how the network would likely become a bottleneck before the VMware stack would.

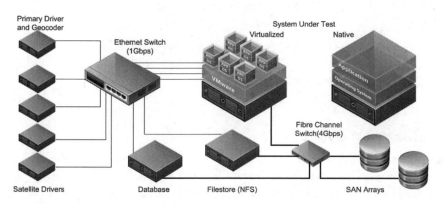

Figure 5-5 The Olio Test Setup

Looking at the Results

In the 90th percentile case, the response-time curves and CPU utilizations for the 2-CPU native and virtualized cases are shown. Below 80% CPU utilization in the VM, the native and virtual configurations have essentially identical performance, with only minimal absolute differences in response times.

Native 2-CPU Versus Virtual 2-vCPU

This section shows the results for the 2-CPU native/physical server versus a 2-vCPU VM. Plotted in Figure 5-6 is the response time (R/T) and CPU utilization. The graph clearly shows that at 80% CPU utilization a threshold is reached. For the response time up to

80%, the response time matches that of the physical server case, and beyond the 80% threshold there is slight divergence, although still within a reasonable difference. As for the CPU utilization, you can see the numbers compare quite well with each other.

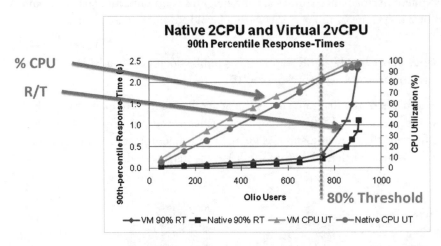

Figure 5-6 Native 2-CPU Versus Virtual 2-vCPU

Native 4-CPU Versus Virtual 4-vCPU

This section shows the results for the 4-CPU native/physical server versus a 4-vCPU VM. Plotted in Figure 5-7 is the response time (R/T) and CPU utilization. The graph clearly shows that at 80% CPU utilization a threshold is reached. For the response time up to the 80%, the response time matches that of the physical server case, and beyond the 80% threshold, there is slight divergence, although still within a reasonable difference. As for the CPU utilization, we see the numbers compare quite well with each other.

Peak Throughput by CPU Count

In Figure 5-8, shown for the 1-CPU case, native was able to achieve 95 ops/sec versus 85 ops/sec for virtual (a 10.5% difference). In the 2-CPU case, it was 179 ops/sec for native versus 169 ops/sec for virtual (a 5.5% difference). In the 4-CPU case, it was 298 ops/sec for native versus 293 ops/sec for virtual (a 1.67% difference). This shows that as the CPU was increased, the throughput tracked well and closer to the native case.

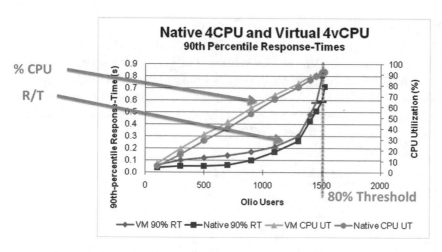

Figure 5-7   Native 4-CPU Versus Virtual 4-vCPU

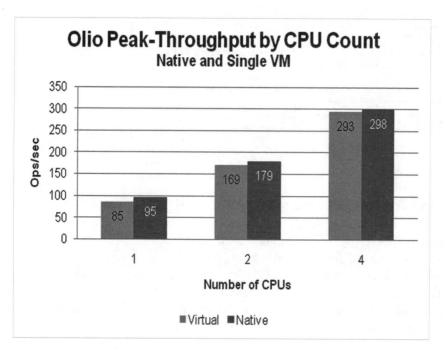

Figure 5-8   Ops/Sec Versus the Number of CPUs as a Measure of Throughput

Comparing 1-vCPU to 4-vCPU Configuration Choices

Figure 5-9 shows three configurations composed of four VMs with one vCPU each, two
VMs with two vCPUs each, and one VM of four vCPUs. The graph has a 90th percentile
response time on the left vertical axis, CPU utilization on the right vertical axis, and the
number of users on the horizontal axis. Here, you see that the 2-vCPU configuration leads
the best-of-breed combination of user throughput for the least amount of heap memory at
a total of 5G across two VMs, or 2.5GB per 2-vCPU VM.

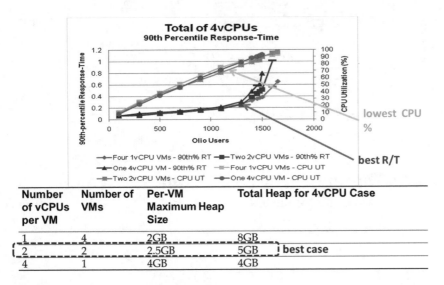

Number of vCPUs per VM	Number of VMs	Per-VM Maximum Heap Size	Total Heap for 4vCPU Case	
1	4	2GB	8GB	
2	2	2.5GB	5GB	best case
4	1	4GB	4GB	

Figure 5-9   Three Configuration Choices: Four Off 1-vCPU VMs, Two Off 2-vCPU VMs, and One
Off 4-vCPU VMs

Figure 5-10 illustrates the peak throughput of the four 1-vCPU VMs, two off 2-vCPU
VMs, and one off 4-vCPU VMs. Again clearly demonstrated is that the two off 2-vCPU
case is the best throughput. Now the reason I chose this as the best result ahead of the
1-vCPU VMs is because for any serious production applications 2-vCPU VMs are what
is most commonly used. If you have a Java application that is fairly busy, you can expect
the garbage collection (GC) to occupy one vCPU, and the second vCPU would be made
available for regular user transactions. If you had a 1-vCPU VM, however, GC and regular
user transactions would be contending for CPU cycles.

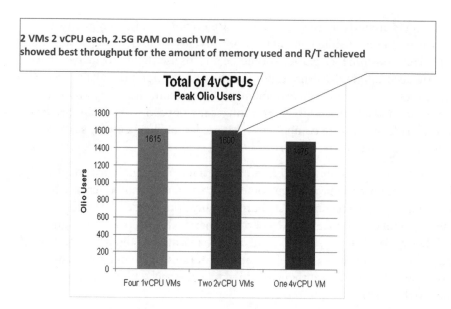

Figure 5-10   Peak Olio Users Versus Various VM vCPU Configurations

SpringTrader Performance Study

In this performance study, the vFabric SpringTrader was put through extensive load testing to establish its scalability, which capacity planners can then use as a guide to how best size a SpringTrader target Java platform. The goal of this workload is to simulate the load placed on the server-side application by users interacting with the application through the browser-based, rich Internet application (RIA). This means that the ordering of calls to the server-side REST application programming interface (API) is restricted to sequences that can be achieved by interacting with the RIA. The workload uses transition probabilities assigned to current operation/next-operation transitions to enable a general specification of possible user flows through the RIA. This approach allows a variety of user profiles and application loads to be implemented by modifying the various transition probabilities. The workload used can be implemented in a fairly direct manner using the version of the Rain workload-driver developed for SpringTrader, supporting asynchronous behaviors, and that make transition decisions based on state information retrieved from the server in previous operations. In the context of SpringTrader, these capabilities allow the implementation of the asynchronous GET request for market summary data and will allow the workload driver to implement sell operations using previously retrieved holdings data.

The extensive performance testing results are used to guide the design and sizing exercise for various vFabric Reference Architecture platform scales, where the performance study can be found (http://www.vmware.com/go/vFabric-ref-arch).

If, for example, designers are looking to size a vFabric Reference Architecture platform for small (100 concurrent user sessions), medium (1000 concurrent user sessions), and/or large (10,000 concurrent sessions) scale, they should be able to use the performance charts to size their platform accordingly. VMware expects architects to extend the vFabric Reference Architecture to suit their own business domain, and as a result, the sizing numbers will be altered to accommodate any architectural changes introduced. The vFabric Reference Architecture is made of software components that are largely horizontally scalable, and extrapolating platform sizes is straightforward.

vFabric SpringTrader (https://github.com/vFabric/springtrader) is a reference application developed by SpringSource to provide customers with an end-to-end reference for developing, provisioning, and managing a distributed application. vFabric SpringTrader is a stock-trading web application that provides services that enable users to create and manage accounts, buy and sell shares of stock, and obtain information about their current portfolio and order history. It is a reimplementation of the DayTrader application originally developed by IBM and currently maintained by the Apache Geronimo project (http://geronimo.apache.org/).

The SpringTrader application has three components: presentation services, application services, and integration services. The presentation services component contains the static content that makes up the RIA that is presented to users in their web browser. The application services component is a Java web application that exposes a REST API that is used by the RIA to execute all operations. The application services directly execute all short running operations, such as user logins and account inquiries. More complex operations, such as processing of buy and sell orders, are passed to the integration services component via an Advanced Message Queuing Protocol (AMQP) messaging backbone. The integration services component is also a Java web application, although it interacts with other components only though AMQP, not HTTP. The integration services also handle updates of pricing data for individual stocks. Both the application and integration services require access to a shared database.

Figure 5-11 shows the SpringTrader topology based on vFabric SQLFire client/server topology discussed earlier in Chapter 2, "Modern Scalable Data Platforms." In the case of SpringTrader, the traditional vFabric SQLFire client/server topology has been slightly modified to accommodate the ability to execute asynchronous messaging of buy and sell stock trading orders through RabbitMQ. In this performance study, SpringTrader is essentially made of the application tier having four SpringTrader applications services deployed on them, and two SpringTrader integration services communicating via RabbitMQ server. In addition, there is a distributed in-memory data management system implemented with vFabric SQLFire containing two nodes in this performance example, shown as the SpringTrader data tier in Figure 5-11.

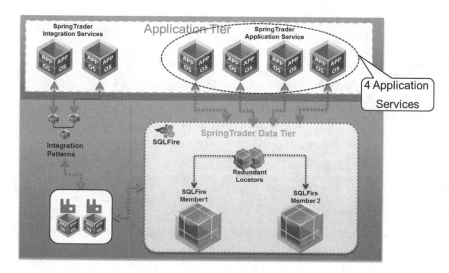

Figure 5-11   SpringTrader Multitier Topology

Application and Data Tier vSphere Configurations

Figure 5-12 shows the infrastructure topology for this performance study, with details in Table 5-2.

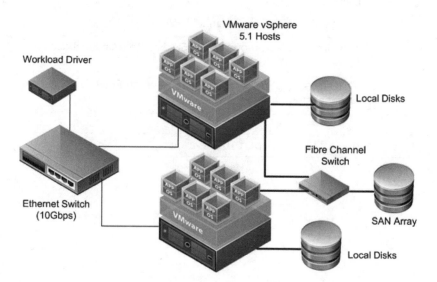

Figure 5-12   SpringTrader Performance Study Platform Topology

Table 5-2   SpringTrader Performance Test vSphere Configurations

Component	Details
Workload Driver	
Operating system	Red Hat Enterprise Linux 6 Update 3, x86_64
System model	Dell PowerEdge R710
Processors	Two Intel Xeon CPU X5680 @ 3.33GHz (total of 12 cores, 24 threads)
Total memory	144GB
Deployment Servers	
Virtualization platform	VMware vSphere 5.1 build 914609
VMware vSphere configuration	The following setting was changed in the Advanced Settings: `/Numa/LocalityWeightActionAffinity = 0`
System model	Dell PowerEdge R720
Processors	Two Intel Xeon CPU E5-2680 @ 2.7GHz (total of 16 cores, 32 threads)
BIOS configuration	Performance profile enabled in the system BIOS
Total memory	192GB
Network controller	Intel 82599EB 10-Gigabit NIC
Storage controller	Dell PERC H710 Mini

QLogic ISP2532 Fibre Channel HBA |
| Storage configuration | SQLFire data stored on VMFS5.58 datastore on local disk. Five-disk RAID 5 LUN

VMs stored in a VMFS5.58 datastore on an EMC CX310 Fibre Channel storage array |
| **Ethernet Switch** | |
| System model | Arista 7124SX 24-port 10GbE switch |

NOTE

The only performance tuning applied to the VMware vSphere 5.1 installation was setting the advanced setting parameter /Numa/LocalityWeightActionAffinity to 0. This setting controls the weight that the CPU scheduler gives to inter-VM communication when making decisions about assigning VMs to Non-Uniform Memory Access (NUMA) nodes. In most cases, leaving this setting at the default value will give the best performance. In this deployment, the high level of communication between the application services VMs and the SQLFire data members (in-memory database) VMs biased the scheduler toward placing these VMs on the same NUMA node. This did not improve performance, and had a negative impact on performance at certain load levels. As a result, the parameter was set to 0 to disable the use of inter-VM communication in scheduling decisions. Careful performance testing should be performed before changing this parameter in a different deployment scenario. You can find more information about this and other scheduler parameters in the technical paper "The CPU Scheduler in VMware vSphere 5.1."

In Figure 5-13, the deployment map (that is, where the VMs are deployed in relation to the underlying vSphere host) is shown. On vSphere Host 1, the Application Service 1, Application Service 3, RabbitMQ 1, Integration Service 1, and SQLFire 1 VMs are deployed. Then on vSphere Host 2, the Application Service 2, Application Service 4, Integration Service 2, RabbitMQ 2, and SQLFire 2 VMs are deployed. Table 5-3 shows the actual VM configurations and sizes for these.

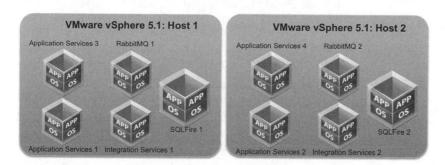

Figure 5-13 VMs and Their Underlying vSphere Hosts for SpringTrader Topology Used in the Performance Test

Table 5-3 shows the VM configurations used for each of the VMs in Figure 5-13.

Table 5-3 VM Configurations

Component	Details
All VMs	
Operating system	Red Hat Enterprise Linux 6 Update 3, x86_64
Virtual NIC	VMXNET 3
SCSI controller	Paravirtual
Application Services VM (Shown in Figure 5-13 as Application Service 1, 2 , 3, and 4)	
Servlet container	VMware vFabric tc Server, Version 2.8.1
vFabric tc Server configuration	Used Tomcat JDBC Connection Pool with max of 111 connections
	Used 100 `maxThreads` in `tomcatThreadPool`
	Used NIO HTTP connector
JVM	Oracle HotSpot JDK 1.6.0_37 64-bit
JVM options	`-Xmx640m -Xms640m -XX:+UseLargePages -XX:+AlwaysPreTouch`
vCPUs	2
Memory	1GB
Integration Services VM (Shown in Figure 5-13 as Integration Service 1 and 2)	
Servlet container	VMware vFabric tc Server, Version 2.8.1
vFabric tc Server configuration	Used Tomcat JDBC connection pool with max of 111 connections
	Used 100 `maxThreads` in `tomcatThreadPool`
	Used NIO HTTP connector
JVM	Oracle HotSpot JDK 1.6.0_37 64-bit
JVM options	`-Xmx256m -Xms256m -XX:+UseLargePages -XX:+AlwaysPreTouch`
Application-level tuning	Increased the number of concurrent consumers on the Spring Integration AMQP inbound channel adapter from 10 to 50.
vCPUs	2
Memory	768MB
AMQP Message Server VM (Shown in Figure 5-13 as RabbitMQ 1 and 2)	
Message server	VMware vFabric RabbitMQ, Version 3.0.1

Component	Details
vCPUs	2
Memory	2GB
RabbitMQ configuration	vm_memory_high_watermark set to 0.7
Other configuration details	SpringTrader AMQP Queues are mirrored for high availability.
	SpringTrader AMQP Queues are durable.
SQLFire VM (Shown in Figure 5-13 as SQLFire 1 and 20)	
Database server	VMware vFabric SQLFire, Version 1.0.3
JVM	Oracle HotSpot JDK 1.6.0_37 64-bit
JVM options	As directed in the *VMware vFabric SQLFire Best Practices Guide*, with the following changes: -Xmx90g -Xms90g -XX:+AlwaysPreTouch.
vCPUs	8
Memory	94GB
Other configuration details	All tables in the SpringTrader database schema are replicated or partitioned with redundancy for high availability.

The SpringTrader Performance Study Results

Figure 5-14 shows the left vertical axis as number of users versus the horizontal axis as the number of application services VMs, and the right vertical axis as the scaling from one application services VM. The results were that 10,400 user sessions, at approximately 3000 transactions per second, were achieved with this configuration. What is even more impressive is that SpringTrader was able to achieve 3000 transactions per second while still maintaining a response time of 0.25 seconds, as shown in Figure 5-15.

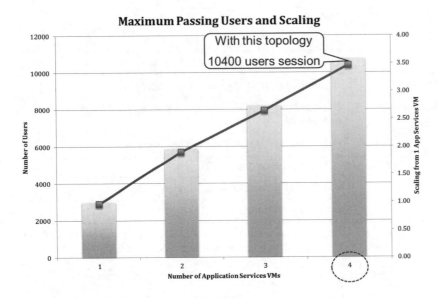

Figure 5-14   SpringTrader Performance Results

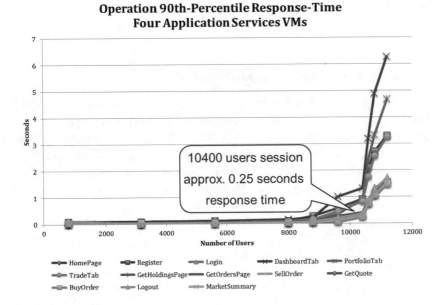

Figure 5-15   Response Time Versus Number of Users

Performance Differences Between ESXi 3, 4.1, and 5

When considering virtualizing large-scale Java platforms, it is important to be on the latest hypervisor. Java platforms will perform on earlier versions; in fact, they perform really well on ESXi 4.1, and have reasonable performance on ESXi 3.5. There have been many improvements that designers should leverage, though.

It is important to be aware of these improvements, but also keep the practicality of applying these limits in check with the reality of the underlying physical hardware. In most cases, these configurations have maximums, particularly with vSphere 5.1, where they are simply ahead of the underlying hardware.

For example, and as shown in Table 5-4, for vSphere 5.1, a VM can be sized as a 64-vCPU VM, but most underlying hardware cannot even present that many cores; the most common hosts that are feasible to purchase range between 16 cores to 40 cores.

Table 5-4   Configuration Maximums Between VI3, vSphere 4, and vSphere 5.1

Feature	VI3	vSphere 4	vSphere 5.1
VM CPU count	4 vCPUs	8 vCPUs	64 vCPUs
VM memory maximum	64GB	255GB	1TB
Host CPU core maximum	32 cores	64 cores	160 cores
Host memory maximum	256 GB	1 TB	2 TB
Powered-on VMs per ESX/ESXi maximum	128	256	512

You might sometimes size a very large VM that essentially represents the entire host. This practice makes sense only during a performance comparison against a physical host to try to determine virtualization overhead. In most cases, the highest number of vCPUs the VM should be configured to have is as many as physical cores are available within a NUMA node. This of course assumes that each vCPU will occupy the entire physical core, because potentially you may have an aggressive workload that is CPU bound. However, if the workload is assumed to be less CPU bound, you can potentially allocate a larger number of vCPUs, greater than the underlying physical or NUMA node; however, because the workload is not as aggressive, the vCPUs may still translate to an equal number of physical cores available within a NUMA node. The extent of the CPU overcommitment will depend entirely on the nature of the workload. At any rate, with hyperthreading (HT) enabled, you should assume that vCPUs = 1.25 pCPUs, where pCPUs is the underlying vSphere host physical cores.

Then a similar argument applies for memory. You should only size VMs with a maximum ceiling configuration that is within the context of a NUMA node, minus the overhead discussed earlier.

The key differences between VI3 and vSphere 4 focused on CPU scheduling and on memory enhancements, as described in the sections that follow.

CPU Scheduling Enhancements

For CPU scheduling, the enhancement highlights are as follows:

- Relaxed coscheduling of vCPUs, introduced in earlier versions of ESX, has been further fine-tuned especially for SMP VMs.

  - The ESX 4.0 scheduler utilizes new finer-grained locking that reduces scheduling overheads in cases where frequent scheduling decisions are needed.

  - The new scheduler is aware of processor cache topology and takes into account the processor cache architecture to optimize CPU usage.

- For I/O intensive workloads, interrupt delivery and the associated processing costs make up a large component of the virtualization overhead. The preceding scheduler enhancements greatly improve the efficiency of interrupt delivery and associated processing.

Memory Enhancements

Hardware-assisted memory virtualization management in VMs differs from physical machines in one key aspect:

- Virtual memory addresses translation. Guest virtual memory addresses must be translated first to guest physical addresses using the guest OS's page tables before finally being translated to machine physical memory addresses. The latter step is performed by ESX by means of a set of shadow page tables for each VM.

- Creating and maintaining the shadow page tables adds both CPU and memory overhead.

This enhancement now uses a hardware-based memory management unit (MMU), greatly improving memory throughput, as illustrated in Figure 5-16. Apache Compile was improved by approximately 55%, Citrix XenApp by 30%, and SQL Server by 12%.

Figure 5-16   Efficiency Improvements Using Hardware-Assisted Memory

There were also significant network driver optimizations in vSphere 4, as shown in Figure 5-17. The network transmit throughput improvements ranged from 18% to 85%, depending on the number of VMs.

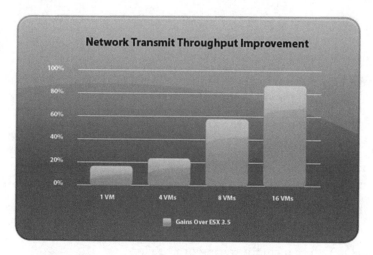

Figure 5-17   Network Transmit Throughput Improvement for vSphere 4

vSphere 5 Performance Enhancements

In vSphere 5, a majority of enhancements focused on improving VMotion throughput. Before inspecting the performance charts on the implemented improvements, it is important to understand the three phases of a VMotion, which are as follows:

- **Phase 1 (guest trace phase):** Traces are placed on the guest memory pages to track any modifications by the guest during migration.

- **Phase 2 (precopy phase):**

  - An initial copy all from source to destination in a preparation phase

  - Iterative copy of changing memory from source to destination

- **Phase 3 (switchover phase):**

  - VM is momentarily quiesced on the source, the last set of memory changes are copied to the target, and the VM is resumed on target.

  - During this phase, the guest briefly pauses processing.

  - Duration is generally less than a second; however, this could cause an abrupt increase in latency.

The improvements are as follows:

- Ability to use multiple network adapters for vMotion

- Latency-aware Metro vMotion that improves performance over long latency and increases round-trip tolerance limit for vMotion from 5msec to 10msec

- Stun During Page Send (SDPS) ensures that vMotion will not fail due to memory convergence issues:

  - In ESXi 4.1, a precopy process would fail to make forward progress due to rapidly changing memory and hence fail the vMotion.

  - ESXi 5 has the enhancement to slow down the memory changes in the source VM, so that the precopy process can converge faster.

- Significant improvements to reduce memory-tracing overhead:

  - In ESXi 5, vMotion is much faster than in ESX 4.1. See the performance paper at http://www.vmware.com/files/pdf/vmotion-perf-vsphere5.pdf and refer to Figure 5-18.

  - SPECWeb2005, 12L users (generated 6Gbps traffic), 4-vCPU VM with 12GB RAM.

  - 37% improvement in vMotion duration.

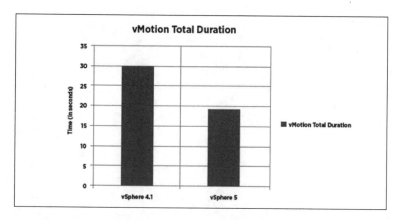

Figure 5-18   vMotion Improvements in vSphere 5 Versus vSphere 4.1

NOTE

There were storage I/O and network I/O enhancements in 5.x, in addition to scheduler improvements to be able to handle 32 vCPUs, especially around reducing the impact of idle CPUs. Finally, a 1 million I/O operations per second (IOPS) per VM in vSphere 5.1 and ~40Gbps network throughput was also achieved.

Chapter Summary

This chapter covered various performance studies, showing that virtualized Java platforms can perform at a high scale. In fact, some virtualized Java platforms execute thousands of transactions per second and run some heavy trading platforms.

Chapter 6

Best Practices

This chapter covers the various best practices for category 1, category 2, and category 3 Java platforms:

- **Category 1 (large number of JVMs):** In this category, hundreds to thousands of Java Virtual Machines (JVM) are commonly deployed on the Java platform, and these are typically JVMs as part of a system that may be servicing millions of users. I have seen some customers with as many as 15,000 JVMs. Whenever you are dealing with thousands of JVM instances, you have to consider the manageability cost and whether opportunities exist to consolidate the JVM instances.

- **Category 2 (JVMs with a large heap size):** This category usually contains fewer JVMs (1 to 20), but the individual JVM heap size is quite large, within a range of 8 to 256GB and potentially higher. These are usually JVMs that have in-memory databases deployed on them. In this category, garbage collection (GC) tuning becomes critical.

- **Category 3:** This is a combination of the first two categories, where perhaps thousands of JVMs are running enterprise applications that are consuming data from category 2 large JVMs in the back end.

Figure 6-1 shows an example of a category 1 workload vSphere cluster, the characteristics of which are as follows:

- Usually made of smaller JVMs, typically with a less-than 4GB heap size, and hence the total Java process memory of 4.5GB and allowing 0.5GB for OS, for a total of 5GB set as virtual memory (VM) memory reservation.

- Usually deployed on vSphere hosts that have less than 96GB of physical RAM, because by the time you stack the many JVM instances, you are likely to reach the CPU boundary before you can consume the entire physical RAM. For example, if instead you chose a vSphere host with 256GB RAM (256 / 4.5GB => 57 JVMs), this would clearly reach the CPU boundary because there are far too many GC cycles, with a potential chance of 57 GC threads to coincide at a particular time and contend for CPU resources.

- Multiple JVMs per VM is a common practice, sometimes referred to as vertical stacking of JVMs on a VM.

- Because category 1 Java platforms can have thousands of JVMs managing compute resource allocation, resource pools can help maintain consistent service level agreements (SLAs). For example, as shown in Figure 6-1, a gold and silver type of resource pool can be set up to service lines of business (LOBs) that have different priority levels. The large scale of that many JVMs makes it necessary to have resource pools.

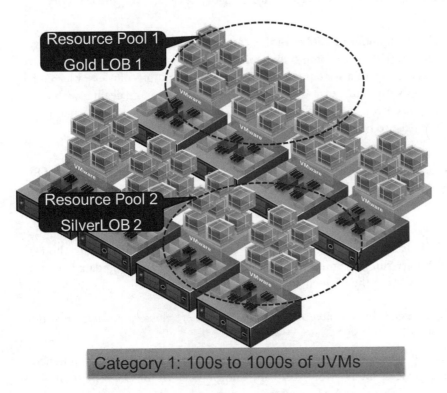

Figure 6-1   Category 1 Java Platform vSphere Cluster Example

Figure 6-2 shows an example of category 2 workload, the characteristics of which are as follows:

- Category 2 vSphere clusters usually consist of fewer than 20 JVMs.

- The JVMs tend to be very large (32 to 128GB).

- Always deploy one VM per Non-Uniform Memory Access (NUMA) node and size to fit perfectly.

- One JVM per VM; avoid JVM stacking on a VM.

- Choose two-socket vSphere hosts and install ample memory (128 to 512GB). This naturally gives you the largest NUMA banks for the same price point on RAM.

- An example of a category 2 workload is an in-memory database, like SQLFire and GemFire.

- Apply latency-sensitive best practices (BPs) by disabling interrupt coalescing at the physical network interface card (pNIC) and the virtual interface card (vNIC).

- A dedicated vSphere cluster should be used, because every vSphere host has to be tuned to disable interrupt coalescing; other workloads sharing the same cluster may not benefit from this. Hence, a dedicated vSphere cluster is advisable.

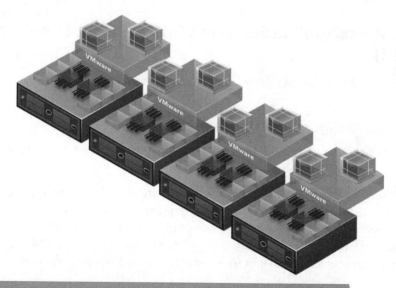

Category 2: a dozen of very large JVMs

Figure 6-2　Category 2 Java Workload vSphere Cluster

In category 3, because a category 1 vSphere cluster is accessing a category 2 Java platform (as shown in Figure 6-3), the respective BPs should be appropriately applied to the vSphere cluster of the category.

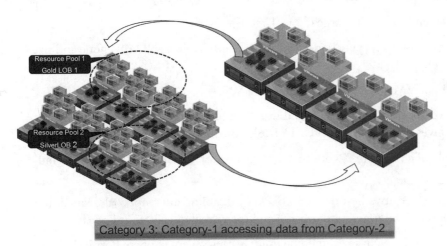

Figure 6-3   Category 3 Java Workload vSphere Cluster

Enterprise Java Applications on vSphere Best Practices (Category 1)

This section outlines the BPs as they pertain to category 1 virtualized Java platforms.

VM Sizing and Configuration Best Practices

Enterprise Java applications are highly customizable, and consequently a performance test has to be conducted to establish best sizing.

It is a best practice to establish the size of your VM in terms of vCPU, memory, and how many JVMs are needed by conducting a thorough performance test that mimics your production workload profile. The resulting VM from the vertical scalability (scale-up) performance test is referred to as the *building block VM*. The building block VM is a good candidate template from which scaled-out (horizontally scaled) VMs can be based.

vCPU for VM Best Practices

Table 6-1 vCPU for VM Best Practices

Best Practice	Description
BP 16: VM sizing and VM-to-JVM ratio through a performance load test.	Establish a workload profile and conduct a load test to measure how many JVMs you can stack on a particular-sized VM. In this test, establish a best-case scenario of how many concurrent transactions you can push through a configuration before it can be safely deemed as a good candidate for scaling horizontally in an application cluster. When in doubt, either due to time pressures or lack of information about the application, assume a 1-JVM to 2-vCPU ratio. You can achieve this by having 1 JVM deployed on 1 VM, or you could have 2 JVMs deployed on a 4-vCPU VM. In either case, the 1-JVM to 2-vCPU ratio is upheld. If indeed the JVM you are deploying is fairly aggressive in terms of how much work it has to get done, you will find that the GC cycle may overall take 1 vCPU and then an additional vCPU is needed for regular user transactions. If after deployment you find that the 1-JVM to 2-vCPU ratio has very low CPU utilization, you can adjust the ratio either by increasing the JVM instances or by reducing the vCPU, or increasing the heap of the JVM. Further, if the CPU utilization is indeed low, it means that you are not fully utilizing the JVM that you have allocated, or you have far too many horizontally scaled-out JVMs and should perhaps look at consolidating some of these JVMs into fewer JVMs with higher heap size.
BP 17: VM vCPU CPU overcommit.	For performance-critical enterprise Java application VMs in production, make sure that the total number of vCPUs assigned to all the VMs does not cause greater than 80% CPU utilization on the ESX host. This best practice is supported by the performance study we saw in the section "The Olio Workload on tc Server and vSphere Performance Study" in Chapter 5, "Performance Studies," where virtualization overhead was negligible compared to physical/native when CPU utilization was up to 80%. Further, when calculating vCPU versus physical CPU (pCPU), always assume 1 vCPU = 1 pCPU, but adjust up or down the vCPU in accordance with the actual pCPU utilization observed/consumed. If hyperthreading is enabled, assume vCPU <= 1.25 pCPU, but approach this with caution; not all workloads will benefit from hyperthreading. Hyperthreading should always be enabled, but it should not figure into the overcommitment calculation unless you were benchmarking to see the absolute ceiling capacity achievable on a vSphere host. Naturally, you would not run a vSphere host in production near ceiling capacity, hence why the conservative approach is taken of not accounting for additional CPU adjustment potentially offered by hyperthreading.

Best Practice	Description
BP 18: For the VM vCPU, do not oversubscribe to CPU cycles that you don't really need.	If your performance load test determines, for example, that 2 vCPUs are adequate up to 70% CPU utilization, but you instead allocate 4 vCPUs to your VM, you potentially have 2 vCPUs idle, which is not optimal. If the exact workload is not known, size the VM with a smaller number of vCPUs initially and increase the number later, if necessary. The optimal sizing of VMs in terms of vCPU is workload dependent, but a good starting point is to size the VMs as large as the underlying cores with a NUMA node/socket. Alternatively, size the VMs smaller than the NUMA node in an evenly subdivisible fashion. For example, if you have a vSphere server with 2 sockets of 8 cores each, your configuration choices are 2 VMs of 8 vCPUs each, or 4 VMs of 4 vCPUs each, or 8 VMs of 2 vCPUs each, or 16 VMs of 1 vCPU. 1-vCPU VMs for production environments with JVMs and VMs of 4GB heap size would probably not scale well, and we often (as mentioned earlier) like to see 2-vCPU VMs for Java applications at a minimum. If under these configurations you find the number of physical cores CPU utilization is low, it means you could potentially increase the number of vCPUs beyond the underlying number of cores, but this practice should be done with caution and careful attention to the workload behavior over the course of its peak cycle.

VM Memory Size Best Practices

To understand how to size memory for a VM, you must understand the memory requirements of Java and various segments within it. Figure 6-4 and Formula 6-1 illustrate these separate memory areas.

Where:

- Guest OS memory. The operating system memory is approximately 0.5 to 1GB (depending on the operating system and other processes).

- -Xms is the initial heap.

- -Xmx is the JVM maximum heap size.

- -Xss is the Java thread stack size. The default depends on the operating system and JVM (usually at 256K on Linux OS, but could be as high as 1MB on Windows).

- Perm Gen, size as -XX:MaxPermSize, is an area additional to the -Xmx (maximum heap) value and contains class-level information. Note that IBM JVMs do not have a Perm Gen area. Instead, the class information within IBM WebSphere is managed like any other heap object with the heap.

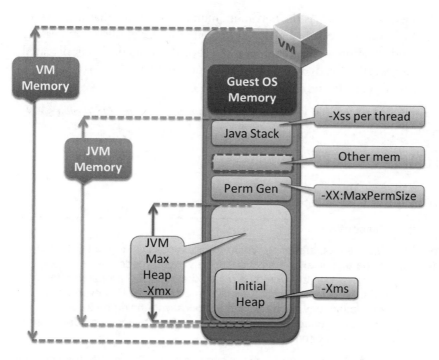

Figure 6-4   Single JVM Deployed on One VM

VM Memory = Guest OS Memory + JVM Memory

JVM Memory =

           JVM Max Heap (-Xmx value) +

           JVM Perm Size (-XX:MaxPermSize) +

           NumberOfConcurrentThreads * (-Xss) + "other Mem"

Formula 6-1   VM and JVM Memory Requirements

- Other Mem is additional memory required for New I/O (NIO) buffers, just-in-time (JIT) code cache, class loaders, socket buffers (receive/send), Java Native Interface (JNI), and garbage collection (GC) internal info. Note that the contents of a direct buffer are allocated from the guest operating system memory instead of from the Java heap and that nondirect buffers are copied into direct buffers for native I/O operations. Load test to appropriately size the effect of these buffers.

- NumberOfConcurrentThreads is the maximum number of threads that will be serviced by the JVM, usually measured as the concurrent number of threads at peak load. Each execution action in Java requires a Java thread allocated. It gets allocated by reserving -Xss worth of native memory that is outside the heap. This is native memory allocated directly from the OS.

- If you have multiple JVMs (*n* JVMs) on a VM, *VM memory = Guest OS memory + N * JVM memory*.

Table 6-2 provides some VM memory size best practices.

Table 6-2   VM Memory Size Best Practices

Best Practice	Description
BP 19: VM memory sizing.	Whether you are using Windows or Linux as your guest OS, refer to the technical specification of the various vendors for memory requirements. It is common to see the guest OS allocated about 0.5 to 1GB in addition to the JVM memory size. However, each installation may have additional processes running on it (for example, monitoring agents), and you need to accommodate their memory requirements as well.
	Figure 6-4 shows the various segments of JVM and VM memory, and Formula 6-1 summarizes VM memory as follows:
	VM memory (needed) = Guest OS memory + JVM memory, where *JVM memory = JVM max heap (-Xmx value) + Perm Gen (-XX:MaxPermSize) + NumberOfConcurrentThreads * (-Xss) + Other Mem*
	The -Xmx value is the value that you found during load testing for your application on physical servers. This value does not need to change when moving to a virtualized environment, especially if this value was previously well established through load testing and extensive production use. Load testing your application when deployed on vSphere will help confirm the best -Xmx value. Note that if you are following some of the recommendations of rationalizing the number of JVM instances, and you plan to collapse additional JVMs, you will need to increase the heap size to accommodate the heap (-Xmx) spaces that pertain to the JVMs that were consolidated.

Best Practice	Description
BP 19: VM memory sizing *(continued)*.	For example, if $-Xmx$ is set to 4GB, as in $-Xmx4g$, the Java process may likely require 4.5GB. (This number included the heap and the off-the-heap section.) Then, allowing at least 0.5GB for the OS, the total memory reservation for the VM that has this single JVM on it is 5GB reservation.

If you have multiple JVMs (*n* JVMs) on a VM, *VM memory = Guest OS memory + N * JVM memory*.

It is recommended that you do not overcommit memory, because the JVM memory is an active space where objects are constantly being created and garbage collected. Such an active memory space requires its memory to be available all the time. If you overcommit, memory ballooning or swapping may occur and impede performance.

An ESX host employs two distinct techniques for dynamically expanding or contracting the amount of memory allocated to VMs. The first method is known as memory *balloon driver* (vmmemctl). This is loaded from the VMware Tools package into the guest OS running in a VM. The second method involves paging from a VM to a server swap file, without any involvement by the guest OS.

In the page swapping method, when you power on a VM, a corresponding swap file is created and placed in the same location as the VM configuration file (VMX file). The VM can power on only when the swap file is available. ESX hosts use swapping to forcibly reclaim memory from a VM when no balloon driver is available. The balloon driver may be unavailable either because VMware Tools is not installed or because the driver is disabled or not running. For optimum performance, ESX uses the balloon approach whenever possible. However, swapping is used when the driver is temporarily unable to reclaim memory quickly enough to satisfy current system demands. Because the memory is being swapped out to disk, a significant performance penalty applies when the swapping technique is used. Therefore, it is recommended that the balloon driver is always enabled; however, monitor to verify that it is not getting invoked as that memory is overcommitted.

Both ballooning and swapping should be prevented for Java applications. To prevent ballooning and swapping, refer to BP 20: Set memory reservation for VM memory needs. |

Best Practice	Description
BP 20: Set memory reservation for VM memory needs.	JVMs running on VMs have an active heap space requirement that must always be present in physical memory. Use the VMware vSphere Client to set the reservation equal to the needed VM memory:
	Reservation memory = VM memory = Guest OS memory + JVM memory
	Set the reservation equal to the total configured memory of the VM.
	If you have multiple JVMs (N JVMs) on a VM, *VM memory = Guest OS memory + N * JVM memory*.
BP 21: Use of large pages.	Large pages have varied results, and they entirely depend on the nature of the workload. Performance of large pages can sometimes vary from –10% degradation to about 20% of improvement.
	Large memory pages help performance by optimizing the use of the Translation Look-aside Buffer (TLB), where virtual to physical address translations are performed. Use large memory pages as supported by your JVM and your guest OS. The operating system and the JVM must be informed that you want to use large memory pages, as is the case when using large pages in physical systems.
	Large pages must be enabled at both the guest OS and JVM level.
	To enable large pages at the JVM level, set the `-XX:+UseLargePages` at the JVM level for Sun HotSpot.
	On the IBM JVM, it is `-Xlp` and `JRockit -XXlargePages`.
	You also need to enable this at the guest OS level. When enabling large pages at OS level, make sure to turn off all processes that may have negative impact due to memory resizing. A clean way of doing this is to shut down major processes that consume a lot of memory.
	To check large pages allocation, use the following:
	`#cat /proc/meminfo	grep Huge`
	HugePages_Total: 0
	HugePages_Free: 0
	HugePages_Rsvd: 0
	Hugepagesize: 4096 kB

Best Practice	Description
BP 21: Use of large pages *(continued).*	This implies that you have 0 large pages allocated and that large pages are sized at 4MB.
	For example, if you want to size 4GB worth of large pages, you set 1000 large pages, because each page is 4MB. To allocate 1000 large pages, use the following:
	`#echo 1000 > /proc/sys/vm/nr_hugepages`
	You should repeat the `#cat /proc/meminfo	grep Huge` to see whether the 1000 pages were indeed allocated. Sometimes, due to the OS not having enough memory, it may not be able to allocate all of these pages. It usually means that there are processes running that are consuming the memory space and that the OS was not able to lock on those pages. The correct action here is to keep shutting down processes until enough memory is available to allocate to large pages.
	Setting large pages should be done with extreme caution, because not all processes can use large pages. Hence, it is best to set a ratio of 60% large pages and 40% smaller pages of the available guest OS memory.
	If you are not using large pages on your current physical Java deployment, you most likely do not have to turn large pages on when virtualizing, but it could benefit performance if large pages are set correctly.
	Large pages can sometimes become an administrative overhead (as new processes, Java and non-Java processes, may be deployed on the VM and hence the guest OS), you have to continuously adjust the large pages allocation to accommodate these new processes. This can sometimes lead to a high administrative cost and is often error prone; well-tuned systems often can do away with having to enable large pages.
	For Windows operating systems, check the user manual; the steps vary from one version to another.

VM Timekeeping Best Practices

Timekeeping can have an effect on Java programs if they are sensitive to accurate measurements over periods of time or if they need a time stamp that is within an exact tolerance (such as a time stamp on a shared document or data item). VMware Tools contains features that are installable into the guest OS to enable time synchronization, and the use of those tools is recommended. Table 6-3 provides a VM timekeeping best practice.

Table 6-3 VM Timekeeping Best Practice

Best Practice	Description
BP 22: Use an NTP source.	Use a common Network Time Protocol (NTP) source to synchronize all systems.
	For a Linux guest OS, the following KB article has a list of settings: http://kb.vmware.com/kb/1006427.
	For a Windows guest OS, the following KB article has a list of settings: http://kb.vmware.com/kb/1318.
	For further reference, see http://www.vmware.com/files/pdf/techpaper/Timekeeping-In-VirtualMachines.pdf.

Vertical Scalability Best Practices

If an enterprise Java application deployed on vSphere experiences heavy CPU utilization and you have determined that an increase in the vCPU count will help resolve the saturation, you can potentially use vSphere hot add to add additional vCPU. Table 6-4 describes a vertical scalability best practice.

Table 6-4 Vertical Scalability Best Practice

Best Practice	Description
BP 23: Hot add or remove CPU/memory.	Check to see whether the guest OS version you are using supports hot add and remove of CPU and memory.
	Because Java processes cannot immediately use all the available CPU, it is probably best to avoid having to use hot add. GC cycles in old generation and the off-the-heap section of the Java process may potentially use hot-added CPU, but this is not very predictable, and not a best practice in production systems. If the VM needs additional CPU cycles outside of the Java processes (for example, for some other process), perhaps CPU hot add can be used.
	Because Java platforms, particularly in category 1, will have lots of horizontally scaled-out copies of an applications in many JVMs, it is best to use the load-balancer layer to cycle the JVM that needs reconfiguration out of the distribution, and then adjust its configuration and place back in the load-balancer pool.
	In the young generation space of the Java heap, `-XX:ParallelGCThreads=<nThreads>` controls the number of executing worker threads that are used in parallel to clean out dead Java objects. If you determine that you need additional threads to allocate here and hence need additional vCPUs, hot add won't work. The reason for this is that any change to the Java command line (for instance, change to `-XX:ParallelGCThreads`) would require a restart of the JVM.
	Changes to memory allocated to Java require a change to `-Xmx`, the max heap size, and hence a restart of the Java process is needed. Therefore, hot memory adds is not recommended, but rather a robust production approach is to cycle the JVM in question out of the load-balancer pool, reconfigure it, and then add it back to the pool.
	VMs with a guest OS that supports hot add CPU and hot add memory can take advantage of the ability to change the VM configuration at runtime without any interruption to VM operations. This proves particularly useful when you are trying to increase the ability of the VM to handle more traffic. With the earlier caveats that if a JVM command-line option reconfiguration is needed, a restart of the JVM is inevitable.
	Plan ahead and enable this feature. The VM must be turned off to have the hot plug feature enabled, but when enabled, you can hot add CPU and hot add memory at runtime without VM shutdown (if the guest OS supports it).

Horizontal Scalability, Clusters, and Pools Best Practices

Enterprise Java applications deployed on VMware vSphere can benefit from using vSphere features for horizontal scalability using vSphere host clusters, resource pools, host affinity, and Distributed Resource Scheduler (DRS). Specifically, in category 1 types of JVM workloads, where there could be hundreds or thousands of JVMs, having the ability to flexibly move VMs around is a key feature that can help you robustly administer such systems. Table 6-5 describes best practices for horizontal scalability, clusters, and pools.

Table 6-5 Horizontal Scalability, Clusters, and Pools Best Practices

Best Practice	Description
BP 24: Use vSphere host clusters.	To enable better scalability, use vSphere host clusters.
	Within category 1 of JVM workload types, if the scale of JVMs is fairly small (for example, fewer than 100 JVMs), this can potentially be a cluster that is shared with other workload types. For customers that have just a few hundred VMs representing their entire footprint, shared clusters are often the norm. However, as you look at a more typical scale of category 1 workloads ranging in the thousands of JVMs and VMs, the need for dedicated vSphere host clusters quickly emerges.
	For larger category 1 type of workloads it is important to consider dedicated vSphere clusters. Within these dedicated vSphere clusters, you can have consistent sizing and various levels of service that will predictably meet SLAs. These are also known as technology-stack-based dedicated vSphere clusters (in this case, Java clusters). These Java vSphere clusters would have a dedicated administrative team that knows the Java application well.
	One way of envisioning the dedicated vSphere clusters is that they map to technology stacks. So, for example, you have dedicated Java vSphere clusters, and then within these clusters you can manage multiple resource pools that act as subclusters mapping to each LOB.

Best Practice	Description
BP 24: Use vSphere host clusters *(continued)*.	When creating clusters, enable VMware high availability (HA) and VMware DRS:
	VMware HA: Detects failures and provides rapid recovery for the VM running in a cluster. Core functionality includes host monitoring and VM monitoring to minimize downtime.
	VMware DRS: Enables vCenter Server to manage hosts as an aggregate pool of resources. Cluster resources can be divided into smaller pools for users, groups, and VMs. It enables vCenter to manage the assignment of VMs to hosts automatically, suggesting placement when VMs are powered on, and migrating running VMs to balance load and enforce allocation policies.
	Enable EVC (for either Intel or AMD). EVC refers to Enhanced vMotion Compatibility. It configures a cluster and its hosts to maximize vMotion compatibility. When EVC is enabled, only hosts that are compatible with those in the cluster may be added to the cluster.
	If feasible, it is always best to dedicate vSphere hosts.
BP 25: Use resource pools.	Multiple resource pools can be used within a cluster to manage compute resource consumption by either reserving the needed memory for the VMs within a resource pool or by limiting/restricting it to a certain level. This feature also helps you meet quality of service and other requirements.
	For example, you can create a Tier 2 resource pool for the less-critical applications and a Tier 1 resource pool for business critical applications.
BP 26: Use affinity rules.	In addition to existing anti-affinity rules, the VM-Host affinity rule was introduced in vSphere 4.1. The VM-Host affinity rule provides the ability to place VMs on a subset of hosts in a cluster. This is very useful in honoring Independent Software Vendor (ISV) licensing requirements. Rules can be created so that VMs run on vSphere hosts in different blades for higher availability. Conversely, limit the vSphere host to 1 blade in case network traffic between the VMs needs to be optimized by keeping them in 1 chassis location.
	Due to specific application server vendor licensing structures, you may need to create smaller vSphere host clusters to contain the cost of licenses. Such vSphere clusters almost always end up as technology-dedicated clusters (that is, Java-based dedicated clusters, with many Java workloads consolidated onto a fewer set of vSphere clusters).

Best Practice	Description
BP 27: Use vSphere-aware load balancers.	vSphere makes it easy to add resources such as host and VMs at runtime. It is possible to provision these ahead of time. However, it is simpler if you use a load balancer that can integrate with vSphere application programming interfaces (APIs) to detect the newly added VMs and add them to its application load-balancing pools without downtime.

Inter-Tier Configuration Best Practices

Much of the discussion has centered on the Java process thus far, but there are other considerations. There are other tiers. In fact, there are four tiers: the load balancer tier, the web server tier, the Java application server tier, and the DB server tier. The configurations for compute resources at each tier must translate to an equitable configuration at the next tier. For example, if the web server tier is configured to handle 100 HTTP requests per second, of those requests you must determine how many Java application server threads are needed, and in turn how many DB connections are needed in the JDBC pool configuration. Table 6-6 describes best practices for inter-tier configuration.

Table 6-6   Inter-Tier Configuration Best Practices

Best Practice	Description
BP 28: Establish appropriate thread ratios that prevents bottlenecks (HTTP threads:Java threads:DB connections ratio).	This is the ratio of HTTP threads to Java threads to DB connections.
	Establish initial setup by assuming that each layer requires a 1:1:1 ratio of HTTP threads:Java threads:DB connections, and then based on the response time and throughput numbers, adjust each of these properties accordingly until you have satisfied your SLA objectives.
	For example, if you have 100 HTTP requests submitted to the web server initially, assume that all of these will have an interaction with Java threads, and in turn, DB connections. Of course, in reality, during your benchmark you will find that not all HTTP threads are submitted to the Java application server, and in turn, not all Java application server threads require a DB connection. That is, you may find your ratio for 100 requests translates to 100 HTTP threads:25 Java threads:10 DB connections, and this depends on the nature of your enterprise Java application behavior. Benchmarking helps you establish this ratio.
	Configure a separate web server pool with adequate number of web server instances that in turn talk to a secondary pool that has Java application server member VMs in it. This will ensure best horizontal scalability at both web server and Java application server layers.

Best Practice	Description
BP 29: Apache web server sizing.	In httpd.conf, you can set any of the directives, such as `StartServers`, `MinSpareThreads`, `MaxSpareThreads`, `ServerLimit`, `MaxClients`, and `MaxRequestsPerChild`. When sizing Apache processes, to determine how much memory to reserve, each of these directives must be understood.
	`MaxClients`: This is the number of concurrent requests that can be serviced by an Apache instance. Requests exceeding this limit will be queued into a queue with length determined by `ListendbackLog` directive.
	`MaxRequestsPerChild`: The `MaxRequestsPerChild` directive sets the limit on the number of requests that an individual child server process will handle. After `MaxRequestsPerChild` requests, the child process will die. If `MaxRequestsPerChild` is 0, the process will never expire.
	`StartServers`: The `StartServers` directive sets the number of child server processes created on startup. Because the number of processes is dynamically controlled depending on the load, there is usually little reason to adjust this parameter.
	`MinSpareThreads`: Minimum number of idle threads to handle request spikes. Different MPMs deal with this directive differently.
	`MaxSpareThreads`: Maximum number of idle threads. Different MPMs deal with this directive differently.
	`ServerLimit`: For the prefork MPM, this directive sets the maximum configured value for `MaxClients` for the lifetime of the Apache process. For the worker MPM, this directive, in combination with `ThreadLimit`, sets the maximum configured value for `MaxClients` for the lifetime of the Apache process. Any attempts to change this directive during a restart will be ignored, but `MaxClients` can be modified during a restart.
	Ideally, you should not mix Apache VMs with Java VMs, although in some cases this may make sense if there is ample compute capacity.
	When sizing VMs for Apache processes, you face the choice of maximum scalability, which implies far more VMs in a scaled-out fashion, or an adequate number of VMs. If you have an adequate number of VMs, it is best to size the VMs fairly large, almost as large as the NUMA node, from a memory and vCPU perspective. Hence, follow the best practice of sizing 1 VM per NUMA node. This in turn will save on the number of memory copies you need to allocate to the guest OS, and instead this now spare memory can be allocated to Apache processes that would service even more requests.

Best Practice	Description
BP 29: Apache web server sizing *(continued)*.	To calculate how much memory is needed for a VM running Apache, use the following: MaxClients = *(Available RAM − Size all non-Apache processes) / Size of Apache process* For example, if you have a vSphere host of 48GB RAM of 2 sockets, 8 cores on each, then by applying Formula 1.2 from Chapter 1: ((48GB * 0.99) − 1GB) / 2 => 23.26GB memory available per VM), you can also allocate 0.5GB to the guest OS. This implies that there is (23.26 − 0.5) => 22.76GB available to be set as memory reservation of the VMs. We are assuming that NUMA perfect VMs are being sized to be deployed on this host. In this case, this means that the host will have 2 VMs with 23.26GB memory reserved and 8 vCPUs on each. Applying the Apache `MaxClients` formula for this example implies (23.26 − *Size all of non-Apache processes) / Size of Apache process*. By taking OS memory requirements into account, the formula translates to (23.26 − 0.5 − *Size all of non-Apache processes) / Size of Apache process*. To find the Apache process size, use the following: `ps -y|C httpd -sort:rss`, to find process size, divide that by 1024 to get Megs To inspect the overall memory and CPU situation on the guest OS, use the following: `free -m` for general overview of buffers/cache `Vmstat 2 5` to display the number of runnable, blocked, waiting, and swap processes Depending on the value from `MaxClients` calculation above (by applying the Apache `MaxClients` formula), because it depends on the memory used by the Apache processes, you can decide on a better `StartServer` value. Let's assume 50 for `StartServer`, and assume 50K concurrent users. Each user thread will use 1 thread, which means 50K threads (worst-case scenario is assumed here, could be lower otherwise): 50K / 16 VMs => 3125 requests to each VM, which means each Apache instance should have 3125 requests going to it and equal number of threads waiting to service the call. This translates to 64 threads, and hence `ThreadsPerChild` = 64, `MaxClients` will be 3125, and `Min` and `Max SpareThreads` is 3125. No doubt these numbers can be adjusted by increasing/decreasing the number of `StartServer`. It will be a choice of having many processes with *x* number of threads or of having fewer processes with more threads. Set `MinSpareThreads` = `MaxSpareThreads`.

Best Practice	Description
BP 29: Apache web server sizing *(continued)*.	Using `mod deflate` may help with improving performance.
	Based on the calculations, you can now plan on how many VMs you will need, typically applying the previously covered sizing approach on a set of VMs and then load testing to verify the numbers and checking memory usage of each process and the maximum amount of memory used at peak. This will help you certify what you can achieve across 2 VMs on 1 vSphere host, and then you can linearly extrapolate from this how many VMs you will need in a scale-out fashion to service the entire traffic set of your application.
	As for `MaxRequestPerChild`, there are 2 schools of thought on this. Many recommend to set it to 0 so that Apache doesn't incur the cost of shutting down and re-creating a process. However, if you have threads within a process that never get cleaned up (which is the effect of setting it to 0), performance will suffer. So, setting this to a max possible value as to the number of requests that it gets per process will help alleviate any memory leakage and so forth. In this case, the peak is assumed to be 50K / 16 VMs and 50 `StartServer` as peak per Apache process. (This is made of 50 `StartServers` * 64 `ThreadsPerChild` => 3200, rounded to nearest hundred.) However, then it needs to be aggregated over a period of 24 hours to determine the total number of processes that a child process (1 of the 50 Apache server processes set up) will get.
	The `ServerLimit` value must be greater or equal to (`MaxClient` / `ThreadsPerChild`). `ServerLimit` is a hard stop on the number of active child processes.
	`ThreadLimit` must be greater than or equal to `ThreadsPerChild`. It is a hard limit on the threads permitted.

Best Practice	Description
BP 30: Load-balancer algorithm choice and VM symmetry.	Use one load-balancer pool for web server VMs and a second pool for Java application server VMs.

When setting up new application nodes, it is advisable to have a minimum of 3 VMs spread across at least 3 vSphere hosts to ensure better availability. The reason for this is that if 1 of the VMs or vSphere hosts becomes faulty, then at least 2 VMs or vSphere hosts are available to provide robust high availability. No doubt, this is a setup for serious production systems, and is a smaller version of the overall active-active architecture approach discussed in the "Active-Active Architectures and Modern Data Platforms" section in Chapter 2, "Modern Scalable Data Platforms." For a comprehensive fault-tolerant and globally available system, review the active-active architecture approach discussed in Chapter 2.

Follow all the design and sizing guidelines discussed thus far in the book, and size the appropriate number of JVMs in 1 pool and then a secondary pool for web servers. Direct traffic from web server pool members to the members of JVM load-balancer pool (that is, the Java application server load-balancer pool).

When directing traffic between web server pool member and JVM pool member, session stickiness may be needed. Most Java applications require session stickiness to fulfill authentication and single sign-on requirements, or sometimes AJAX calls also need stickiness.

Take into account the available algorithms of your load balancer. Make sure that when using the scale-out approach that all of your VMs are receiving an equal share of the traffic. Some industry standard algorithms are round-robin, weighted round-robin, least connections, and least response time. You may want to initially default to least connections and then adjust as you see fit in your load test iterations.

Keep your VMs symmetrical in terms of the size of compute resource. For example, if you decide to use 2-vCPU VMs as a repeatable, horizontally scalable building block, this helps with your load-balancing algorithm, working more effectively than if there were a pool of nonsymmetrical VMs for 1 particular application. That is, mixing 2-vCPU VMs with 4-vCPU VMs in 1 load-balancer-facing pool is nonsymmetrical and the load balancer has no notion of weighing this unless you configure for it at the load-balancer level, which is time-consuming.

High-Level vSphere Best Practices

It is important to follow the best practices for vSphere, http://www.vmware.com/pdf/ Perf_Best_Practices_vSphere5.1.pdf. Table 6-7 provides a summary of some of the key networking, storage, and hardware best practices that are commonly followed.

Table 6-7 High-Level vSphere Best Practices

Best Practice	Description
BP 31: vSphere 5.1.	The generic vSphere best practices are well documented at http://www.vmware.com/pdf/Perf_Best_Practices_vSphere5.1.pdf.
BP 32: vSphere networking.	Separate infrastructure traffic from VM traffic. You can achieve this by either using separate physical network adapters or separate VLANs that can potentially share the same underlying physical switch and network. Ensure that you trunk all VLANs used on all pNIC ports.
	Use NIC teaming for availability and load balancing. Always connect virtual switch to 2 or more pNICs.
	The NetIOC concept revolves around resource pools concept in much the same way as for CPU and memory resource pools. NetIOC classifies traffic into six predefined classes: vMotion, iSCSI, FT logging, Management, NFS, and Virtual Machine Traffic.
	When using bandwidth allocation, select "shares" instead of "limits," because shares would have more flexibility in redistribution of spare capacity. If you are concerned about a certain traffic class creating a performance bottleneck and causing the traffic classes to suffer, you can use limits in those cases. Consider vMotion, for example; you could set a limit on multiple vMotions that might saturate the physical network.
	If EtherChannel is configured on the physical side, note that only static is supported and that Link Aggregation Control Protocol (LACP) (dynamically negotiated EtherChannel) should not be used.
	If EtherChannel is configured on the physical side, on the virtual side you have to configure IP hash on the virtual switch or the virtual distributed switch.
	Enable link-state tracking on the physical switch if it is available. If it is not available, consider beacon probing on the virtual switch.

Best Practice	Description
BP 33: vSphere storage.	**Note:** Typically, category 1 type of Java workloads are more CPU and memory bound and less storage bound, unlike databases. In category 2, for example, in-memory databases will track both like a Java workload and a database workload, hence CPU, memory, and storage best practices are key.
	VMware recommends a minimum of four paths from an ESX host to a storage array, which means the host requires at least two HBA ports.
	Follow vSphere storage best practices, refer to http://www.vmware.com/files/pdf/techpaper/ SAN_Design_and_Deployment_Guide.pdf
BP 34: vSphere host.	Disable any other power-saving mode in the BIOS.
	NUMA considerations: IBM (X-Architecture), AMD (Opteron-based), and Intel (Nehalem) Non-Uniform Memory Access (NUMA) systems are supported by vSphere. On AMD Opteron-based systems, such as the HP ProLiant DL585 Server, BIOS settings for node interleaving determine whether the system behaves like a NUMA system or like a Uniform Memory Accessing (UMA) system.
	By default, vSphere NUMA scheduling and related optimizations are enabled only on systems with a total of at least 4 CPU cores and with at least 2 CPU cores per NUMA node.
	VMs with a number of vCPUs equal to or less than the number of cores in each NUMA node are managed by the NUMA scheduler and have the best performance.
	Hardware BIOS: Verify that the BIOS is set to enable all populated sockets, and enable all cores in each socket.
	Enable turbo mode if your processors support it.
	Make sure hyperthreading is enabled in the BIOS.

SQLFire Best Practices and SQLFire on vSphere Best Practices (Category 2 JVM Workload Best Practices)

The best way to understand best practices in category 2 workloads is to consider an actual example. In this case, we assume vFabric SQLFire as the category 2 workload. Typical SQLFire workloads have a dozen JVMs in a cluster, but these are of fairly large heap size (for example, 32 to 128GB per JVM, across 8 to 12 JVMs in any given cluster).

The best practices discussed previously for category 1 workloads apply equally to category 2 workloads, but with some notable differences. Category 1 workloads almost always are made of one or more vSphere clusters, dedicated or shared across other workloads. Obviously, if the density of JVMs is high (500+), these are likely dedicated clusters at any rate; however, in category 1, workloads are always run within one dedicated vSphere cluster and are never shared with other workloads. This category 1 rule refers to one SQLFire data fabric (data grid/cluster) mapped to fit within one dedicated vSphere cluster. The reason for the dedicated cluster is because the latency-sensitive tuning best practices applied to category 2 workloads may hurt category 1 workloads in some instances. The other reason has to do with administration and the series classification of category 2 workloads. Think of how you guard your virtualized RDBMS (typically dedicated and in a highly protected administrative zone); in vFabric SQLFire and category 2 workloads, this rule also applies. You only want your Java DevOps (Java DBAs) to administer and care about this cluster, and not some other less workloads that may have a different access pattern and hence workload lifecycle behavior.

The other major distinguishing factor is that it is likely that category 1 workloads would have a much higher number of JVMs and hence VMs, and in some cases you can have multiple JVMs within one VM. In contrast, category 2 workloads are always configured one JVM to one VM. Category 2 workloads are always latency sensitive and memory bound, and that is why we want to configure the largest JVM and VM combination that fits with a NUMA node. Category 1 workloads, however, are likely to track CPU bound simply because of the high density of JVMs (that is, thousands of JVMs, each with its own GC cycle, that can demand lots of CPU cycles at peak times). This is why it is common to see category 1 workloads deployed on four-socket vSphere hosts, while category 2 workloads are always configured on two-socket hosts. The four-socket vSphere hosts would likely have more CPU cores (when compared to two-socket hosts) to help category 1 workloads by providing ample CPU to the thousands of GC cycles, while category 2 workloads are aided by having very large NUMA banks with two-socket servers. These are usually NUMA memory banks that category 2 workloads can fully consume.

Finally, category 1 workloads usually have much smaller JVM sizes than category 2, but this is not a cast-in-stone rule. Suffice it to say, however, that the amount of JVM tuning effort within category 1 is much less than in category 2. This is especially true when you consider that most category 1 workloads will fit nicely within a scaled set of 4GB heap JVM instances (where 4GB is a unique and automatically 32-bit compressed space even though it is still running within the 64-bit JVM, and hence requires vastly less tuning to get a good SLA). However, in category 2 workloads, we size as big a JVM as we can afford to fit within NUMA node to reduce the number of JVM instances within the SQL data cluster. The fewer JVMs in the cluster, the fewer potential network hops or less chatter. It is also easier to administer the cluster when you have a handful of JVMs, even though they are large JVMs. This is a memory-bound workload, and it benefits from being able to quickly access as much local memory as possible for the fewest number of JVM instances.

SQLFire Best Practices

This section covers SQLFire best practices, highlighting JVM tuning and sizing examples that provide optimal performance. See Table 6-8 for further details.

Table 6-8   SQLFire Best Practices

Best Practice	Description
BP 35: JVM version.	Use JDK 1.6.0_29 or the latest JDK. As of this writing, JDK 1.6.0_43 is also available and can be used; or if you run JDK 7, the use of JDK 1.7.0_25 is also possible.

BP 36: Use parallel and CMS GC policy combination.	`java -Xms64g -Xmx64g -Xmn21g -Xss1024k`
	`-XX:+UseConcMarkSweepGC`
	
	`-XX:+UseParNewGC`
	`-XX:CMSInitiatingOccupancyFraction=75`
	
	`-XX:+UseCMSInitiatingOccupancyOnly`
	`-XX:+ScavengeBeforeFullGC`
	
	`-XX:TargetSurvivorRatio=80 -XX:SurvivorRatio=8`
	
	`-XX:+UseBiasedLocking`
	
	`-XX:MaxTenuringThreshold=15 -XX:ParallelGCThreads=4`
	
	`-XX:+OptimizeStringConcat`
	
	`-XX:+UseStringCache -XX:+DisableExplicitGC`
	
	Set `-XX:+UseConcMarkSweepGC` to use the concurrent low-pause GC in the old generation and the parallel young generation collector (`-XX:+UseParNewGC`). The low-pause collector sacrifices some throughput to minimize stop-the-world GC pauses for the old generation. It requires more headroom in the heap, so increase the heap size to compensate. The configuration shown here has `-XX:ParallelGCThreads=4`, which implies that the size of the VM that this JVM resides on is at least 8 vCPUs.

Best Practice	Description
BP 36: Use parallel and CMS GC policy combination *(continued)*.	When setting −XX:ParallelGCThreads, size it at 50% of the available number of underlying vCPU or CPU cores initially, and then adjust progressively upward if you need to or if you are seeking better performance and the system still has ample CPU cycles. In the example in Figure 4-18 in Chapter 4, "Designing and Sizing Large-Scale Java Platforms," 1 JVM is configured to run on 1 VM that resides on 1 socket that has 8 underlying CPU cores, and therefore 50% of the CPU compute resource is allocated to potentially be consumed by −XX:ParallelGCThreads. The other 50% on the socket remains for regular application transactions. That is, 4 vCPUs are consumed by the ParallelGCThreads, and the remaining 4 are available to service application threads, concurrent old generation activity, off-the-heap activity, and any other workload that might be running on the VM, such as a monitoring agent.
	One minor caveat here is that in the very short pausing phases of the initial mark (aside from the other concurrent phases) it is single threaded but finishes rather quickly, and then the re-mark is multithreaded. The initial mark being single threaded does not use any of the −XX:ParallelGCThreads allocated, but the re-mark phase being multithreaded uses some of the parallel threads allocated. Because re-mark is a very short phase, it uses negligible parallel thread cycles. You can tune −XX:ParallelGCThreads to below 50% allocation and give more threads back to your applications. If you attempt this and it does not hurt overall response time, it might be prudent to reduce −XX:ParallelGCThreads. Conversely, if you have exhausted young generation size tuning, −Xmn, and have ample CPU cycles, consider increasing beyond the 50% mark progressively in 1-thread increments. Load test and measure response times for the application to confirm the benefits of the incremental adjustment.

Best Practice	Description
BP 36: Use parallel and CMS GC policy combination *(continued)*.	When considering reducing $-XX:ParallelGCThreads$, the minimum should be 2. Any lower than this can negatively impact the behavior of the parallel collector. When sizing large-scale JVMs for vFabric SQLFire types of workloads (for example, 8GB and greater), it requires at least a 4-vCPU VM configuration, because 2 vCPUs are taken by $-XX:ParallelGCThreads$, and the other 2 vCPUs are taken by the application threads. This configuration rule is shown for both the JVM configuration in Figure 2-16 in Chapter 2 (the 4-vCPU VM has 2 *ParallelGCThreads*) and Figure 2-18 in Chapter 2 (an 8-vCPU VM has 4 *ParallelGCThreads* allocated). This is 50% of the available vCPUs in both cases. Further, when using a CMS type of configuration, you should always use VMs with 4 vCPUs or more. The 50% rule is a starting point, and if you have ample CPU cycles left and want to improve GC, consider raising $-XX:ParallelGCThreads$. This should never be set greater than the number of underlying cores available on the VM. The reason why we set this to 505 is because we want to leave CPU cycles for other activities, such as the old generation GC, off-the-heap activity, and any other process that may be running on the VM in addition to the Java process. Set $-XX:CMSInitiatingOccupancyFraction=75$ for high-throughput latency-sensitive applications that generate large amounts of garbage in the old generation, such as those that have high rates of updates, deletes, or evictions. This setting tells the concurrent collector to start a collection when tenured occupancy is at the given percentage. With the default setting, a high rate of tenured garbage creation can outpace the collector and result in an OutOfMemory error. A setting too low can affect throughput by doing unnecessary collections. Conversely, a collection too late can lead to concurrent mode failure, which should be avoided by lowering the percentage. Test to determine the best setting. For a definition of each JVM option and further guidance, refer to Table 3.1 in Chapter 3, "Tuning Large-Scale Java Platforms." Follow steps outlined in the section, "GC Tuning Approach," from Chapter 3 for the GC tuning approach should you want to conduct further tuning.
BP 37: Set initial heap equal to maximum heap.	Set $-Xms$ (initial heap) to $-Xmx$ (maximum heap). **Note** Without this setting, performance can suffer if the initial heap setting is not adequate and the JVM responds by increasing the memory allocated, causing overhead at runtime.

Best Practice	Description
BP 38: Disable calls to `System.gc()`.	Set `-XX:+DisableExplicitGC` to disable GC. This causes calls to `System.gc()` to be ignored, hence avoiding the associated long latencies.
BP 39: New generation size.	Set the `-Xmn` value to be large enough to avoid the new generation filling up. Making the new generation large enough avoids the cost of copying objects into the old generation, which can impact performance.
	A common approach is to set the `-Xmn` size to approximately 33% of the heap's maximum size (that is, 33% of `-Xmx` for heap sizes less than 8GB). For heap sizes from 8 to 100GB, the 33% rule might be too high; usually, 10% to 15% of the maximum heap size for these is adequate. To establish the best size for your application, you must load test and measure how often the new generation fills up. Based on this, decide whether to adjust the `-Xmn` value. Start at 33%, and then adjust down only if you notice large minor GC durations or pauses that are negatively impacting the application transaction response times. If no negative impact is noticed at 33% of `-Xmx` initially, leave `-Xmn` at 33% of `-Xmx`.
	For smaller heaps, if the heap is less than 8GB, set `-Xmn` < 33% of `-Xmx`. For larger heaps, if the heap is much greater than 8GB, set `-Xmn` < 10% to 15% of `-Xmx`. However, it is difficult to apply this rule consistently on varied workload behavior.
	A further rule to consider when sizing `-Xmn` is that partitioned tables most likely have higher numbers of short-lived objects and therefore can require a larger `-Xmn` value. Compare this with replicated tables where the rate of change is minimal and not many short-lived objects are created, and therefore a lower `-Xmn` is adequate.
	Note This guidance has a caveat that depends on the behavior of the application. For example, if the application requires many query calls, configure a size at the upper end of the `-Xmn` range described. For mostly insert or update calls, configure a size in the middle of the range.
BP 40: Using 32-bit addressing in a 64-bit JVM.	When memory is constrained, set the `-XX:+UseCompressedOops` JVM option. This uses a 32-bit pointer address space within a 64-bit JVM for heap sizes up to 32GB. This can save substantial memory space (in some cases up to 50%), although the savings varies based on the Java types used within the application.

Best Practice	Description
BP 41: Stack size.	In most cases, the default `-Xss` stack is adequate, ranging in size from 256KB to 1MB depending on the JVM and operating system. However, latency-sensitive workloads can benefit from having a large Java stack if the objects within a thread do not escape to other threads. Setting the Java stack to a larger value reduces the number of concurrent threads you can fit into the available RAM. This can improve transaction response times, which might be what you are more concerned with (as opposed to packing more, smaller stack threads within the same memory space). Setting the `-Xss` stack to a range of 1 to 4MB is common practice for memory-bound latency-sensitive workloads.
BP 42: Perm size.	It is a common best practice to set `-XX:MaxPermSize` in the range from 128 to 512MB, although the actual size can vary for your application, and appropriate testing should be conducted. The `PermSize` is where class-level information is kept. In the HotSpot JVM, this is allocated outside the heap (that is, in addition to the `-Xmx`).
BP 43: Table placements in a JVM.	Place both replicated and partitioned tables within 1 JVM instance (that is, within 1 data management node). This provides the best scalability and performance. By default, vFabric SQLFire partitions each data point into a bucket using a hashing policy on the key. The physical location of the key/value pair is abstracted away from the application. In addition, no default relation exists between data stored in different partitioned tables. To run transactions on partitioned tables, you must colocate all data accessed in any single transaction on the same data host. In addition, in many cases you can get better performance if you colocate similar data within a table and between tables.

For example:

A query run on a patient, the related health records, and the insurance and billing information is more efficient if all of the data is grouped in a single JVM.

A financial risk analytical application runs more quickly if all trades, risk sensitivities, and reference data associated with a single instrument are located together.

Colocation generally improves the performance of data-intensive operations. You can reduce network hops for iterative operations on related data sets. You can usually significantly increase overall throughput for compute-heavy, data-intensive applications. You specify colocation through specialized vFabric SQLFire DDL keywords during table definition. |

vFabric SQLFire Best Practices on vSphere

vFabric SQLFire and vSphere provide a robust complement to deliver data faster and more reliably using cost-effective x86 commodity hardware and vSphere. Table 6-9 describes some recommended best practices when virtualizing vFabric SQLFire. These would also apply to any latency-sensitive in-memory workloads (in-memory databases) that have excessive network traffic and are memory bound.

Table 6-9   vFabric SQLFire Best Practices on vSphere

Best Practice	Description
BP 44: Enable hyperthreading and do not overcommit CPU.	Always enable hyperthreading.
	Do not overcommit CPU; vFabric SQLFire applications are typically latency sensitive that are CPU bound. Size these based on the available physical cores.
	For most production vFabric SQLFire servers, always size with a minimum of 2-vCPU VMs. However, larger 8-vCPU VMs might be necessary in some cases to achieve your SLAs.
	Apply NUMA locality by sizing VMs to fit within the NUMA node. If you suspect the VM has poor NUMA locality, inspect the N%L counter from esxtop. With good NUMA locality, this should be 100%.
	Note The terminology of NUMA node is equivalent to 1 CPU socket. So, for a server with 2 sockets, there are 2 NUMA nodes. Therefore, the available number of physical CPU cores and RAM are divided equally among the NUMA nodes. This is critical when sizing VMs to fit within one NUMA node. Refer to Figure 4.9 in Chapter 4 and the discussion of NUMA locality.
	For example, a 2-socket 16-core (8 cores on each socket) server with 192GB RAM has two NUMA nodes, each with 8 physical cores (CPUs) and 96GB RAM (192 / 2). When sizing VMs, it is important not to exceed the limits of 8 vCPUs and 96GB RAM. Exceeding any of these CPU and RAM maximums of each NUMA node can force the VM to fetch memory from a remote location, impacting performance. There are many vSphere CPU scheduler enhancements to avoid this, but following this example can help.

Best Practice	Description
BP 44: Enable hyperthreading and do not overcommit CPU *(continued)*.	If somehow the VMs are not sized perfectly to have 1 VM in each NUMA node, it might be that vSphere will determine scheduling additional VMs on the same NUMA node would help, but this is not always a good assumption by vSphere. This sometimes can happen if you are intermixing smaller-size JVMs and VMs with large JVMs and VMs being deployed on the same vSphere host. For example, if you have a topology setup such as the one shown in Figure 2.4 in Chapter 2, it is possible that the VMs from the client tier, such as Enterprise App 1 and SQLFire Member 1, may end up on the same NUMA node simply because vSphere scheduler detects that these 2 VMs have a high amount of chatter between them. Ideally, you should avoid this, either by using */Numa/LocalityWeightActionAffinity* set to 0, or not mix smaller JVM and VMs on the same vSphere hosts. Ideally, you should have only SQLFire member VMs on vSphere hosts that fit perfectly into the NUMA nodes so that they don't allow other VMs to be scheduled in, and the entire VM that fits within the NUMA node avoiding any other VM being scheduled in there. The enterprise application services/client tier type of JVMs can be placed on separate vSphere hosts.
	Note In VMware vSphere 5.1, there is an advanced setting parameter, and you can set this to 0: */Numa/LocalityWeightActionAffinity*. This setting controls the weight that the CPU scheduler gives to inter-VM communication when making decisions about assigning VMs to NUMA nodes. In most cases, leaving this setting at the default value will give the best performance. But if you happen to mix client applications with server applications on the same vSphere host, this setting will perhaps improve scalability. In the SQLFire client/server topology, client VMs mixed with server VMs have a high level of communication between them. This biased the scheduler default algorithm toward placing these VMs on the same NUMA node. This behavior will impede performance, and will have a negative impact on performance at certain load levels. As a result, the parameter was set to 0 to disable the use of inter-VM communication in scheduling decisions in the default algorithm.
	As further note on NUMA, know that one advantage of virtualizing workloads over physical is the NUMA optimizations that vSphere offers. In the case of Java workloads that are memory intensive, especially in category 2 workloads, if not virtualized and deployed on physical systems, one would have to resort to using `numactl` command for NUMA pinning, which is a static task that constantly needs to be updated as the workload's behavior changes over time— not a great thing to have to administer on a daily basis, while also not likely to perform as well as an advanced NUMA algorithm that vSphere provides.

Best Practice	Description
BP 45: CPU cache sharing.	You can set `sched.cpu.vsmpConsolidate = "true"`, as described in "Consolidating vCPUs for an SMP Virtual Machine Can Improve Performance for Some Workloads" (http://kb.vmware.com/kb/1017936). On the current vSphere5.1 this is on by default, for earlier vSphere check the above KB article. This instructs the ESXi scheduler to place the vCPUs of an SMP VM into the fewest last-level cache (LLC) as possible. This policy results in better cache sharing.
BP 46: vFabric SQLFire member server, JVM, and VM ratio.	Have 1 JVM instance per VM. This is not usually a requirement, but because vFabric SQLFire JVMs can be quite large (up to 128GB), it is advisable to adhere to this rule. Increasing the heap space to service more data demand is better than installing a second instance of a JVM on a single VM. If increasing the JVM heap size is not an option, consider placing the second JVM on a separate newly created VM, thus promoting more effective horizontal scalability. As you increase the number of vFabric SQLFire servers, also increase the number of VMs to maintain a 1:1:1 ratio among the vFabric SQLFire server, the JVM, and the VMs. It is important to size for a minimum of 4-vCPU VMs with 1 vFabric SQLFire server running in one JVM instance. This allows ample CPU cycles for the garbage collector and the rest for user transactions.
BP 47: VM placement.	Because vFabric SQLFire can place redundant copies of cached data on any VM, it is possible to inadvertently place two redundant data copies on the same vSphere host. This is not optimal if a host fails. To create a more robust configuration, use VM1-to-VM2 anti-affinity rules to indicate to vSphere that VM1 and VM2 can never be placed on the same host (because they hold redundant data copies).
BP 48: Set VM memory reservation.	Set memory reservation at the VM level so that vSphere provides and locks down the needed physical memory upon VM startup. Once allocated, vSphere does not allow the memory to be taken away. Follow the sizing example shown in Figure 4-17 in Chapter 4. If you choose this kind of sizing, your reservation should be set at 68GB, as shown in the diagram. If you choose lower or higher JVM sizes, adjust all the relative sizes shown in the example accordingly, but maintain the relative ratios. If you choose a different size than the example, set the appropriate reservation level for the full size of the memory in the VM you have configured. Do not overcommit memory for vFabric SQLFire hosts. For optimal performance, when sizing memory for vFabric SQLFire server within 1 JVM on 1 VM, the total reserved memory for the VM should not exceed what is available within 1 NUMA node. Refer to BP 44 for further NUMA discussion and considerations.

Best Practice	Description
BP 49: vMotion, DRS cluster, and vFabric SQLFire server.	When you first commission the data management system, place VMware vSphere Distributed Resource Scheduler (DRS) in manual mode to prevent an automatic VMware vSphere vMotion operation that can impact response times.
	vMotion can complement vFabric SQLFire features during scheduled maintenance to help minimize downtime impact due to hardware and software upgrades. It is a best practice to trigger vMotion migrations over a 10 Gigabit Ethernet network interface to speed up the vMotion migration process.
	Do not allow vMotion migrations with vFabric SQLFire locator processes; the latency introduced to this process can cause other members of the vFabric SQLFire servers to falsely suspect that other members are dead.
	Use dedicated vFabric SQLFire vSphere DRS clusters. This is especially important when you consider that the physical NIC and virtual NIC are specifically tuned to disable interrupt coalescing on every NIC of an ESXi host in the cluster. This type of tuning benefits vFabric SQLFire workloads, but it can hurt other non-vFabric SQLFire workloads that are memory throughput bound as opposed to latency sensitive as in the case of vFabric SQLFire workloads.
	If using a dedicated vSphere DRS cluster is not an option, and vFabric SQLFire must run in a shared DRS cluster, make sure that DRS rules are set up that do not perform vMotion migrations on vFabric SQLFire VMs.
	If the restriction to have vFabric SQLFire members to be excluded from vMotion migrations, it is preferred that all vMotion migration activity of vFabric SQLFire members happens over 10GbE, during periods of low activity and scheduled maintenance windows.
	Note In some cases, a vMotion migration might not succeed and instead fails back because of a rapidly changing volatile memory space, which can be the case with partitioned tables and in some cases of replicated tables. The failback is a fail-safe mechanism to the source VM, and it does not impact the source VM. vMotion makes this failback decision based on the time it takes to complete the iterative copy process that captures changes between the source VM to the destination VM. If the changes are too rapid and vMotion is not able to complete the iterative copy within the default 100 seconds, it checks whether it can failsafe to the running source VM without interruption. Therefore, vMotion transfers the source VM to the destination only if it is certain that it can complete the memory copy.

Best Practice	Description
BP 50: VMware HA and vFabric SQLFire.	vFabric SQLFire VMs should have vSphere HA disabled. If this is a dedicated vFabric SQLFire DRS cluster, you can disable HA across the cluster. However, if this is a shared cluster, it is important to exclude vFabric SQLFire VMs from vSphere HA. **Note** Set up anti-affinity rules between the vFabric SQLFire VMs that will not cause any two vFabric SQLFire servers to run on the same ESXi host within the DRS cluster.
BP 51: Guest OS.	Red Hat Enterprise Linux 5 and earlier versions incur higher virtualization overhead because of the high-frequency timer interrupts, frequent access to virtual PCI devices for interrupt handling, and an inefficient Linux timekeeping mechanism. By selecting a more current version of Linux, such as SUSE Linux Enterprise Server 11 SP1 or Red Hat Enterprise Linux 6 based on 2.6.32 Linux kernels, or Windows Server 2008, you can minimize these causes of virtualization overhead. In particular, Red Hat Enterprise Linux 6 has a tickless kernel that does not rely on a high-frequency interrupt-based timer and is therefore much friendlier to virtualized latency-sensitive workloads. Refer to "Timekeeping Best Practices for Linux Guests" (http://kb.vmware.com/kb/1006427) and "Timekeeping in VMware Virtual Machines" (http://www.vmware.com/files/pdf/Timekeeping-In-VirtualMachines.pdf).

BP 52: Physical NIC.	Most 1 Gigabit Ethernet or 10 Gigabit Ethernet network interface cards (NICs) support a feature called interrupt moderation or interrupt throttling, which coalesces interrupts from the NIC to the host so that the host does not spend all of its CPU cycles processing interrupts. However, for latency-sensitive workloads, the time that the NIC delays the delivery of an interrupt for a received packet or for a packet that has successfully been sent on the wire is time adding to the latency of the workload.
	
	Most NICs also provide a mechanism, usually with the `ethtool` command, to disable interrupt coalescing. VMware recommends to disable physical NIC interrupt moderation on the vSphere ESXi host as follows:
	
	`# ethtool -C vmnicX rx-usecs 0 rx-frames 1`
	`   rx-usecs-irq 0 rx-frames-irq 0`
	
	Where `vmnicX` is the physical NIC as reported by the ESXi command:
	
	`# esxcli network nic list`

Best Practice	Description
BP 52: Physical NIC *(continued)*.	You can verify that your settings have taken effect by issuing the following command:
	`# ethtool -c vmnicX`
	Note that although disabling interrupt moderation on physical NICs is extremely helpful in reducing latency for latency-sensitive VMs, it can lead to some performance penalties for other VMs on the ESXi host, in addition to higher CPU utilization to deal with the higher rate of interrupts from the physical NIC.
	Disabling physical NIC interrupt moderation can also defeat the benefits of large receive offloads (LROs), because some physical NICs (such as Intel 10 Gigabit Ethernet NICs) that support LRO in hardware automatically disable it when interrupt moderation is disabled, and the ESXi implementation of software LRO has fewer packets to coalesce into larger packets on every interrupt. LRO is an important offload for driving high throughput for large message transfers at reduced CPU cost. So, consider this tradeoff carefully. Refer to "Poor TCP Performance May Occur in Linux Virtual Machines with LRO Enabled" (http://kb.vmware.com/kb/1027511).
	If the vSphere host is restarted, the above configurations must be reapplied.
BP 53: Virtual NIC.	Follow the best practices highlighted in the "Best Practices for Performance Tuning of Latency-Sensitive Workloads in vSphere Virtual Machines" (http://www.vmware.com/resources/techresources/10220).
	ESXi VMs can be configured to have one of the following types of virtual NICs: Vlance, VMXNET, Flexible, E1000, VMXNET2 (Enhanced), or VMXNET3. This is described in "Choosing a Network Adapter for your Virtual Machine" (http://kb.vmware.com/kb/1001805).
	Use VMXNET3 virtual NICs for your latency-sensitive, or otherwise performance-critical, VMs. It is the latest generation of paravirtualized NICs designed for performance, and is not related to VMXNET or VMXNET2 in any way. It offers several advanced features, including multiqueue support, receive-side scaling, IPv4/IPv6 offloads, and MSI/MSI-X interrupt delivery. Modern enterprise Linux distributions based on 2.6.32 or newer kernels, like Red Hat Enterprise Linux 6 and SUSE Linux Enterprise Server 11 SP1, ship with built-in support for VMXNET3 NICs, so it is unnecessary to install VMware Tools to get VMXNET3 drivers for these guest operating systems.

Best Practice	Description
BP 53: Virtual NIC *(continued)*.	VMXNET3 by default also supports an adaptive interrupt coalescing algorithm, for the same reasons that physical NICs implement interrupt coalescing. This virtual interrupt coalescing helps drive high throughputs to VMs with multiple vCPUs with parallelized workloads (for example, multiple threads), while also striving to minimize latency of virtual interrupt delivery.

However, if the workload is extremely sensitive to latency, VMware recommends that you disable virtual interrupt coalescing for VMXNET3 virtual NICs as follows.

Use VMware Programmatic APIs to add the special VM configuration options as defined in "VMware vSphere Web Services SDK Documentation" (http://www.vmware.com/support/developer/vc-sdk/). Refer to the vSphere API Reference, under the VirtualMachine Managed Object Type, for the `OptionValue[]` `extraConfig` property of the `VirtualMachineConfigInfo` configuration property.

To do so manually, first power off the VM. Edit your VM's .vmx configuration file and locate the entries for VMXNET3, as follows:

`ethernetX.virtualDev = "vmxnet3"`

`ethernetX.coalescingScheme = "disabled"`

Power on the VMs for the virtual interrupt coalescing settings to take effect.

This new configuration option is available only in ESXi 5.0. |
| BP 54: Trouble-shooting SYN cookies. | When troubleshooting performance problems, verify that you are not impacted by SYN cookies. *SYN cookies* are the key element of a technique used to guard against SYN flood attacks. Daniel J. Bernstein, the technique's primary inventor, defines SYN cookies as "particular choices of initial TCP sequence numbers by TCP servers." In particular, the use of SYN cookies allows a server to avoid dropping connections when the SYN queue fills up. Instead, the server behaves as if the SYN queue had been enlarged. The server sends back the appropriate SYN+ACK response to the client but discards the SYN queue entry. If the server then receives a subsequent ACK response from the client, the server is able to reconstruct the SYN queue entry using information encoded in the TCP sequence number. |

Best Practice	Description

BP 54: Trouble-shooting SYN cookies *(continued)*.	To check for the presence of SYN cookies, use the following:
	
	`grep SYN /var/log/messages Aug 2 12:19:06 w1-vFabric-g1 kernel: possible SYN flooding on port 53340.`
	
	`Sending cookies.`
	
	`Aug 2 12:54:38 w1-vFabric-g1 kernel: possible SYN flooding on port 54157.`
	
	`Sending cookies.`
	
	`Aug 3 10:46:38 w1-vFabric-g1 kernel: possible SYN flooding on port 34327.`
	
	`Sending cookies.`
	
	To determine whether SYN cookies are enabled (1 is on, 0 is off), use the following:
	
	`$ cat /proc/sys/net/ipv4/tcp_syncookies`
	
	`1`
	
	To temporarily disable SYN cookies (changes at reboot), use the following:
	
	`# echo 0 > /proc/sys/net/ipv4/tcp_syncookies`
	
	To permanently disable SYN cookies, add/modify the following in /etc/sysctl.conf:
	
	`# Controls the use of TCP syncookies`
	
	`net.ipv4.tcp_syncookies = 0`

Best Practice	Description
BP 55: Storage.	Use the PVSCSI driver for I/O-intensive vFabric SQLFire workloads.
	Align disk partitions at the VMFS and guest OS levels.
	Provision VMDK files as `eagerzeroedthick` to avoid lazy zeroing for vFabric SQLFire members.
	Use separate VMDKs for vFabric SQLFire persistence files, binary, and logs.
	Map a dedicated LUN to each VMDK.
	As of the Linux 2.6 kernel, the default I/O scheduler is completely fair queuing (CFQ). The scheduler is an effective solution for nearly all workloads. The default scheduler affects all disk I/O for VMDK and RDM-based virtual storage solutions. In virtualized environments, it is often not beneficial to schedule I/O at both the host and guest layers. If multiple guests use storage on a file system or block devices managed by the host operating system, the host might be able to schedule I/O more efficiently because it is aware of requests from all guests and knows the physical layout of storage, which might not map linearly to the guests' virtual storage. Testing has shown that NOOP perform better for virtualized Linux guests. ESX/ESXi uses an asynchronous intelligent I/O scheduler, and for this reason virtual guests should see improved performance by allowing ESX/ESXi to handle I/O scheduling. For further information, see "Linux 2.6 Kernel-Based Virtual Machines Experience Slow Disk I/O Performance" (http://kb.vmware.com/kb/2011861).

Category 3 Workloads Best Practices

As defined earlier, category 3 Java workloads are a combination of category 1 JVMs accessing category 2 JVMs. Therefore, the best practices for category 3 are a collective of best practices for both category 1 and category 2 discussed thus far in this chapter.

IBM JVM and Oracle jRockit JVMs

Thus far, all the tuning guidance has been for Oracle HotSpot JVM (formerly Sun JVM); however, there are some differences that we want to highlight. Knowing these differences will help you choose the right GC policy.

In Figure 6-5, an IBM JVM deployed on one VM is shown with the various memory segments. The JVM is similar to the Oracle HotSpot JVM discussed earlier, with one caveat. The caveat is that the PermGen area is managed like any other object within the heap. This is why the PermGen is omitted from Formula 6-2, as it is part of the value of –Xmx for IBM JVMs because it is inside the heap. The PermGen area, as explained earlier, is not a separate area within the heap. It is simply a linked list that gets managed like any other object in the heap. This is one of the key sizing differences between Oracle HotSpot JVM and IBM JVM. This also implies that the PermGen area in IBM JVM is dynamically managed and that it doesn't have to be statically set like in the Oracle HotSpot JVM. The key advantage here is that you do not have to statically guess the best value for the PermGen every time that new code is released.

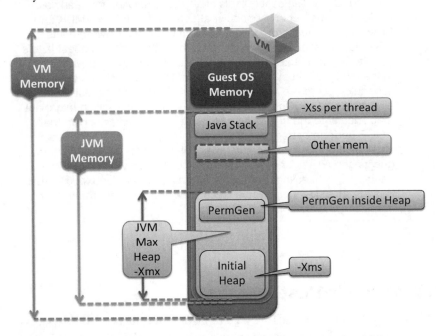

Figure 6-5   Memory Segments of One IBM JVM Deployed on One VM

VM Memory for Websphere = Guest OS Memory + JVM Memory for IBM JVM

JVM Memory for IBM JVM =

JVM Max Heap (-Xmx value) +
NumberOfConcurrentThreads * (-Xss) + "other Mem"

Formula 6-2   VM Memory for WebSphere

Figure 6-6 shows one jRockit JVM deployed on one VM memory segment. As you can see, the key difference is that the PermGen area as known in the Oracle HotSpot JVM is called Metadata and is managed outside the heap in the off-the-heap section of the Java process. This, again, is not statically sized as in the Oracle HotSpot JVM and so provides many benefits of not having to continuously maintain it. The Metadata section is, however, accounted for in Formula 6-3, because this area has to be sized within the overall memory requirements of the Java process. One significant note is that because jRockit takes an approach of JIT-all, meaning that it assumes that all code segments are hot and hence all code paths are precompiled, jRockit may potentially use considerably more memory than Oracle HotSpot in an apples-to-apples comparison basis. If you load test properly to determine whether –Xmx is set appropriately, this should provide you decent guidance to complete the calculation shown as Formula 6-3.

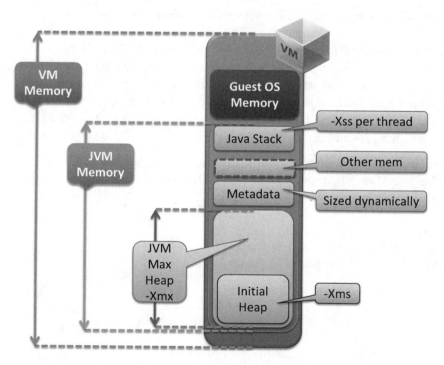

Figure 6-6   Memory Segments of One jRockit JVM Deployed on One VM

VM Memory for jRockit = Guest OS Memory + JVM Memory for jRockit

JVM Memory for jRockit =

JVM Max Heap (-Xmx value) +

Metadata +

NumberOfConcurrentThreads * (-Xss) + "other Mem"

Formula 6-3   VM Memory Segments for jRockit

GC Policy Selection

Having seen much GC tuning guidance and various memory sizing considerations, it is important to pause for a minute and summarize. There are many GC policies from the various vendors, such as Oracle (HotSpot JVM and jRockit) and IBM (J9 JVM), but all offer similar GC policies, but with slight variations. Almost all of these policies compromise between the impact of reducing latency to yield better response time but at the cost of memory throughput reduction, or conversely increase the impact of latency and thus response time for the benefit of pushing better memory throughout. Figure 6-7 shows this comparison and lists a few pros and cons.

Within the Oracle HotSpot JVM, there are essentially four policies, as shown in Table 6-10. The most significant are the throughput parallel collectors and CMS. Both of these are used on enterprise class category 1 and 2 workloads.

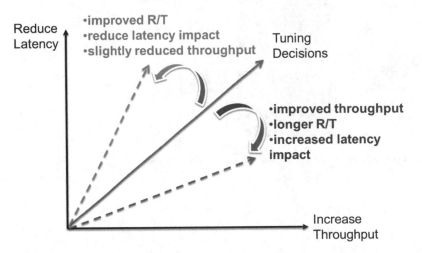

Figure 6-7   GC Tuning Is a Balancing Act Between Reduction in Latency Versus an Increase in Memory Throughput

Table 6-10   Oracle HotSpot JVM Policy Types

GC Policy Type	Description
Serial GC	Mark, sweep, and compact algorithm. Both minor and full GC are stop-the-world threads. Stop-the-world GC means that the application is stopped while GC is executing. Not very scalable algorithm. Suited for smaller < 200MB JVMs (for example, client machines).
Throughput GC (ParNewGC)	Parallel GC. Similar to serial GC, but uses multiple worker threads in parallel to increase throughput. Both young and old generation collection are multithread, but still stop-the-world. The number of threads allocated by `-XX:ParallelGCThreads=<nThreads>`. *Not* concurrent, meaning that when the GC worker threads run, they will pause your application threads. If this is a problem, move to CMS, where GC threads are concurrent.
Concurrent GC (CMS)	Concurrent mark and sweep. Note that this is not a compacting collector. Concurrent implies that when GC is running it doesn't pause your application threads; this is the key difference from throughput/parallel GC. Suited for applications that care more about response time than throughput. CMS does use more heap when compared to throughput/ParallelGC. CMS works on the old generation concurrently, but the young generation is collected using ParNewGC, a version of the throughput collector. Has multiple phases: Initial mark (short pause) Concurrent mark (no pause) Precleaning (no pause) Re-mark (short pause) Concurrent sweeping (no pause)
G1	Only in J7 and mostly experimental; it is equivalent to CMS + compacting.

IBM GC Choices

Table 6-11 shows the IBM JVM GC policies. The default often has to be changed to -Xgcpolicy:Optavgpause or -Xgcpolicy:Gencon when moving applications from development to production environments. Leaving it at default can cause scalability issues. This detail is often overlooked when promoting development configurations to production.

Table 6-11   IBM JVM GC Policies

-Xgc:mode	Usage	Example
-Xgcpolicy:Optthroughput (Default)	Performs the mark and sweep operations during GC when the application is paused to maximize application throughput. Mostly not suitable for multi CPU machines.	Apps that demand a high throughput but are not very sensitive to the occasional long GC pause
-Xgcpolicy:Optavgpause	Performs the mark and sweep concurrently while the application is running to minimize pause times; this provides best application response times. There is still a stop-the-world GC, but the pause is significantly shorter. After GC, the app threads help out and sweep objects (concurrent sweep).	Apps sensitive to long latencies transaction-based systems where response time are expected to be stable
-Xgcpolicy:Gencon	Treats short-lived and long-lived objects differently to provide a combination of lower pause times and high application throughput. Before the heap is filled up, each app helps out and marks objects (concurrent mark).	Latency-sensitive apps, objects in the transaction don't survive beyond the transaction commit

Oracle jRockit GC Policies

Table 6-12 shows the Oracle jRockit GC Policies.

Table 6-12   Oracle jRockit GC Policies

-Xgc:mode	Usage	Example
`-Xgc:throughput` (Default) `-Xgc:genpar` `-Xgc:singlepar` (non-gen) `-Xgc:parallel` (non-gen)	Optimizes for max throughput.	Apps that demand a high throughput but are not very sensitive to the occasional long GC pause

`-Xgc:pausetime`
 	
`-Xgc:gencon`
 	
`-Xgc:singlecon` (non-gen)
 	
-Default pause target is 500ms
	Optimizes for short and even pause times.
	
	Can use `-XpauseTarget:time`. The pause target affects the application throughput. A lower pause target inflicts more overhead on the memory management system.
		Apps sensitive to long latencies transaction-based systems where response times are expected to be stable

`-Xgc:deterministic`	Optimizes for very short and deterministic pause times. Can use `-XpauseTarget:time`.	Apps with deterministic latencies and transaction-based applications such as brokerage

Chapter Summary

This chapter covered category 1, 2, and 3 best practices, with best practices for hardware, vSphere, and the JVM highlighted. Keep in mind that the single most important best practice is to set memory reservation. On the JVM side of things, you want to size the JVM correctly and select the correct GC policy. In category 2 workloads, NUMA becomes extremely important.

Chapter 7

Monitoring and Troubleshooting Primer

The key to troubleshooting Java workloads is to understand the critical four technology tiers shown in Figure 7-1: the load balancer tier, the web server tier, the Java application server tier, and the DB server tier.

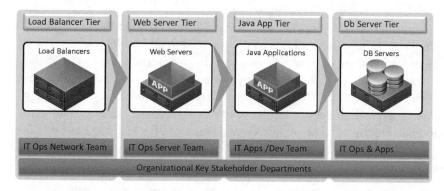

Figure 7-1   Four Key Technology Tiers and Stakeholders

When troubleshooting Java application issues, many often assume that a garbage collection (GC) problem exists at the Java application tier. However, problematic issues could be present in any one of these tiers. Complicating troubleshooting efforts is the fact that teams from multiple operational divisions within an organization usually manage their own distinct technology tier, without a single administrator of the platform who has a holistic view. In addition to the technology challenges large-scale virtualization may present, organizational challenges resulting from these traditional siloed technical approaches must be confronted:

- The network operations team manages the load balancer tier. Although that team might have adequate load-balancer knowledge, load balancers are often just a part-time hobby for them. This somewhat dilettante approach creates an opportunity for Java architects and DevOps engineers to take the initiative and learn about the various vendor-specific load-balancer configurations, balancing algorithms, and monitoring consoles.

- The web server tier is managed by Linux administrators (if it is Apache) or by the Windows Server team (if Internet Information Services [IIS] is used). These Linux/Windows administrators may not have deep knowledge about how to best tune web servers. As a Java architect, or DevOps engineer, it is important that you specialize in this area and understand all the design and sizing requirements of each web server. For example, you need to know how to determine how many web servers are needed. So, you must learn to analyze peak traffic reports from the load balancer, and then based on the size of each transaction, determine how many and what size web server instances are needed. See Chapter 4, "Designing and Sizing Large-Scale Java Platforms," and Chapter 6, "Best Practices," for more information.

- The Java application server tier is heavily architected by the development/applications team, and often the operations team has little control over the design of the overall deployment topology. This is where the seed of all problems often lies, because the application team designs a system that the operations team has to operate and support. It is often prudent for the operations team to have sufficient application knowledge to be able to vet the design and rationalize the deployment topology. These rationalization techniques are similar to those discussed in earlier chapters (for example, rationalizing the number of Java Virtual Machines [JVMs], the number of virtual machines [VMs], and various other sizing and tuning considerations that can help to ensure a successful management of Java platforms).

- The DB server tier is, naturally, managed by both the operations and the applications teams because the design of the schema construct is dictated by the developers. However, the operations team often includes database administrators (DBAs), who can then manage the operational aspects of the database. Having deep database (DB) operations knowledge is key to troubleshooting and tuning the DB.

As a Java architect who might need to deal with both the operations and application teams when diagnosing critical Java issues, you need to be aware of the various teams managing the platform and the four key technology tiers shown in Figure 7-1. Invariably, a good Java architect becomes the force that drives change and facilitates better design through effective communication and collaboration across all of these tiers. In many ways, the Java architect is the glue that holds these four tiers together.

The good news is that (we hope) all of these tiers are fully virtualized. Therefore, you have one common runtime platform on VMware vSphere that unites these tiers and forces all teams involved to come to the discussion table. Because all of these tiers are on VMware vSphere, you can generate performance charts from vCenter; in some extreme cases, you can use esxtop. In addition, because all four tiers are virtualized, you can effectively size the entire platform within one design and sizing context, an impossibility if half the platform is virtualized and the rest is on physical.

Open a Support-Request Ticket

If you suspect the VMware vSphere is not configured optimally and is the cause of a bottleneck, file a support request (http://www.vmware.com/support/contacts/file-sr.html). In addition, you might want to do the following:

- Follow the troubleshooting steps outlined in the performance-troubleshooting guide for ESX4.0: http://communities.vmware.com/docs/DOC-10352.

- Verify that you have applied all the best practices discussed in Chapter 6.

- Run the `vm-support` utility to collect necessary information so that VMware can help diagnose the problem. It is best to run this command when the symptoms first occur.

> **NOTE**
>
> In VMware environments, you can refer to the following paper for troubleshooting using vCenter Operations Manager: "How to Troubleshoot vSphere 5.x Performance Issues Using vCenter Operations" (http://communities.vmware.com/servlet/JiveServlet/previewBody/23094-102-1-30667/vsphere5x-perfts-vcops.pdf).

Collecting Metrics from vCenter

When troubleshooting any issues with the Java platform, you want to collect vCenter performance metrics for each of the four tiers mentioned in Figure 7-1. For Java platforms with primarily category 1 types of workloads, it is important to collect CPU, memory, network charts, and disk usage.

When looking at vCenter charts, you can inspect performance by selecting the Performance tab and adjusting the time range after clicking the Advanced button. vCenter provides three different memory counters (Consumed, Granted, and Active), as illustrated in Figure 7-2.

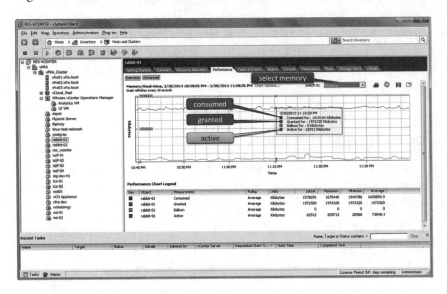

Figure 7-2   vCenter Performance Chart for Memory

When reading these counters, keep the following in mind:

- **Consumed memory:** This is the amount of guest physical memory consumed by the VM for guest memory allocation. This does not include overhead memory. However, if you apply the design and sizing guidelines introduced in Chapter 4, you should be able to apply a small overhead calculation to the amount of consumed memory and thus determine the actual memory used by the VM. For the most part, the overhead number is insignificant, usually on the order of 1%. The consumed memory can be calculated as shown in Formula 7-1.

> Consumed Memory = granted memory – memory saved due to memory sharing

Formula 7-1   Consumed Memory

- **Granted memory:** This is the actual physical memory granted by vSphere to be mapped to the guest operating system of the VM.

- **Active memory:** This is the amount of guest operating system in use by the VM. This value is often much lower than consumed memory and granted memory.

NOTE

When sizing VMs for JVMs deployment, follow the guidance in Chapter 4. If you find after consistent peak usage that the consumed memory is substantially less than the reserved memory (refer to the calculations in Figure 4-3, where the total reservation is 5GB), you can progressively adjust the reservation amount to a lower value. It is always best to set the reservation memory to the granted value, and the granted value must always be larger than the Java heap (-Xmx), by approximately 25% plus any guest OS memory requirements. Refer to Formula 4-1 for the actual calculation. You might sometimes be tempted to use active memory as a guide for sizing; however, this practice may potentially lead to memory over-commitment within the environment, which will hurt the performance of Java workloads in general. Specifically, these practices are not recommended for production-level workloads that run critical applications, with the caveat that some development or lower-priority QA environment may attempt to overcommit, but with extreme sizing caution.

The CPU (%) graph shown in Figure 7-3 presents the VM CPU usage and ready values, as described in the list that follows.

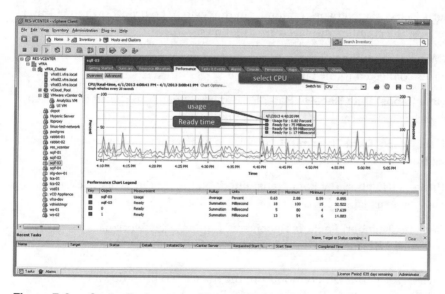

Figure 7-3   vCenter Performance Charts for CPU

- **Usage:** This is the amount of actively used virtual CPU as a percentage of total available CPU. It is the average usage over all available vCPUs configured on the VM. If a vCPU shows 100%, this implies that it has consumed 100% of an underlying physical core. Formula 7-2 shows the calculation to determine vCPU usage.

> Virtual CPU Usage = usage in MHz / (vCPUs* core frequency)

Formula 7-2   vCPU Usage

- **Ready time:** Ready time refers to the amount of time during which the VM was ready but could not get a scheduled time slice on the underlying physical core. If the CPU ready time is high and there are ample CPU cycles on the host, you most likely have far too many VMs allocated on this host, or perhaps a Non-Uniform Memory Access (NUMA) imbalance exists, where a majority of the VMs are running on just one NUMA node. Reducing the number of vCPUs in use by all VMs on the host might address the problem. Alternatively, you might want to revisit the design and sizing of the VMs to ensure that they are fitting correctly into the NUMA nodes. Our guideline for ready time is that it should not be more than 5% (for production applications) or 1000ms per vCPU per 20s sampling period as taken from vCenter. Ready time can also be caused by a CPU limit on a VM or on a resource pool that impacts a VM.

For network charts (select the Network option from the Switch To drop-down in vCenter shown in Figure 7-3), the counters displayed are as follows:

- **Network (Mbps) Usage:** Sum of the data transmitted and received across all virtual NIC instances connected to the virtual machine

- **Network Rate (Mbps) Data Receive Rate:** Rate at which data is received across each virtual network interface card (NIC) instance on the VM

- **Network Rate (Mbps) Data Transmit Rate:** Rate at which data is transmitted across each virtual NIC instance of the VM

- **Network Packets (Number) Packets Transmitted:** Number of network packets transmitted across each virtual NIC instance on the VM

- **Network Packets (Number) Packets Received:** Number of network packets received across each virtual NIC instance on the VM

For disk-usage charts (select the Disk option from the Switch To drop-down in vCenter shown in Figure 7-3), the counters displayed are as follows:

- **Allocated:** Total amount of logical datastore space provisioned on the VM

- **Used:** Amount of physical datastore space in use by the VM

- **Not shared:** Amount of datastore space that belongs only to this VM and is not shared with other VMs

The following note describes how to navigate vCenter advanced performance charts.

> **NOTE**
>
> You can view CPU, memory, disk, and network statistics for an object in the advanced performance charts. These charts support additional data counters not supported in the overview performance charts.
>
> When connected directly to an ESX/ESXi host, the advanced performance charts display only real-time statistics and past-day statistics. To view historical data, the vSphere Client must be connected to a vCenter Server system.
>
> To access the advanced performance charts, follow these steps:
>
> 1. Select a host, cluster, resource pool, or VM in the Inventory panel.
>
> 2. Click the Performance tab.
>
> 3. Click Advanced.
>
> 4. To view a different chart, select an option from the Switch To list. The default charts are configured to show the following information:
>
>   - **CPU:** Shows the CPU usage in megahertz (MHz). Available for clusters, resource pools, hosts, and VMs.
>
>   - **Memory:** Shows the amount of memory granted. Available for clusters, resource pools, hosts, and VMs.
>
>   - **Disk:** Shows the aggregated storage performance statistics. Available for hosts and VMs.
>
>   - **Network:** Shows the aggregated network performance statistics. Available for hosts and VMs.
>
> The amount of historical data displayed in a chart depends on the collection interval and collection level set for vCenter Server.

Troubleshooting Techniques for vSphere with esxtop

For extended troubleshooting beyond what vCenter performance charts offer, you can use esxtop.

Table 7-1 describes the most common metrics used during troubleshooting.

Table 7-1 Common esxtop Metrics

Display	Metric	Threshold	Description
CPU	%RDY	5	Overprovisioning of vCPU, excessive usage of virtual symmetric multiprocessing (vSMP), or a limit (check %MLMTD) has been set. This %RDY value is the sum of all vCPU's %RDY for a VM. For example, if %RDY is 20 for a 1-vCPU VM, this is problematic because it means 1 vCPU is waiting 20% of the time for the VMkernel to schedule it. In contrast, if %RDY is 20% for a 4-vCPU VM, this is probably okay, because on average only 5% of the time the CPU cores were not available. You should investigate any threshold %RDY value of 10% or higher.
CPU	%CSTP	3	Percentage of time a resource spends in a ready, co-schedule state. Values beyond 3 indicate excessive usage of vSMP. Decrease the number of vCPUs for this particular VM.
CPU	%MLMTD	0	Percentage of time the ESXi VMkernel deliberately did not run the resource pool, VM, or world because doing so would violate the resource pool, VM, or world's limit setting. Because the resource pool, VM, or world is ready to run when it is prevented from running in this way, the %MLMTD (max limited) time is included in %RDY time. If larger than 0, the worlds are being throttled. One possible cause is a limit on CPU.
CPU	%SWPWT	0	Percentage of time a resource pool or world spends waiting for the ESXi VMkernel to swap memory. The %SWPWT (swap wait) time is included in the %WAIT time (the VM waiting on swapped pages to be read from disk). You may have overcommitted memory. Any value greater than 0 is problematic.

Display	Metric	Threshold	Description
MEM	MCTLSZ	1	Amount of physical memory reclaimed from the resource by way of ballooning. If larger than 0, the host is forcing the VM to inflate the balloon driver to reclaim memory because the host is overcommitted.
MEM	SWCUR	1	Current swap usage by this resource pool or VM. If larger than 0, the host has swapped memory pages in the past. You may have overcommitted.
MEM	SWR/s	1	Rate at which the ESXi host swaps in memory from disk for the resource pool or VM. If larger than 0, the host is actively reading from swap. This is caused by excessive memory overcommitment.
MEM	SWW/s	1	Rate at which the ESXi host swaps resource pool or VM memory to disk. If larger than 0, the host is actively writing to swap. This is caused by excessive memory overcommitment.
MEM	N%L	80	Current percentage of memory allocated to the VM or resource pool that is local. If less than 80, the VM experiences poor NUMA locality. If a VM has a memory size greater than the amount of memory local to each processor, the ESX scheduler does not attempt to use NUMA optimizations for that VM.
NETWORK	%DRPTX	1	Percentage of transmit packets dropped. If dropped packages are transmitted, the hardware is overworked due to high network utilization.
NETWORK	%DRPRX	1	Percentage of receive packets dropped. If dropped packages are received, the hardware is overworked due to high network utilization.
DISK	GAVG	10	Average VM operating system latency per command, in milliseconds (ms). Look at DAVG and KAVG as GAVG = DAVG + KAVG.
DISK	DAVG	10	Average device latency per command, in milliseconds. At this level, you have disk latency that is likely to be caused by a storage array.

Display	Metric	Threshold	Description
DISK	KAVG	0.1	Average ESXi VMkernel latency per command, in milliseconds. Disk latency is caused by the VMkernel. High KAVG usually means queuing. Check QUED.
DISK	QUED	1	Number of commands in the ESXi VMkernel that are currently queued. This statistic applies only to worlds and devices. Queue has maxed out. Possibly queue depth is set too low. Check with your array vendor for the optimal queue value.
DISK	ABRTS/s	1	Aborts issued by the VM because storage is not responding. For Windows VMs, this happens after a 60-second default. Can be caused by path failure or the storage array not accepting I/O.
DISK	RESET/s	1	The number of command resets per second.

NOTE

If you are on ESXi that doesn't have Service Console, you can use vSphere Management Assistant (vMA), which you can find at http://www.vmware.com/support/developer/vima/. In addition, you can access a handy resxtop vCLI reference from https://www.vmware.com/pdf/vsphere4/r41/vsp4_41_vcli_inst_script.pdf.

Java Troubleshooting Primer

Beyond troubleshooting the virtual environment discussed thus far, you want to have tools at hand that can help you diagnose Java issues. Many commercial products are available, the extent of which is beyond the scope of this book. A good starting-point tool comes free with Java, called JConsole. Under the JAVA_HOME/bin directory, you can launch JConsole. By doing so, you launch the application shown in Figure 7-4. From the drop-down list, you can select a running JVM process to monitor.

NOTE

A prerequisite for understanding this section is to read through the best practices and tuning advice provided in Chapters 1 through 6.

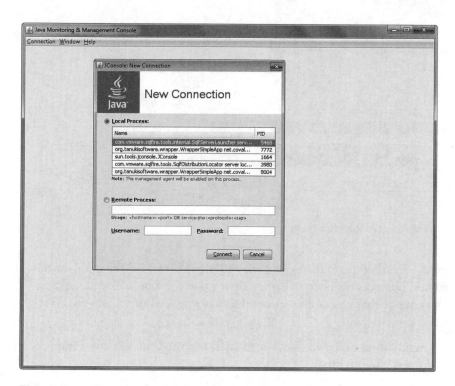

Figure 7-4 JConsole for Monitoring Java

Figure 7-5 shows the various areas of the Memory tab of JConsole.

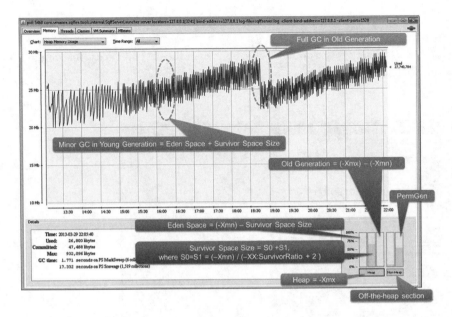

Figure 7-5   JConsole Memory Graph for Java

The chart in Figure 7-5 shows the following, which will prove useful as you apply various tuning advice and best practices outlined in earlier chapters in this book. As you make an adjustment, it is imperative that you double-check the values against the charts shown in Figure 7-5:

- In the lower-right corner of Figure 7-5, the Heap (-Xmx) and the Off-the-Heap memory sections are highlighted.

- The Heap section contains three subsections: the Eden Space, Survivor Space, and Old Generation. The young generation is made up of Eden space and survivor spaces (two survivor spaces); refer to Formula 7-3.

Young Generation = Eden Space + Survivor Space Size

Formula 7-3   Young Generation Size

- The Eden space is sized as per Formula 7-4, where -Xmn is the young generation size.

$$\boxed{\text{Eden Space} = (-Xmn) - \text{Survivor Space Size}}$$

Formula 7-4   Eden Space Size

You can calculate survivor space size as shown in Formula 7-5, where S0 and S1 are the first and second survivor spaces, young generation has two survivor spaces that are equal in size, and collectively they make up the entire survivor space.

$$\boxed{\begin{array}{c} \text{Survivor Space Size} = S0 + S1 \\ \text{Where } S0=S1=(-Xmn) \,/\, (-XX{:}SurvivorRatio + 2\,) \end{array}}$$

Formula 7-5   Survivor Space Size

- The chart also shows the old generation, as calculated according to Formula 7-6, where -Xmx is the Java heap and -Xmn is the young generation.

$$\boxed{\text{Old Generation} = (-Xmx) - (-Xmn)}$$

Formula 7-6   Old Generation Size

- The chart in Figure 7-5 also shows the frequency of minor GC as it applies to the Young Generation section and full GC as applied to the Old Generation section of the heap.

> **NOTE**
> Another handy tool to use is VisualVM, which you can download from http://visualvm.java.net/download.html.

The following sections explain how to begin troubleshooting. You'll learn about some severe Java application problems that are related to GC or memory leakage and some that are related to thread contention. For Java Database Connectivity (JDBC)-based errors, refer to the JDBC driver provided to you by the database vendor. Of particular importance for performance are OutOfMemory, StackOverflow, and Thread Deadlock errors.

Troubleshooting Java Memory Problems

Consider an example where you observe load increases and decreases over a period of time. If memory continues to build without reclamation (in the worst case), or a GC reclamation occurs but not everything is reclaimed, you might have a memory leak. This is very likely if these symptoms persist to a point where the application suffers from an OutOfMemory error. In this case, you need to investigate the GC frequency and settings:

- To turn on GC verbose mode:

  - `verbose:gc`: Prints basic information about GC to the standard output

  - `-XX:+PrintGCTimeStamps`: Prints the times that GC executes

  - `-XX:+PrintGCDetails`: Prints statistics about different regions of memory in the JVM

  - `-Xloggc:<file>`: Logs the results of GC in the specified file

> **NOTE**
>
> To get a graphical representation of the GC log, you can use the GCViewer, which you can download from http://www.tagtraum.com/gcviewer-download.html.

- Re-inspect the `-Xmx`, `-Xms`, `-Xss` settings. Double-check each of these values and make sure that you have the right syntax. You can specify in gigabytes (GB) as `-Xmx4g` or `-Xmx4096m`. Both are basically 4GB of heap. In production environments, always set `-Xms` equal to `-Xmx` and avoid any heap repaging costs at runtime.

- If you're using Java Development Kit (JDK) 6, you can use a tool called `jmap` on any platform. Running `jmap` may add additional load on your environment, so plan for the best time to run it. You can also use the VisualVM tool or the Memory Analysis Tool (MAT, http://www.eclipse.org/mat/downloads.php). The MAT tool has a leak analyzer that often proves quite useful, as discussed at http://help.eclipse.org/kepler/index.jsp?topic=/org.eclipse.mat.ui.help/welcome.html.

- You can add `-XX:+HeapDumpOnOutOfMemoryError` to the Java command line to generate a heap dump file. You can learn more about various heap dump generation approaches at http://wiki.eclipse.org/index.php/MemoryAnalyzer.

- The general approach to reproduce a memory leak during debugging is to do the following:

  - Run GC manually to clean the application.

- Execute a list of methods that you suspect, and then run GC again. Calculate the difference in object count between before and after GC in this step, and compare the numbers. Repeat this several times and look for code segments that have a higher percentage of object generation to others in relative terms. For example, if during the first few iterations all code sections correlate with each other consistently in terms of object creation, and object count, but all of the sudden one code segment pulls ahead and starts to create lots of objects, essentially diverging from correlating with the other related methods in its call hierarchy, this is the suspected leak.

- Repeat the two preceding points, and take heap dumps or use the MAT to analyze. String concatenation, long-running threads, usage of thread pools, custom JDBC pools, custom class loaders, custom cache (especially home-brewed caching mechanisms), and ThreadLocal usage are often suspect code areas for memory leaks.

- If you're using JDK 5, remember the following:

  - If you're running Linux with JDK 5, you can use `jmap`.

  - If you're using JDK 5 Update 14 or later, you can use the `-XX:+HeapDumpOnCtrlBreak` option when starting JVM, and then use the Ctrl+Break key combination on Windows to dump the heap.

Troubleshooting Java Thread Contentions

If you suspect that your enterprise Java application is suffering from long pauses, or just has general response-time issues to the point where the JVM needs to be restarted to resolve the issue, you might also need to inspect the Java thread dump. You can obtain a Java thread dump by pressing Ctrl+Break for a Windows OS or in Linux by issuing `Kill -3` on the Java process ID. It is important to take the thread dump right at the point where problematic symptoms appear. This holds especially true if you are conducting a benchmark load test. In that case, take the thread dump at max peak load, and then inspect the behavior of the various application threads.

Many widely used thread-analysis tools are available that interpret the thread dump and highlight in red the hot threads or threads waiting for a lock. You can begin your code investigation from that point and follow the call stack.

NOTE

You can also use VisualVM to inspect thread dumps. Synchronized methods are the most notorious for creating blocking situations, and eventually application crashes. In addition, the pessimistic locking of resources when communicating with a database in a non-thread-safe manner can cause multiple threads to contend and interlock on resources. This is especially true when there aren't enough DB connections to service the number of concurrent Java threads, and even more serious when DB connections are shared across threads when not intended to.

Chapter Summary

Although monitoring and troubleshooting Java platforms warrants an entire book in its own right, this chapter outlined the key tools that can help you to monitor and diagnose issues with virtualized Java platforms. For the vSphere environment, this chapter highlighted both vCenter and esxtop. For the Java environment, the chapter outlined JConsole and various command-line options.

FAQs

"We have virtualized our WebSphere environment and we are now considering open source applications server alternatives. What options do we have in this space?"

The first point of inspection is whether the customer application uses Enterprise Java-Beans (EJBs). If it does not use EJBs, you can migrate to vFabric tc Server relatively easily. However, if it does use EJBs, you can leverage the Spring Migration Analyzer (SMA) to guide you through the migration process.

You can obtain the SMA tool from https://github.com/SpringSource/spring-migration-analyzer. The installation and usage is quite simple.

You can run the SMA tool using the following command; shown is the execution of SMA against the daytrader-ear-1.1.ear:

```
$ ./migration-analysis.sh daytrader-ear-1.1.ear -o report
```

This will generate a report located in file:///<SMAInstallDir>/spring-migration-analyzer-1.0.0.M2/bin/reports/daytrader-ear-1.1.ear.migration-analysis/index.html.

The report will show each major code section and what the impact analysis is. You can use this information to plan a code refactoring effort. Generally speaking, the code sections to address fall into the following categories:

- No code changes are required for migrating Java Database Connectivity (JDBC) data source transactions; here you may want to consider using Spring JdbcTemplate and transaction management to simplify the code.

- Minimal migration impact is required for Java Message Service (JMS) code because it can be used in tc Server. To simplify this impact, consider using Spring JMS support, such as JMSTemplate.

- Minimal migration impact on Java Naming and Directory Interface (JNDI) code because it can be easily ported to tc Server.

Table A-1 shows the impact analysis summary comparing DayTrader and non-EJB solutions with Spring-like implementations.

Table A-1   SMA Tool Comparison of DayTrader to Non-EJB Solution

DayTrader	Non-EJB Approach
Utilizes the JMS API	Little or no migration is usually required because JMS can be used within tc Server. Consider using Spring JMSTemplate.
Utilizes the JNDI API	JNDI is available in tc Server, and therefore no work is required to migrate the application.
	It may be worth considering using Spring <jee-jndi-lookup> support to perform any JNDI lookups, rather than using the JNDI API directly.
Utilizes the JTA	Use of the Java Transaction API (JTA) is usually covered under programmatic transaction demarcation; tc Server does not include a transaction manager implementation supporting the JTAs.
	The most direct migration approach, often requiring no code-level changes, is to plug in an external transaction manager (such as Atomikos). Or refactor code away from JTA (for example, the Spring programmatic TransactionTemplate).
Many classes that use data source transactions	No code changes are usually required. However, during the migration, you may want to consider using the Spring JdbcTemplate and transaction management to simplify the code.
Uses stateless session beans	Stateless session beans can be easily migrated to a Spring-managed component.

DayTrader	Non-EJB Approach
Message-driven beans (MDBs)	Assuming that an external JMS provider is available, the migration of each MDB is straightforward. Such beans are usually migrated to a Spring message-driven Plain Old Java Object (POJO) facilitated by a message listener container.
MDBs that use declarative JTA transactions	Default MDB configuration uses declarative transactions (which is not necessary).
	If the transaction does not involve any external resources, the transaction was not actually necessary.
	The bean can be easily migrated to a Spring message-driven POJO with no declarative transaction configuration.

"Are there any customer testimonies from customers who have virtualized and tuned large-scale Java platforms that follow the recommendations you provide?"

"With our OrderExpress project, we upgraded our Middleware Services, Commerce, Portal, WCM, Service Layer, DB2 Database; migrated from AIX to Linux; virtualized on VMware; moved the application into a three-tier DMZ; increased our transactions by over 150%; and added significant new capabilities that greatly improved the customer experience. Changing such a wide range of technology components at once was a huge challenge. However, using VMware vSphere and additional architectural changes, we were successful in improving performance by over 300%; lowered costs in the millions; improved security, availability, and scalability; and now we plan to continue evolving this application to maintain greater than 30% yearly growth."

—Jeff Battisti, Senior Enterprise Architect at Cardinal Health

"I'm afraid that performance will suffer if I virtualize the enterprise Java application."

It has been demonstrated many times that when running Java applications in native mode versus running on vSphere the performance is comparable. Performance does not suffer. To back up the best practices outlined in this book, Figure A-1 shows a performance study that was conducted by HP using an EJB-based DayTrader application deployed on both a physical and virtualized IBM WebSphere application server for a side-by-side comparison. The chart quickly shows very good performance on the virtualized IBM WebSphere application server when compared with the physical case, and with a particular optimal virtual machine (VM) configuration of two and four vCPUs. You can reference the full study at http://www.vmware.com/resources/techresources/10095.

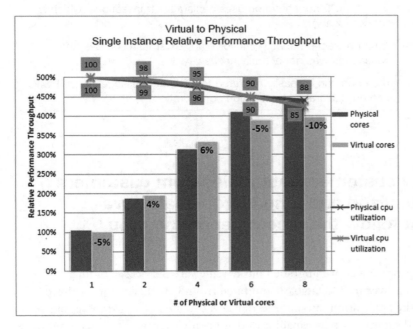

Figure A-1   A Performance Graph of Throughput Versus Number of CPUs or vCPUs (Conducted by HP)

"I looked at virtualization, and in my environment I can only get a three-to-one server-consolidation ratio, so I don't think it's worth it."

Consolidation is only one of the many benefits of virtualization. Many VMware customers use virtualization to perform faster and more confident upgrades, maximize application service levels, and improve manageability and recoverability.

"Where can I get support?"

See VMware support: http://www.vmware.com/support/; or contact your application server vendor. VMware support will guide you through any of the application servers, including WebLogic and WebSphere.

"Why would I choose to virtualize enterprise Java applications?"

You can improve the efficiency and availability of IT resources and applications through virtualization.

Start by eliminating the old "one server, one application" model and run multiple VMs on each physical machine. Free your IT administrators from spending so much time managing servers rather than innovating. About 70% of a typical IT budget in a nonvirtualized data center goes toward just maintaining the existing infrastructure, with little left for innovation.

"Are there any performance issues?"

No. Refer to a case study conducted by HP running WebSphere on vSphere: http://www.vmware.com/resources/techresources/10095. Depending on the number of cores or vCPUs allocated, the VMware vSphere in some cases exceeds the performance of a physical environment, as shown in two-core and four-core configurations of about 4% and 6%, respectively. See Chapter 5, "Performance Studies," for various performance studies.

> **NOTE**
>
> Some of the world's largest financial trading platforms run on vSphere, often using in-memory databases such as vFabric GemFire and SQLFire with multiple JVMs in a cluster that is in the terabytes range. When tuned correctly and in accordance with the best practices laid out in this book, the performance is excellent on these types of systems.

In a recent performance study conducted as part of the vFabric Reference Architecture project, impressive transactional numbers were achieved with the vFabric SQLFire-based client/server topology shown in Figure A-2.

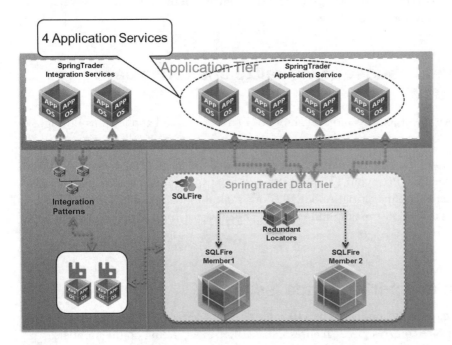

Figure A-2   vFabric Reference Architecture

The topology is made of a vFabric SQLFire client/server topology morphed into the application tier communicating back with the SpringTrader data tier. Here is the topology that was used for the 10,000-user test: In the application tier, four SpringTrader application services VMs were used, along with two integration services, two RabbitMQ servers, and two SQLFire members. Each of the four SpringTrader application services had two vCPUs and 1GB of memory, the two SpringTrader integration services had two vCPUs and 768MB, the two RabbitMQ servers had two vCPUS and 2GB allocated, and the two SQLFire members had eight vCPUs each and 94GB allocated to the SQLFire member of the SpringTrader data tier.

Figure A-3 shows the scalability test results with the left vertical axis showing the number of users, the normalized scaling from one application service VM on the right vertical axis, and the number of application service VMs used in the scale test shown on the horizontal axis. The result of 4 VMs along the horizontal axis and 10,400 users along the left vertical axis are the results for the configuration shown in Figure A-2. For fewer than 10,400 users, the figure shows the number of application services VMs needed. In this test, the number of application services VMs is variable along the starting point (from one VM to four VMs). However, the RabbitMQ servers (two VMs), integration services (two VMs), and SQLFire (two VMs) were all kept constant at two VMs.

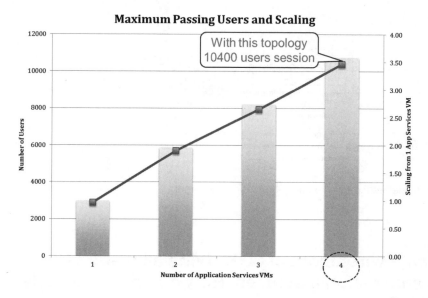

Figure A-3   vFabric Reference Architecture Maximum Passing Users and Scaling

The response time for the configuration shown in Figure A-4 is approximately 0.25 seconds at 10,400 users, and approximately 3000 transactions/second. These types of transactional numbers showcase how virtualized systems in combination with an in-memory data management system, such as vFabric SQLFire, can achieve very high scalability and performance.

For further information about this performance test, see Topic-3 of the vFabric Reference Architecture page: http://www.vmware.com/go/vFabric-ref-arch.

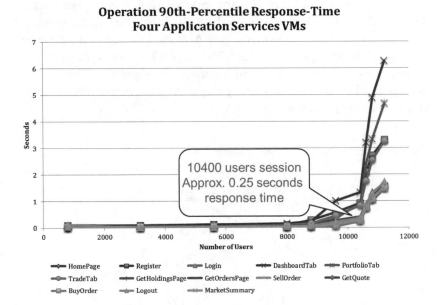

Figure A-4   vFabric Reference Architecture Response Time Graph

"We have an environment of 8000 JVMs all made of WebLogic application instances. How could we possibly virtualize this?"

It is important to consider first the possibility of being able to consolidate JVMs, and then determine what ratio of JVMs to VMs you will deploy and how many VMs you will deploy on each vSphere host. See Chapter 4, "Designing and Sizing Large-Scale Java Platforms," for sizing guidelines. The key guidance is to establish your current level of memory and CPU utilization for the existing physical farm of 8000 WebLogic servers, and then map that to a virtual environment. If you don't know what to assume or where to start, consider all the best practices in this book, and specifically start with a one JVM to two vCPU ratio assumption, and then size your environment that way. Perform a small load test across several VMs on a few vSphere hosts in a cluster to verify your assumptions.

NOTE

If you cannot consolidate JVMs because of application constraints, this is fine, and you can always consider a one-to-one WebLogic managed server to one VM. However this is usually not feasible. In this case, you can consider deploying multiple JVMs on a VM while keeping the vCPU and memory utilization in mind. The ratio of one JVM to two vCPU applies only to WebLogic managed servers. However, a WebLogic admin server can be deployed on any VM, whether that VM has a WebLogic managed server on it or not; it doesn't really matter. WebLogic admin servers don't consume a lot of resources.

With WebLogic managed servers, you have to ensure that the WebLogic admin server is sufficiently high availability (HA) protected with a vSphere cluster.

"What technology tools and runtime services are contained in vFabric?"

Table A-2 describes the various vFabric tools and runtime components.

Table A-2   vFabric Tools and Runtime Services

Component	Description
Spring Tools Suite	STS provides the best Eclipse-powered development environment for building Spring-powered enterprise applications. STS supplies tools for all the latest enterprise Java, Spring, Groovy, and Grails-based technologies. Included with STS is the developer edition of vFabric tc Server, the drop-in replacement for Apache Tomcat that is optimized for Spring. With its Spring Insight console, vFabric tc Server Developer Edition (http://www.springsource.com/developer/tcserver) provides a graphical real-time view of application-performance metrics that enables developers to identify and diagnose problems from their desktops. STS supports application targeting to local, virtual, and cloud-based servers. It is freely available for development and internal business operations use with no time limits.

Component	Description
Spring Framework	The Spring Framework contains numerous features for the creation of web applications. The features are implemented in the following modules: **Spring Inversion of Control (IoC):** Configures application components and manages the Java objects. **Spring Aspect-Oriented Programming (AOP):** Enables implementation of cross-cutting routines. **Spring Data:** Works with relational database management systems on the Java platform using Java Database Connectivity (JDBC) and object-relational mapping tools. **Transaction Management:** Unifies several transaction management application programming interfaces (APIs) and coordinates transactions for Java objects. **Spring Web Model View Controller (MVC):** A Hypertext Transfer Protocol (HTTP) and servlet-based framework that provides hooks for extension and customization, with web flows and JavaServer Faces. **Mobile Application Development:** Tools for making web applications suitable for use on a mobile device and for creating native clients that communicate with Spring back ends. **Spring Remote:** Configurative Remote Procedure Call (RPC)-style export and import of Java objects over networks supporting Remote Method Invocation (RMI), Common Object Request Broker Architecture (CORBA), and HTTP-based protocols, including Simple Object Access Protocol (SOAP) web services. **Spring Batch:** A framework for high-volume processing featuring reusable functions that include logging and tracing, transaction management, job processing statistics, job restart, skip, and resource management. **Spring Security:** Configurable security processes that support a range of standards, protocols, and tools through the use of the Spring Security subproject. **Remote Management:** Configurative exposure and management of Java objects for local or remote configuration with Java Management Extensions (JMX).

Component	Description
Spring Integration	Spring Integration provides an extension of the Spring programming model to support the well-known Enterprise Integration Patterns (http://www.eaipatterns.com/). It enables lightweight messaging within Spring-based applications and supports integration with external systems using declarative adapters. These adapters provide a higher level of abstraction over Spring support for remoting, messaging, and scheduling. Spring Integration's primary goal is to provide a simple model for building enterprise integration solutions while maintaining the separation of concerns essential for producing maintainable, testable code.
vFabric tc Server	vFabric tc Server provides enterprise users with a lightweight server that has operational management, advanced diagnostics, and mission-critical support capabilities businesses need. Designed to be a drop-in replacement for Apache Tomcat, vFabric tc Server enables a seamless migration path for existing custom-built and commercial software applications already certified for Tomcat.
vFabric Web Server	vFabric Web Server is based on the popular Apache web server (http://httpd.apache.org/docs/2.2/), providing a familiar, proven foundation for the web tier. Unlike Apache, vFabric Web Server is precompiled, preconfigured, and prepatched, reducing deployment times from a typical 3 days to 30 minutes. It has a consistent installation process and structure across all supported operating systems, and installation is through a self-extracting archive with no requirements for install location and no dependencies on graphics libraries. You can patch and upgrade multiple instances for further reduction in deployment and support costs.
vFabric EM4J	VMware vFabric Elastic Memory for Java (EM4J) enables memory to be shared dynamically among Java Virtual Machine (JVM) instances without sacrificing performance.
	Automatically allocate Java heap memory to the JVMs that need it most.
	Deploy more application server VMs on each vSphere host, increasing server consolidation.
	Reduce the likelihood of out-of-memory errors that can cripple applications.

Component	Description
vFabric RabbitMQ	vFabric RabbitMQ is a complete and highly reliable enterprise messaging system based on the emerging Advanced Messaging Queuing Protocol (AMQP) standard. It is licensed under the open source (http://www.rabbitmq.com/mpl.html) and has a platform-neutral distribution in addition to platform-specific packages and bundles for easy installation. It is an efficient, highly scalable, and easy-to-deploy queuing software that makes handling message traffic effortless. vFabric RabbitMQ is portable across major operating systems and developer platforms. Unlike other messaging products, vFabric RabbitMQ is protocol based, enabling it to connect with a wide range of other software components and making it an ideal messaging solution for cloud computing.
vFabric SQLFire	vFabric SQLFire is an in-memory distributed data management platform that can be spread across many VMs, JVMs, and vFabric SQLFire servers to manage application data. Using dynamic replication and partitioning, vFabric SQLFire offers the following features in the platform: Data durability Trigger-based event notification Parallel execution High throughput Low latency High scalability Continuous availability WAN distribution
vFabric vPostgres	vFabric Postgres (http://www.vmware.com/products/application-platform/vfabric-postgres/overview.html) is an enterprise-class ANSI SQL relational database optimized for VMware vSphere. It is fully compatible with proven open source PostgreSQL (http://www.postgresql.org/). Lowered database total cost of ownership (TCO) and increased agility within vSphere environments. Elastic database memory to share database memory pools rather than overprovisioning. Smart configuration to reduce tuning time after resizing VMs. Leverage existing standard PostgreSQL tools.

Component	Description
vFabric Application Director	Accelerate and automate the configuration and deployment of multitier applications. vFabric Application Director is a cloud-enabled application provisioning solution that simplifies how to create and standardize application deployment topologies across cloud services. vFabric Application Director is optimized for vFabric components but is extensible to other components that might be a part of a Spring application. Starting with an intuitive drag-and-drop canvas, application architects can quickly create complete deployment blueprints, or visual deployment topologies, that can be saved and later deployed onto any cloud with tight control over installation dependencies, configuration changes, and editable scripts.
vFabric Data Director	Improve agility and drastically reduce database TCO through database-aware virtualization and self-service lifecycle management with vFabric Data Director. Securely automate routine tasks, including database provisioning, HA, backup, and cloning. vFabric Data Director is a unified platform for heterogeneous databases, currently supporting Oracle Database 10g Release 2 and 11g Release 2 and VMware vFabric Postgres 9.0 and 9.1 (http://www.vmware.com/products/application-platform/vfabric-postgres/overview.html). Enterprise-grade security, flexibility, control, and compliance enable users to benefit from the agility of public cloud database services.
	Reduce database hardware and license costs through database-aware virtualization on vSphere.
	Increase agility through automated database lifecycle management.
	Accelerate application development through policy-based self-service.

"Do I have to code Java differently when running on vSphere?"

Coding practices don't change for Java on vSphere versus Java on native.

All tuning that you would have done for your Java on native is reusable for Java on vSphere.

Most Java workloads virtualize readily, but in some instances, for very large transactions, CPU and memory constraints may apply. See Chapter 3, "Tuning Large-Scale Java Platforms," and Chapter 4, "Designing and Sizing Large-Scale Java Platforms," for further detail.

"Are there any Java best practices for vSphere?"

Yes. See the best practices in Chapter 6, "Best Practices."

"How would you achieve vertical scalability of Java applications running on vSphere?"

Vertical scalability features of vSphere allow for compute resources to be adjusted at any time without need for redesign. Depending on the situation and supportability of the guest operating system, you can adjust CPU and memory. However, if you adjust the Java heap size, a JVM restart is usually required.

"How would you achieve horizontal scalability of Java applications running on vSphere?"

Horizontal scalability enables you to rapidly create new VMs and have them service traffic to meet your demands. Creating VMs is easy, but to truly create a burst scale-out capacity of your application, the newly created VM must be easily introduced into the load balancer pool to service additional traffic.

"How would you guard against server hardware failure when running Java applications on vSphere?"

VMware high availability (HA) can relocate the Java application server to another host that is active, thus minimizing downtime and disruption to service levels. Now because Java workloads are typically horizontally scaled out, it implies that there is always more than one copy to service transactions, so when you power cycle one JVM, other JVMs are still up and servicing transactions. It is true, however, that the JVM that you have just restarted would have lost transactions that were midstream. In such cases, you can consider a fault-tolerant persistence mechanism at the application level to guard against this.

"How would you achieve high availability of Java applications running on vSphere?"

You can achieve optimal HA via VMware Distributed Resource Scheduler (DRS), which can be used to balance workloads automatically. VMware HA and DRS with minimal configuration changes can provide a robust availability solution.

"How many JVMs can I stack on a single VM, and how many vCPUs should the VM use?"

This depends on your application's transactional throughput. VMware recommends that you performance load test your application to determine your optimal ratio for the number of JVMs, number of VMs, and number of vCPUs on each VM. Also refer to Chapter 3 and Chapter 4.

"Which application servers have been proven on vSphere in production?"

No specific application server works better with vSphere; all are good candidates. As many VMware customers have demonstrated, their Java environments virtualize well in dev, test, and production. We find the most commonly used application servers are Oracle WebLogic, IBM WebSphere, JBoss, Tomcat, and vFabric tc Server, which are all good examples of easily virtualized application servers, along with many others.

"What kind of testing has been done to validate running WebLogic on vSphere?"

We have several customers that have done independent performance testing of WebLogic running on vSphere in the insurance and hospitality industries. The results they achieved were equal to native in the cases of apples-to-apples comparisons, and in some cases performance was even better due to slight re-architecture of the deployment, Java version upgrade, and hardware upgrade.

"Which web servers have been proven on vSphere in production?"

It has been demonstrated that both Apache Web Server and Microsoft Internet Information Services (IIS) run well on vSphere and in production.

"Java applications platforms are multitier. Which tiers make sense to virtualize first?"

At a high level, we classify the enterprise Java applications platform into the following tiers:

- Load balancer tier
- Web server tier
- Java application server tier
- DB tier

We do not recommend any particular order, and some VMware customers virtualize all the tiers. However, we do see a growing trend where migrations are done in phases, as follows:

- **Phase one:** Migrate the web server tier to run on vSphere.
- **Phase two:** Migrate the Java application server tier to run on vSphere.
- **Phase three:** Migrate the DB server tier to run on vSphere.
- **Phase four:** Optionally migrate the load balancer tier to run on vSphere via load-balancer third-party virtual appliances that run on vSphere.

"How does vSphere help with business continuity for enterprise Java applications?"

VMware vCenter Site Recovery Manager does the following:

- Provides failover to secondary site
- Automates your recovery plans
- Allows a fast storage-replication adapter
- Recovers multiple sites into a single shared recovery site
- Simulates and tests the recovery plan
- Provides a powerful API for further scripting (http://www.vmware.com/support/developer/srm-api/srm_10_api.pdf)

"If I have a problem with Oracle WebLogic Server running on VMware virtual infrastructure, who should I call for support?"

Oracle provides best-effort support for WebLogic Server running on VMware software. Customers can initiate a support call with either Oracle for WebLogic-related issues or with VMware support for VMware virtualization-related issues. The best and quickest way to isolate a problem is to have VMware and Oracle support teams working together jointly to resolve an issue.

"If I have a problem with IBM WebSphere Server running on VMware vSphere, who should I call for support?"

General software support for IBM SWG products in a VMware environment: http://www-01.ibm.com/support/docview.wss?&uid=wws1e333ce0912f7b152852571f60074d175

VMware product support information for IBM WebSphere Application Server products: http://www-01.ibm.com/support/docview.wss?uid=swg21242532

"What about licensing?"

- For vSphere licensing, contact VMware Sales at http://www.vmware.com/contact/contact_sales.html.

- For licensing and application servers, contact the specific application-server vendor.

- For Oracle WebLogic, the following provides additional information on support, licensing, and pricing.

  General software support for Oracle products in a VMware environment; MetaLink 269212.1 on the Oracle partner website: http://myoraclesupport.oracle.com or http://metalink.oracle.com. You must be registered as a support user to get to the MetaLink document.

- IBM WebSphere:

  Pricing policies for IBM software on virtualized platforms, including VMware: http://www-01.ibm.com/software/lotus/passportadvantage/Counting_Software_licenses_using_specific_virtualization_technologies.html

  Contact IBM for pricing.

"Are there any customer references?"

Here is a partial list of VMware customers who have already successfully virtualized applications on WebLogic Server:

- **First American Financial Group:** https://www.vmware.com/files/pdf/partners/first_american_corp_cs_091207.pdf
- **I2 Technologies India:** https://www.vmware.com/files/pdf/customers/apac_in_08Q1_ss_vmw_i2_technologies_english.pdf
- **VMware Session on Oracle E-Business Suite from VMworld 2009 (viewable without a password):** http://www.vmworld.com/docs/DOC-3624

Here is a partial list of VMware customers who have already successfully virtualized applications on WebSphere Application Server:

- **Ohio Mutual Insurance Group (OMIG):** http://www.vmware.com/files/pdf/customers/08Q4_isv_vmw_OMIG_english.pdf
- **T-Systems Austria:** http://www.vmware.com/files/pdf/customers/06Q4_cs_vmw_T-systems_Austria_English.pdf
- **First Marblehead:** http://www.vmware.com/files/pdf/customers/09Q2_cs_vmw_First_Marblehead_english.pdf

"What decisions must be made because of virtualization?"

You must determine the size of the repeatable building-block VM. This is established by benchmarking, along with total scale-out factor. Determine how many concurrent users each single vCPU configuration of your application can handle, and extrapolate that to your production traffic to determine the overall compute-resource requirement. Having a symmetrical building block (for example, every VM having the same number of vCPUs) helps keep load distribution from your load balancer even. Essentially, your benchmarking test helps you determine how large a single VM should be (vertical scalability) and how many of these VMs you will need (horizontal scalability).

You must pay special attention to scale-out factor, and see up to what point it is linear within your application running on top of VMware. Java applications are multitiered, and bottlenecks can appear at any point along the scale-out performance line and quickly cause nonlinear results. The assumption of linear scalability may not always be true, and it is essential to load test a preproduction replica (production to be) of your environment to accurately size for you traffic.

"I have conducted extensive GC sizing and tuning for our current enterprise Java application running on physical. Do I have to adjust anything related to sizing when moving this Java application to a virtualized environment?"

No. All tuning that you would perform for your Java application on physical is transferable to your virtual environment. However, because virtualization projects are usually about driving a high-consolidation ratio, it is advisable that you conduct adequate load testing to establish your ideal compute-resource configuration for individual VMs, the number of JVMs within a VM, and the overall number of VMs on the ESX host.

In addition, because this type of migration involves an OS/platform change as well as a JVM vendor change, it is advisable to read through Chapter 3 and Chapter 4.

"How many and what size virtual machines will I need?"

This depends on the nature of your application. We most often see two-vCPU VMs as a common building block for Java applications. One of the guidelines is to tune your system for more scale out as opposed to scale up. This rule is not absolute; it depends on your organization's architectural best practices. Smaller, more scaled-out VMs may provide better overall architecture, but you will incur additional guest OS licensing costs. If this is a constraint, you can tune toward larger four-vCPU VMs and stack more JVMs on them.

"What is the correct number of JVMs per virtual machine?"

There is no one definite answer. This largely depends on the nature of your application. The benchmarking you conduct can determine the limit of the number of JVMs that can be stacked up on a single VM.

The more JVMs you put on a single VM, the more JVM overhead and cost of initializing a JVM is incurred. Alternatively, instead of stacking up multiple JVMs within a VM, you can instead increase the JVM size vertically by adding more threads and heap size. This can be achieved if your JVM is within an application server such as Tomcat. Then, instead of increasing the number of JVMs, you can increase the number of concurrent threads available and resources that a single Tomcat JVM services for your n number of applications deployed and their concurrent requests per second. The limitation of how many applications you can stack up within a single application server instance/JVM is bounded by how large you can afford your JVM heap size to be and performance. The tradeoff of very large JVM heap size beyond 4GB needs to be tested for performance and GC-cycle impact. This concern is not specific to virtualization; it applies equally to physical server setup.

"We would like to use the full logical CPU capacity of a host and take full advantage of HT."

Let's take the example of a Dell server R810, dual eight-core machine with hyperthreading (HT) enabled. It means there are 16 physical CPUs, and with HT enabled the count is 32 logical CPUs. The ideal case here is to configure multiple VMs, choosing from various available vCPU configurations, such as two vCPU, four vCPU, or eight vCPU. Aim at adhering to the following equation:

Total vCPUs = Physical CPUs + 25%

In our example here, this means we have

16 physical CPUs + 25% * 16 = 20 vCPUs approximately

Now this is not a cast-in-stone rule, and you can actually go higher than this in terms of adding, for example, 3 VMs with each being at 8-vCPU, for a total of 24 vCPUs, and you may find the overall host CPU utilization still within the acceptable range for your setup. But anything beyond this and you will start to encroach on the limits of the host.

> **NOTE**
>
> Even though the processor has HT, scheduling more frequently does not guarantee that the VM will catch up. This is because the amount of CPU resources received by the vCPU is affected by the activity on the other logical processor on the same physical core. To guarantee the vCPU that is behind can catch up, ESX will sometimes not schedule VMs on the other logical processor, effectively leaving it idle. See http://kb.vmware.com/kb/1020233.

"We have a monitoring system that is a single JVM heap of 360GB. Can we tune this?"

The first question you should ask is why the monitoring system has only one JVM. Wouldn't it be a concern that there is a single point of failure? Perhaps you can defer this question back to the vendor of the monitoring system. Here are things to keep in mind:

- In the meantime, you can at least virtualize it and get the benefits of VMware HA, just in case it needs to be restarted somewhere else during a potential failure situation (so at least this way you have some level of protection).

- The main trick to sizing such large JVMs is the size of the underlying Non-Uniform Memory Access (NUMA) nodes. As usual, always choose two-socket vSphere hosts; those will yield the largest NUMA nodes

- If you have 1TB of memory on the host, sizing the monitoring system JVM process that is in question would be quite straightforward because the entire process would fit into a NUMA node. However, that amount of memory is usually pricy, and not many customers have it, and certainly in this case the customer only has 512GB across the vSphere host.

- Because there is only 512GB on the vSphere host, we have to take into account certain aspects of the Java process that will run across two NUMA nodes.

- The main thing here is to try to fit at least one entire section of the Java heap within one NUMA node. In this case, if you apply the best practice that the young generation (-Xmn) should be 33% of the Java heap (-Xmx), this implies 0.33 * 360GB => 118.8, rounded to 118GB. This should fit into one of the NUMA nodes, but let's next double-check this.

- The vSphere host is made of 512GB RAM and 2 sockets of 10 cores each. If we apply overhead calculation, then per NUMA node memory => ((0.99 * 512) – 1) / 2 => 252.94, rounded up to 253GB, is the amount of local NUMA memory.

- Based on this NUMA bank of about 253GB, the young generation and parts of the old generation will fit nicely into the first NUMA node, and some will interleave to the next NUMA node, because the young generation is 118GB, and the old generation is 360 – 118 => 242GB. All of the young generation 11 * GB will fit into the NUMA node, and a partial section of the 242GB old generation will interleave across two NUMA nodes. This, of course, can be problematic, but your customer might have just gotten used to the type of performance offered by such a setup and accepted it.

- Assuming that you really need a JVM that is 360GB, you would size a single VM with 360GB + 1GB for OS + 25% * 360GB for off-the-heap overhead => 360GB + 1GB + 90GB = 451GB possible memory will be used by the Java process. Because this is a single VM, the vSphere NUMA scheduler will do its best to localize the execution to the local NUMA bank. It can also apply NUMA client methodology where the singular VM is actually split underneath to manage NUMA interleaving situations.

- Figure A-5 illustrates one potential configuration for the 360GB JVM.

```
java -Xms360g -Xmx360g -Xmn118g -Xss1024k -XX:+UseConcMarkSweepGC
-XX:+UseParNewGC -XX:CMSInitiatingOccupancyFraction=75

-XX:+UseCMSInitiatingOccupancyOnly -XX:+ScavengeBeforeFullGC

-XX:TargetSurvivorRatio=80 -XX:SurvivorRatio=8

-XX:+UseBiasedLocking -XX:MaxTenuringThreshold=15

-XX:ParallelGCThreads=10 -XX:+OptimizeStringConcat

-XX:+UseCompressedStrings -XX:+UseStringCache -XX:+DisableExplicitGC
```

Figure A-5   JVM Configuration of a Monitoring System for a 360GB Heap

NOTE
Every attempt should be made to size down the Java process heap to fit within the NUMA node (as is often possible) because most heap spaces of this magnitude are underutilized. The other reason is that the efficiency enhancement in terms of better memory throughput gained from local NUMA memory for both young generation and old generation space easily exceeds the need to have a heap that is larger than the NUMA node. An alternative to the configuration in Figure A-5 is the configuration shown in Figure A-6, where we have reduced the heap size to fit within the NUMA node. The NUMA node is 253GB, allowing for 1GB for the guest OS. This implies the total Java process can have 252GB worth of memory, now allocating 10% in this case to an off-the-heap section. It implies that the Java heap can be 0.9 * 252GB => 226GB. Then we applied a young generation size of 33% of 226GB => 0.33 * 226GB => 74.5GB, rounding to 74GB. This also assumes that you will size down the VM memory reservation to 253GB so that the entire VM process, and hence the entire JVM, fits into one NUMA node. Note that the advantage of virtualizing such a process is to leverage all the high availability, scalability, and VMotion benefits of vSphere. Additionally, vSphere NUMA optimization algorithm is available by default; this algorithm

is always attempting to optimize balancing and locality of the VM in a manner that yields the best memory throughput. VMware vSphere will take care of NUMA optimization so that you don't have to worry about it, as opposed to in physical deployments, where you must do this manually by using a guest OS numactl command to pin the Java process to the NUMA node, a practice that can get quite complicated quickly. This type of NUMA optimization offered by vSphere is one major reason for virtualizing large VM and JVMs, in addition to all of the flexibility, high availability, and reliability features of vSphere.

```
java -Xms226g -Xmx226g -Xmn74g -Xss1024k -XX:+UseConcMarkSweepGC
-XX:+UseParNewGC -XX:CMSInitiatingOccupancyFraction=75

-XX:+UseCMSInitiatingOccupancyOnly -XX:+ScavengeBeforeFullGC

-XX:TargetSurvivorRatio=80 -XX:SurvivorRatio=8

-XX:+UseBiasedLocking -XX:MaxTenuringThreshold=15

-XX:ParallelGCThreads=10 -XX:+OptimizeStringConcat

-XX:+UseCompressedStrings -XX:+UseStringCache -XX:+DisableExplicitGC
```

Figure A-6   JVM Configuration of a Monitoring System for a 226GB Heap

"We are on the DevOps team, and we get challenged about our JVM knowledge by the developers. Can you help us with some preliminary information about the JVM internals and how it needs to be sized?"

Note that if you have read through this book, and specifically Chapter 3 and Chapter 4, you have all the information you need to convince the Java architects of how JVMs need to be sized. However, if you want to equip yourself with some more background information on how the internals of the JVM works, in addition to what is discussed in these chapters, see Figure A-7. The left side of the diagram shows the VM memory and JVM memory diagram that has been used throughout this book. The right side of the diagram is an expanded view of the internals of the heap. Chapter 4 covered in depth how to tune JVMs, and it was assumed that you have some background knowledge about the various sections of the JVM. The expanded view shows the Java heap configured with -Xmx, and then in turn the Java heap is split between the young generation (YoungGen) and old generation (OldGen).

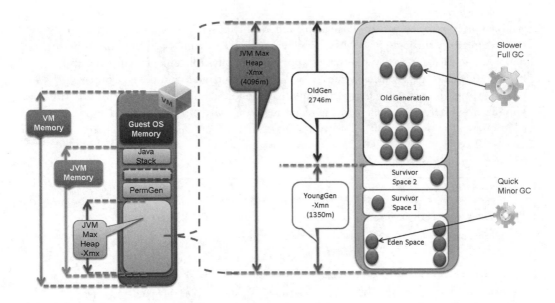

Figure A-7   Expanded View of the Java Heap

In the example, the Java heap size is 4096m, the YoungGen is 33% of the heap at 1350m, and the OldGen is simply the difference between the heap size and the YoungGen (2746m, 67% of the heap -Xmx). With this common configuration, the YoungGen has plenty of space for object churn. The YoungGen, in turn, has a section called the Eden space and two survivor spaces, survivor space 1 and 2.

Objects in Java applications are created in the Eden space, and then if they are not referenced anymore, the next minor GC cycle will garbage collect these. However, if the objects are live and being referenced, they will get copied to the first survivor space. This cycle continues, and if objects continue to survive in survivor space 1, they are moved to survivor space 2 in the next cycle. Furthermore, if objects continue to survivor space 2, objects then will eventually be promoted to the OldGen; note that some iterations of copying between survivor spaces will take place multiple times before finally the threshold is crossed and objects are copied over to the old generation. In the YoungGen, minor garbage collections are relatively quick, but still pausing; in the OldGen, full garbage collection shouldn't occur as much (every few hours) and lasts in the minutes range depending on the size of the OldGen.

Glossary

AMQP The Advanced Message Queuing Protocol (AMQP) is an open standard application layer protocol for message-oriented middleware. The protocol has features such as messaging, queuing, routing both point to point and publish and subscribe, in addition to reliability and security.

ballooning Ballooning is the name given to the memory-reclamation process invoked by the balloon driver. The balloon driver, also known as the vmmemctl driver, collaborates with the server to reclaim pages that are considered least valuable by the guest operating system. It essentially acts like a native program in the operating system that requires more and more memory. The driver uses a proprietary ballooning technique that provides predictable performance that closely matches the behavior of a native system under similar memory constraints. This technique effectively increases or decreases memory pressure on the guest operating system, causing the guest to invoke its own native memory management algorithms. You can refer to the following vSphere memory management paper for additional details: http://www.vmware.com/files/pdf/perf-vsphere-memory_management.pdf.

CPU overcommit This is where you are allocating more virtual CPU (vCPU) resources than what is physically available on the ESX host. For further information, see the vSphere Best Practices paper: http://www.vmware.com/pdf/Perf_Best_Practices_vSphere4.0.pdf.

dependency injection Dependency injection is a specific form of inversion of control where the concern being inverted is the process of obtaining the needed dependency. The term was first coined by Martin Fowler to describe the mechanism more clearly. Dependency injection in object-oriented programming is a technique that is used to supply an external dependency or reference to a software component. In technical terms, it is a design pattern that separates behavior from dependency resolution, thus decoupling highly dependent components. Instead of components having to request dependencies, they are given, or injected, into the component.

DRS   The vSphere Distributed Resource Scheduler continuously balances computing capacity in resource pools to deliver the performance, scalability, and availability not possible with physical infrastructure. DRS uses VMotion to move virtual machines (VMs) around to more fairly distribute workloads.

guest OS   This is either the Linux-based or Windows-based operating system that is installed on the VM.

host   A host in VMware terminology is server hardware that is running VMware's ESX bare-metal hypervisor. It is a "host" for VMs to run on.

IoC   In software engineering, inversion of control (IoC) is an abstract principle describing an aspect of some software architecture designs in which the flow of control of a system is inverted in comparison to procedural programming. In traditional programming, the flow of the business logic is controlled by a central piece of code that calls reusable subroutines that perform specific functions. Using inversion of control, this "central control" design principle is abandoned. The caller's code deals with the program's execution order, but the business knowledge is encapsulated by the called subroutines.

In practice, IoC is a style of software construction where reusable generic code controls the execution of problem-specific code. It carries the strong connotation that the reusable code and the problem-specific code are developed independently, which often results in a single integrated application.

large memory pages   In addition to the usual 4KB memory pages, ESX also makes 2MB memory pages available (commonly referred to as *large pages*). By default, ESX assigns these 2MB machine memory pages to guest operating systems that request them, giving the guest operating system the full advantage of using large pages. The use of large pages results in reduced memory management overhead and can therefore increase hypervisor performance. If an operating system or application can benefit from large pages on a native system, that operating system or application can potentially achieve a similar performance improvement on a VM backed with 2MB machine memory pages. Consult the documentation for your operating system and application to determine how to configure them each to use large memory pages. You can find more information about large page support in the resource titled "Large Page Performance" at http://www.vmware.com/resources/techresources/1039.

memory overcommit   Memory overcommit occurs when you have allocated more RAM than is physically available on the host.

memory reservation   Memory reservation refers to the minimum amount of physical memory guaranteed to be made available to the VM at all times. If this requested reserved memory is not available upon VM startup, the VM will simply not start. A successful startup of the VM means the required memory was reserved.

NUMA   Non-Uniform Memory Access (NUMA) is a computer memory design used in multiprocessors, where the memory access time depends on the memory location relative to a processor. Under NUMA, a processor can access its own local memory faster than nonlocal memory (that is, memory local to another processor or memory shared between processors).

vApp   A vApp is a collection of VMs (and potentially other vApp containers) that are operated and monitored as a unit. From a management perspective, a multitiered vApp acts a lot like a virtual machine object. It has power operations, networks, datastores, and its resource usage can be configured.

virtual machine (VM)   A virtual machine is a software implementation of a machine (that is, a computer that executes programs like a physical machine would). VMs can be created with variant compute resources, such as virtual CPU, referred to as vCPU, RAM, and storage.

vMotion   vMotion technology, deployed in production by 80% of VMware customers, leverages the complete virtualization of servers, storage, and networking to move an entire running VM instantaneously from one server to another. vMotion uses the VMware cluster file system to control access to a VM's storage. During a vMotion, the active memory and precise execution state of a VM is rapidly transmitted over a high-speed network from one physical server to another, and access to the VM's disk storage is instantly switched to the new physical host. Because the network is also virtualized by the VMware host, the VM retains its network identity and connections, ensuring a seamless migration process.

VMware ESX/ESXi   Like its predecessor ESX, ESXi is a "bare-metal" hypervisor, meaning that it installs directly on top of the physical server and partitions it into multiple VMs that can run simultaneously, sharing the physical resources of the underlying server. VMware introduced ESXi in 2007 to deliver industry-leading performance and scalability while setting a new bar for reliability, security, and hypervisor management efficiency.

VMware vCenter Server   VMware vCenter Server is the simplest, most efficient way to manage VMware vSphere (whether you have ten VMs or tens of thousands of VMs). It provides unified management of all the hosts and VMs in your data center from a single console with an aggregate performance monitoring of clusters, hosts, and VMs. VMware vCenter Server gives administrators deep insight into the status and configuration of clusters, hosts, VMs, storage, the guest OS, and other critical components of a virtual infrastructure—all from one place.

Both architectures use the same kernel to deliver virtualization capabilities, but the ESX architecture also contains a Linux OS, called *Service Console*, that is used to perform local management tasks such as executing scripts or installing third-party agents. The Service Console has been removed from ESXi, drastically reducing the hypervisor codebase footprint (less than 150MB versus ESX's 2GB) and completing the ongoing trend of migrating management functionality from the local command-line interface to remote management tools.

VMware vSphere   VMware vSphere, (prior name, VMware Infrastructure 4) is VMware's first cloud operating system, able to manage large pools of virtualized computing infrastructure, including software and hardware.

Index

vmware PRESS

Virtualizing and Tuning
Large-Scale
Java Platforms

Emad Benjamin

FREE
Online Edition

Your purchase of *Virtualizing and Tuning Large-Scale Java Platforms* includes access to a free online edition for 45 days through the **Safari Books Online** subscription service. Nearly every VMware Press book is available online through **Safari Books Online**, along with thousands of books and videos from publishers such as Addison-Wesley Professional, Cisco Press, Exam Cram, IBM Press, O'Reilly Media, Prentice Hall, Que, and Sams.

Safari Books Online is a digital library providing searchable, on-demand access to thousands of technology, digital media, and professional development books and videos from leading publishers. With one monthly or yearly subscription price, you get unlimited access to learning tools and information on topics including mobile app and software development, tips and tricks on using your favorite gadgets, networking, project management, graphic design, and much more.

Activate your FREE Online Edition at
informit.com/safarifree

STEP 1:   Enter the coupon code: COZWDDB.

STEP 2:   New Safari users, complete the brief registration form.
            Safari subscribers, just log in.

If you have difficulty registering on Safari or accessing the online edition,
please e-mail customer-service@safaribooksonline.com

  Adobe Press  ALPHA Cisco Press FT Press FINANCIAL TIMES IBM Press. Microsoft Press New Riders O'REILLY

 Peachpit Press PRENTICE HALL Que Redbooks SAMS SAS Publishing vmware PRESS WILEY WROX